Living Through Breast Cancer

What a Harvard doctor and survivor
wants you to know about getting the best
care while preserving your self-image

Carolyn M. Kaelin M.D., M.P.H.

with Francesca Coltrera

616.994
KAE

McGraw·Hill

New York   Chicago   San Francisco   Lisbon   London   Madrid   Mexico City
Milan   New Delhi   San Juan   Seoul   Singapore   Sydney   Toronto

Library of Congress Cataloging-in-Publication Data

Kaelin, Carolyn.
    Living through breast cancer : what a Harvard doctor and survivor wants you to know about getting the best care while preserving your self-image / by Carolyn Kaelin with Francesca Coltrera.
       p.   cm.
    Includes index.
    ISBN 0-07-144463-7
    1. Breast—Cancer—Popular works.   I. Coltrera, Francesca.   II. Title.

RC280.B8K33   2005
616.99′499—dc22

                                                 2005000932

1 2 3 4 5 6 7 8 9 0   DOC/DOC   0 9 8 7 6 5

ISBN 0-07-144463-7

Art credits can be found on page 363 and should be considered an extension of this copyright page.

McGraw-Hill books are available at special quantity discounts to use as premiums and sales promotions, or for use in corporate training programs. For more information, please write to the Director of Special Sales, Professional Publishing, McGraw-Hill, Two Penn Plaza, New York, NY 10121-2298. Or contact your local bookstore.

The information contained in this book is intended to provide helpful and informative material on the subject addressed. It is not intended to serve as a replacement for professional medical advice. Any use of the information in this book is at the reader's discretion. The author, publisher, and the President and Fellows of Harvard College specifically disclaim any and all liability arising directly or indirectly from the use or application of any information contained in this book. A health care professional should be consulted regarding your specific situation.

This book is printed on acid-free paper.

⊙

⊙

CONTENTS

◉

Part III

REGAINING YOUR BALANCE: EXERCISE, NUTRITION,
SEXUALITY, AND MORE

PREFACE

◉

MANY WOMEN'S LIVES are touched by breast cancer, either through their own diagnosis or that of a friend or loved one. If you have picked up this book, chances are you are one of those women. As a breast cancer surgeon—and as of last year, a breast cancer patient as well—I, too, am one of those women.

Recent advances have greatly pared down the cosmetic and emotional impacts of breast cancer and its treatment. Breast cancer is being diagnosed earlier and tissue sampling is more precise and less traumatic, thanks to new biopsy techniques. Emerging therapies have extended and improved the lives of women faced with this disease, and improved surgical and radiation procedures leave less of an imprint than older treatments. Most importantly, today women are less likely than ever to die of breast cancer.

Still, from up close, breast cancer can seem as frightening and overwhelming as it did thirty years ago. Not only is your life suddenly on the line, but so is your *way* of life. And your sense of self.

I wanted to offer women facing breast cancer information based on my work as a breast cancer surgeon and some hard-won insight drawn from my experiences as a breast cancer patient. Francesca Coltrera, an exceptional health writer, worked with me to present this information in an accessible way and helped bring these pages alive. I also drew upon the invaluable expertise of many colleagues at Brigham and Women's Hospital and Dana-Farber Cancer Institute, as well as the knowledge of many others who spend their days supporting women with breast cancer. Much of the information on surgery and reconstruction was developed in concert with clinical staff working on the Brigham and Women's Hospital booklet *Breast Surgery: A Guide for Patients and Families*.

It is our hope that *Living Through Breast Cancer* will serve as a valuable guide through a challenging time and help you anchor your sense of self during treatment and afterward. By providing up-to-date and clear information, it will help you understand your diagnosis and think through your treatment options. Its pages also detail ways to ease or erase lingering aftereffects.

While any errors and omissions in the book are our responsibility, we would like to gratefully acknowledge those who shared their expertise and very valuable time.

At Brigham and Women's Hospital and Dana-Farber Cancer Institute, Ann H. Partridge, M.D., M.P.H.; Julia S. Wong, M.D.; and Eric P. Winer, M.D., were especially heroic. Elizabeth S. Ginsburg, M.D.; Charles A. Hergrueter, M.D.; Jennifer A. Ligibel, M.D.; Stacy Kennedy, M.P.H., R.D./L.D.N.; Darrell N. Smith, M.D.; Janet Kunsman, R.N., N.P.; Barbara Silver; Peter Mauch, M.D.; Sanaz Ghazal; Larry Raymond; and Julie L. Durmis, director of Friends Boutique, were enormously helpful as well.

Cheri Bishop, D.M.D., of Hammond Pond Dental Associates, and dermatologists Lynn Baden, M.D., M.P.H., and Leslie Lucchina, M.D., graciously shared their time and expertise. We also owe a debt to the expertise of Walter C. Willett, M.D., Dr. P.H., Chair of the Department of Nutrition at the Harvard School of Public Health, for the nutrition information provided in this book.

We further wish to thank Reebok Master Trainers Josie Gardiner and Joy Prouty; Kathleen Gill Bazazi, general manager of Images at Massachusetts General Hospital; Patricia A. Wrixon and Christine Lafferty at The Salon at 10 Newbury and Lynn Groff, manager, Diego for expertise on wigs and hair; Brian Brady, makeup director, Guiliano Day Spa; and Holly Metcalf, founder and executive director of the Row as One Institute. Special heartfelt thanks to my dear friends Barbara Rodriguez, writer and assistant professor of literature at Tufts University, who has long been an inspiration to me and has thoughtfully supported me during the writing of this book; Marcia Gregg, who was there for my children (and me) at every deadline while I was cloistered away; and Suzy Marden, who has shared her own life experiences with me and has taught me how to live in the moment, which is where I needed to be with each word of this book.

We would like to extend our heartfelt gratitude to our editor at McGraw-Hill, Judith McCarthy, who championed this project and guided us through it.

At Harvard Health Publications, Dr. Anthony Komaroff, editor in chief, supported us from the book's conception to its completion. Managing editor Nancy Ferrari poured countless hours into making this book shine and was truly a pleasure to work with at every step. Assistant editors Christine Junge and Raquel A. Schott and interns Jessica Gottlieb, Gareth A. Hughes, Jonah B. Leshin, and Vered Schreiber were especially helpful as well. Shaneen Washington kept us organized and on track. Thanks also to the artists who contributed to this work, including Doron Ben-Ami, Harriet B. Greenfield, Raoul Kim, Scott Leighton, and Patrick Scullin.

This book has been brought to life through the many patients, friends, and acquaintances and their partners who unstintingly shared with us their experiences with breast cancer. We salute their generosity, inspiration, grit, and humor. As their stories unfold, perhaps you will recognize situations that echo your own.

Finally, we would also like to acknowledge our partners, children, and parents who were so very patient and helpful. Our love always.

INTRODUCTION

◉

IN 2004, THE American Cancer Society estimated that 215,990 women would learn that they had invasive breast cancer. Another 59,390 would be told that they had in situ breast cancer—a collection of cells that might one day tumble into an invasive cancer but which were identified before they were able to infiltrate surrounding tissues. If you are reading this book, odds are good that you or someone you love has reluctantly joined this sisterhood. While the news may seem terrible from where you stand, the outlook has never been brighter. The surgeries, drugs, and radiation techniques used to control breast cancer are more precisely targeted than ever. Women with breast cancer are living longer, often better lives than was possible even just a decade ago.

Yet there is no escaping the fact that the very treatments that lengthen lives have rippling effects that are nowhere near that beneficial. This book is dedicated to changing that equation for the better whenever possible. It is based on authoritative research and offers nitty-gritty guidance drawn from my experience as a breast cancer surgeon who has also been a patient. Part I can help you get your bearings during the early months when medical terms and treatment choices whiz at you with lightning speed. Part II presents a broad spectrum of ways to handle minor and major challenges to your body and deepest sense of self that stem from breast cancer treatments. Part III, which embraces new thinking in exercise and nutrition and responds to concerns surrounding fertility, sexuality, menopause, and the mind, will help you regain your balance so that you emerge from this experience as strong and healthy as possible.

The pages that follow resound with the voices of many women who have been treated for breast cancer as well as the voices of experts in the field and would not have been possible without their thoughtful contributions. To protect their privacy, the names of the women who spoke with us have been changed, but their heartfelt insights remain untouched.

PART I

GETTING YOUR BEARINGS: DIAGNOSIS, TREATMENT, AND DRAWING TOGETHER YOUR MEDICAL TEAM

I

UNDERSTANDING YOUR DIAGNOSIS

◉

Practically every woman diagnosed with breast cancer finds the first few moments after those words are uttered heart-stopping. Once her doctor told her she had breast cancer, said Annette, she barely heard anything else during the rest of the appointment. She felt grateful her husband was there to listen, a simple act that seemed impossible that day. "I walked out of there so overwhelmed. My doctor said, 'cancer, mastectomy, and chemotherapy,' and I really don't remember any other words."

Understanding a breast cancer diagnosis can be tricky even without the emotional buzz that blocks out normal comprehension. If you're not a health professional, you may feel you've plunged into a crash course full of confusing language and unintelligible statistics. This chapter will help you navigate this unfamiliar territory during a difficult time in your life.

THE STARTING LINE

As a breast cancer surgeon and director of the Comprehensive Breast Health Center at Brigham and Women's Hospital in Boston, I understood the intricacies of breast cancer quite well. Yet in 2003 my own diagnosis ushered me through the mirror and into a world more familiar to breast cancer patients than to their doctors. I had spent the spring and summer of that year training for the Pan-Mass Challenge, a 190-mile bike ride that raises research dollars for Dana-Farber Cancer Institute in Boston. One sunny July day, while taking off my cycling jersey after a twenty-five-mile training ride, I noticed the tiniest, most subtle area of skin pulling inward on my right breast. Everything felt fine. There was no lump. The mammogram I had the following day looked fine, too. An ultrasound picked up many small breast cysts, suspended like tiny water balloons, which are normal variations of breast tissue.

But there was one dim shape that looked a bit funny. I asked a colleague to take a sample of this tissue with a large, hollow needle. The next morning, the chief of breast pathology came to my office holding my pathology slides in her hand to gently and regretfully break the news. I had breast cancer. The irony was unmistakable.

In the final eleven days before the Pan-Mass Challenge, I had many x-rays and two surgeries. The night before the ride, I searched for a sports bra that didn't require me to raise my arms over my head to wriggle into it. I found two and wore both to make biking less uncomfortable. The next morning, I set out on a shorter version of the full 190-mile route I had planned to ride. I began in the rain and ended in the heat seventy-five miles later at the last water stop. It wasn't the finish line I'd hoped to reach.

That day I stopped a little short of my goal. Today, after three lumpectomies (breast-conserving surgeries) ultimately followed by a mastectomy, chemotherapy, and reconstructive surgery, I can see the finish line. It's my hope that this book will smooth the journey for other women facing a breast cancer diagnosis and for those who love and support them.

ANATOMY OF A BREAST

Over the ages, the breast has been lauded for beauty as well as its ability to nourish a baby. Between the soft outer skin of the breast and the underlying pectoral (chest) muscles covering the ribs lies a landscape of fat interwoven with milk-producing glandular tissue. The milk glands are shaped like stalks of broccoli. The fluffy ends of the stalks, which are called *lobules*, produce the milk. The stalks themselves are the *ducts* that carry milk from the lobule to the nipple during breast-feeding. (See Figures 1.1 and 1.2.)

Intricate networks carve pathways between the glands and through the fatty portions of the breast. Nerves richly endow the breast skin, nipple, and areola with sensation. Arteries, veins, and smaller blood vessels deliver oxygen and nutrients to the tissues and cart off waste products. Lymphatic vessels carry thin, milky fluid called *lymph* to small bean-shaped organs called *lymph nodes* that appear in clusters near the outer breast in the *axilla* (underarm), around the collarbone, and in the

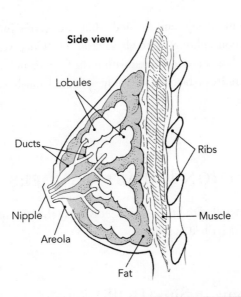

Figure 1.1 The breast is composed primarily of fat and breast tissue and also has nerves, arteries, veins, and lymphatic vessels that carry lymph fluid to the lymph nodes. The lobules are milk-producing glands and the ducts carry the milk from the lobules to the nipple during breast-feeding. Breast cancer usually starts inside the gland and in time it may break through the gland wall and spread through the lymph channels or blood vessels to other parts of the body.

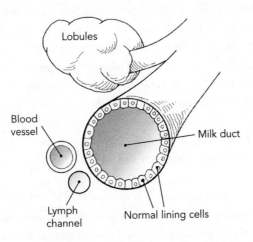

Figure 1.2 Normal duct. Normal cells line the milk duct in the breast. The lobules of the breast, where milk is produced, are lined with normal cells.

chest. As part of the immune system, the nodes filter out germs and foreign matter and produce infection-fighting white blood cells. The blood vessels and lymphatic channels of the breast are contained within the fatty tissue surrounding the ducts and lobules. There are no blood vessels or lymphatic channels within the ducts and lobules themselves.

COMMON BREAST CANCERS

If you have been diagnosed with breast cancer, it is likely that you have one of the more common forms, described as follows.

Ductal Carcinoma in Situ (DCIS)

Cancer is said to be in situ if it is contained within one or more ducts in the breast and has not spread beyond those confines. While ductal carcinoma in situ has not invaded the surrounding tissues of the breast, it might eventually do so if neglected. Because it doesn't have access to the blood vessels or lymphatic channels outside the glands, it can't migrate to other organs in the body and is considered breast cancer at its earliest stage (Stage 0). At screening centers, about one in every five new breast cancers diagnosed is DCIS, while the remaining four out of five are invasive.

On a mammogram, DCIS typically appears as a huddle of irregularly shaped, tiny white specks that look like grains of sand. The clustered specks represent calcifications within a duct. (See Figure 1.3.) The mammography report may note that the calcifications are pleomorphic (irregularly shaped) and linearly arranged up and down the duct. Roughly 15 percent of women with DCIS have a larger hazy spot (density) associated with the calcifications. In 10 percent a density appears without any calcifications. In a relative handful of cases, doctors find DCIS incidentally on a biopsy specimen without having seen any sign of it on the mammogram or during a physical exam.

In the era of modern mammography, it is unusual for DCIS to be noticed during a breast exam. Rarely, the condition appears as a palpable, wedge-shaped thickening in the breast where the cancer cells have congested a single duct; as spontaneous, single duct nipple discharge; or as an erosion of the nipple skin by cancer cells percolating up the duct, a condition termed *Paget's disease*.

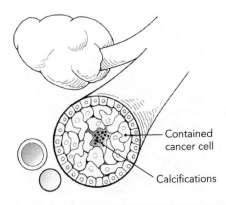

Figure 1.3 Ductal carcinoma in situ. Breast cancer may begin with the mutation of a single cell in a duct of a normal breast. When cancer cells begin to multiply but stay contained inside the duct, the condition is known as ductal carcinoma in situ (DCIS). This often appears as a cluster of white dots (calcifications) on a mammogram.

The cells of an invasive cancer have broken out of the gland and thus potentially have access to the blood vessels and lymph channels within the breast. If DCIS is left untreated, it is difficult to predict whether or not it might become an invasive breast cancer and how slowly or quickly this might occur. Several long-term studies have looked at women whose biopsies were initially interpreted as benign but were found to contain a small amount of DCIS during subsequent review. After ten or more years of follow-up, 14 to 80 percent of these women had received a diagnosis of invasive cancer.

Certain molecular markers common to both DCIS and invasive breast cancer suggest that DCIS falls in the first stretch of a path leading toward invasion. Low-grade DCIS (Grade I), in which the worrisome cells have fewer abnormal features, may be closer to the starting line. High-grade DCIS (Grade III), which is marked by increasingly abnormal cells, appears to be many steps down the path to invasive cancer. Intermediate-grade DCIS (Grade II) lies somewhere in between.

Invasive (Infiltrating) Ductal Carcinoma (ID)

The most common form of breast cancer is invasive ductal (ID), accounting for about four out of five invasive breast cancers. This cancer has broken through the

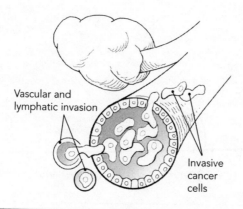

Figure 1.4 Invasive ductal carcinoma. This type of cancer exists when cancer cells break through the wall of the duct and enter the surrounding tissue. The cells may invade the blood vessels and lymph channels of the breast, increasing the likelihood that the cancer will spread (metastasize) to other parts of the body.

duct wall and invaded the surrounding fatty tissue of the breast. From there it may spread to other parts of the body through the blood vessels or lymph channels (lymphatic-vascular invasion, or LVI). (See Figure 1.4.)

Invasive (Infiltrating) Lobular Carcinoma (IL)

Roughly 10 percent of invasive breast cancers are this type. The cancer cells have grown through the lobule wall and can spread to other parts of the body via the lymphatic channels or bloodstream.

LESS COMMON BREAST CANCERS

Far less often, women learn they have one of the forms of breast cancer described as follows.

MICROSCOPIC WARNING FLAGS, NOT CANCER

Certain microscopic changes in breast cells are sometimes found in tissue removed during a biopsy. Although the affected cells look different from normal cells, they are *not* malignant (cancerous), and in most women they do not progress to cancer. However, they are warning flags of an increased susceptibility for breast cancer. These noncancerous changes in breast cells include the following:

- **Lobular carcinoma in situ (LCIS):** Despite the misleading name chosen in the 1940s and never updated, LCIS is not cancer. LCIS is an irregular growth of the cells lining the wall of a lobule that does not penetrate the gland wall. Because it cannot be felt and usually does not appear as an abnormality on a mammogram, this tissue change is generally detected incidentally during a biopsy. LCIS is like a little red flag—a marker—in the breast indicating that a woman has an increased risk of developing breast cancer when compared to the general female population. This risk is approximately 1 percent per year, or up to 35 percent over a lifetime. A woman with LCIS should have a mammogram annually and an examination by a breast specialist every six to twelve months. Because tamoxifen (Nolvadex) has been shown to reduce the risk of invasive breast cancers in women with LCIS by approximately 50 percent, it is worth asking your doctor about the potential risks and benefits of this option (see Chapter 5).
- **Atypical lobular hyperplasia (ALH) and atypical ductal hyperplasia (ADH):** These microscopic changes in breast tissue are extra cells (hyperplasia) growing in the lobules or ducts that appear unusual or atypical. Such hyperplasias are sometimes found by mammography. The Nurses' Health Study, which has followed more than 120,000 nurses since 1976, has found that women who have atypical hyperplasias confirmed by biopsy have a moderately higher risk of developing breast cancer compared to women without these tissue changes and a somewhat lower risk than those with LCIS. The risk is highest among premenopausal women. ALH is more strongly linked to premenopausal breast cancer than is ADH. Women who have either ALH or ADH should have an annual mammogram and a clinical breast examination once or twice a year. Because tamoxifen has been shown to reduce the risk of invasive breast cancers in women with either ALH or ADH (particularly those with ADH), it is worth discussing the potential risks and benefits of this option with your physician (see Chapter 5).

Medullary Carcinoma

Looking much like the pink color of brain tissue (the medulla), this cancer has a relatively well-defined, distinct boundary between tumor and normal breast tissue. It accounts for 1 to 7 percent of all breast cancers, and its prognosis is better than that for invasive forms of lobular or ductal carcinoma.

Tubular Carcinoma

Named for cells that look like little tubes, tubular carcinoma accounts for 1 to 2 percent of breast cancers. Although it is an invasive cancer, it rarely *metastasizes* (spreads), even when there are signs that the original tumor has spread to the lymph nodes. Thus, it has a better prognosis than invasive forms of lobular or ductal carcinoma.

Papillary Carcinoma

The cells of this uncommon breast cancer stick out like little papules, or fingerlike projections. This form of cancer is most commonly in situ. On occasion it also contains an invasive component. Both lymph node involvement and metastatic disease are rare. The National Surgical Adjuvant Breast and Bowel Project study found that 2.5 percent of invasive breast cancers were invasive papillary carcinoma.

Inflammatory Breast Cancer (IBC)

In this more advanced form of breast cancer, invasive cancer cells have traveled through the lymphatic channels of the breast and into the lymphatic network of the skin. The cancer cells clog these channels, blocking lymph fluid drainage and causing breast swelling and red, warm skin. Other than skin thickening, frequently there is no other sign, such as a distinct lump or finding on mammography. At first, IBC may look like an infection. Infections usually respond to antibiotic treatment, so a woman who has a breast inflammation that *doesn't* clear up or that clears up only temporarily after one to two weeks of antibiotics should see a breast surgeon. Typically, this cancer is diagnosed with a skin biopsy. This is an aggressive form of breast cancer, and chemotherapy usually precedes surgery.

Paget's Disease of the Breast

First appearing as a reddened sore with flaking skin that mimics eczema on the nipple, this rare cancer progresses to crustiness and oozing that fails to improve. One difference between Paget's disease and eczema is that eczema almost always affects only the areola, the dark area around the nipple, and spares the nipple. A biopsy of the nipple skin will show cancer cells growing up through the ducts and onto the nipple skin. Usually an underlying cancer is discovered. If it is invasive, prognosis is based on the stage of that lesion.

DIAGNOSIS: BREAST CANCER

Shortly before Thanksgiving, Sloan, a forty-three-year-old mother of two, was doing a breast self-exam when she felt a lump she had never noticed before. She was certain it was cancerous. "I knew right away," she said. When she went for a mammogram, that lump turned out to be fine, but the x-ray showed another suspicious area that proved to be an invasive cancer. A definitive diagnosis required a biopsy and several more very anxious days spanning the holiday.

WHAT ABOUT THE OTHER BREAST?

If you have been diagnosed with cancer in one breast, what is the likelihood of developing it in the other breast? Uneasiness surrounding this question bothers many women. Whether you had DCIS or invasive breast cancer, your lifetime risk for a cancer in the other breast can lie between 10 and 25 percent or possibly higher. Those at highest risk are women who have one or more of the following attributes:

- were first diagnosed at a young age
- have a strong family history of breast cancer or known hereditary breast cancer mutation
- have tumors in several areas of the breast
- have an invasive lobular cancer

Taking tamoxifen reduces this risk by roughly 50 percent. Talk with your doctor about this and other risk reduction measures.

While the wait for results is always difficult, as Sloan found, it is standard procedure to do certain imaging tests as well as a biopsy before making a definitive diagnosis of breast cancer.

IMAGES OF CANCER: THE FIRST STEP

Radiologic imaging tests are not perfect, but they often help detect breast cancer at an earlier stage when it is easier to treat. Most likely, you have had one or more of the following imaging tests.

Mammogram

Best known of these tests is the mammogram, an x-ray of the breast. A *screening mammogram* is done when a clinical breast exam is normal. It consists of two views of each breast: an up-and-down view (cranial-caudal, or CC) and a side-to-side view (medial-lateral-oblique, or MLO). A *diagnostic mammogram* is performed to evaluate an abnormality found during a breast exam (a lump, changes in the skin, or nipple discharge) or an irregularity on the screening mammogram. In addition to the standard CC and MLO views, the radiologist also may perform views at other angles, magnification, or compression views.

On a mammogram, interior breast structures appear in shades ranging from white to black. The white areas are mainly milk ducts. The hazy gray and black areas are fat tissue. Abnormalities appear as an opaque white haze called *densities* when they can be seen easily with the naked eye or *calcifications* when they are tiny and best viewed using a magnifying glass. A density with a starburst shape, dubbed *spiculated*, often indicates cancer. Noncancerous densities usually appear as a light spot with a smooth outline and no radiating arms.

Calcifications look like tiny, bright white dots the size of grains of sand. Benign calcifications are usually scattered randomly through both breasts, almost like a snowstorm. Sometimes, benign calcifications that are similar in size and possibly coarse looking are clustered in a small space. When calcifications appear as tiny dots of different sizes and shapes (*pleomorphic*) in a line (*linearly* arranged), they

CLINICAL SIGNS OF BREAST CANCER

A woman may notice abnormalities while touching her breasts or doing a self-exam, or her doctor or another health care professional might find some of these warning signs during a clinical breast exam:

- A lump or mass
- A thickening apparent in one breast and absent in the other
- Skin dimpling (*retraction*) that appears as a pulling in of the skin
- Skin irritation, redness, scabbing, or erosion
- Swelling of the breast with or without redness on the skin
- New nipple inversion (nipple turning inward); many women are born with inverted nipples, which is normal for them
- A reddened or scaly nipple
- Spontaneous discharge other than breast milk from a nipple
- A lump beneath the arm

If you or anyone you know would like information on doing a breast self-exam, contact the American Cancer Society (cancer.org or 800-ACS-2345).

are likely to be inside a duct and generally indicate cancer. Keep in mind that suspicious calcifications will turn out to be benign 70 to 80 percent of the time.

Breast Ultrasound

This test is usually the next step when assessing a suspicious density found on a mammogram or when further evaluating a palpable breast mass. Ultrasound can visualize only small areas of the breast accurately, which is one reason why it is not used as a screening test. High-density sound waves create a picture called a *sonogram* that helps doctors evaluate whether a density is a fluid-filled cyst, a solid mass, or a variation of normal breast tissue. A cyst, which shows up on the sonogram as a black hole or spot because sound waves go through the fluid, is usually benign.

A solid mass appears as a white spot because sound waves echo off it. Generally, a benign mass is horizontally aligned with smooth borders, and one that is malignant is vertically oriented with irregular borders.

Breast MRI

Breast MRI (magnetic resonance imaging) offers a high-resolution method to visualize the breast without radiation. Usually, MRI is used when a woman has a swollen underarm lymph node that is found to contain breast cancer cells, but the cancer cannot be located by physical exam or mammography. (This is called an *occult* breast cancer.)

Sometimes, doctors use MRI to examine the muscles of the chest wall for suspected cancer, because this area can be hard to reach with mammography. MRI has other uses as well. One is to determine the size and extent of a known tumor, particularly for invasive lobular breast cancers, which can be much larger than they appear during a physical exam or on a mammogram. MRI can also reveal whether anticancer drugs being administered to shrink a tumor before surgery (*neoadjuvant chemotherapy*) are working. In addition, breast MRI may be used to check for recurrences after lumpectomy and radiation treatment.

Breast MRI is an expensive and somewhat complex technology that requires special equipment and radiologists who are experienced in interpreting the images. It can produce a false positive result in which a benign abnormality might resemble cancer. Nevertheless, major medical centers are finding that breast MRI, when used with mammography and ultrasound, can be a powerful tool for certain women. Although it can only identify DCIS in 50 percent of patients—and thus isn't useful for routine screening of women at low or average risk for breast cancer—it appears to be more sensitive than mammography alone in women who carry the mutated gene BRCA1 or BRCA2 (see the sidebar "Genetic Tests" later in this chapter).

Breast Ductogram

Occasionally, a specialized type of mammography called *ductography* (or *galactography*) is used to evaluate spontaneous nipple discharge from a single duct in one breast. A doctor inserts a soft, slender, blunt-tipped catheter into the duct and injects a small amount of dye, or contrast medium, that will show up on an x-ray. The procedure must be performed at a time when discharge from the nipple is evident in order to find and check the correct duct.

BIOPSY: THE NEXT STEP

Breast cancer is never diagnosed with imaging tests alone. One or more biopsy techniques are necessary. During a biopsy, a physician removes a tissue sample from a worrisome area so that it can be evaluated under a microscope by a specially trained doctor called a *pathologist* or *cytologist*.

Ask your doctor if it is possible to have a core needle biopsy rather than an open surgical biopsy. That preserves the option, when appropriate, of using chemotherapy before surgery to shrink a tumor enough to allow a lumpectomy rather than mastectomy, if a woman wishes.

Fine Needle Aspiration Biopsy

A doctor uses a slender needle to *aspirate* (draw out) fluid from a cyst or a small amount of tissue from a solid mass. This may be done in the doctor's office. This tissue sample is examined under the microscope to determine whether cancer is present (fluid may also be evaluated this way, particularly if it contains blood).

If the cells prove to be cancerous, the doctor may recommend a large core needle biopsy or open surgical biopsy to learn more about important characteristics of the tumor, such as whether it has estrogen and progesterone receptors, which are explained later in this chapter.

Image-Guided Large Core Needle Biopsy

During a *core needle biopsy*, a doctor numbs the skin and uses a hollow needle the thickness of a pen tip to remove samples of breast tissue. Since the early 1990s, image-guided large core needle biopsy has become the method of choice to evaluate breast abnormalities that are visible on a mammogram or ultrasound but not easily felt by hand.

Calcifications are typically sampled using mammography to guide the needle. Densities can be sampled by ultrasound guidance or mammography, depending on which imaging system can best visualize the density. The procedures are explained in the following sections.

Stereotactic Core Needle Biopsy Using Mammography

During this procedure, the woman lies face down on a specially designed table. Her breast hangs through a hole in the table. Two clear Plexiglas plates compress and stabilize the breast. A hole in one of the plates exposes the breast skin. The doctor numbs the skin and deeper breast tissue, makes an incision the size of a robust freckle, and then inserts the biopsy needle. Using computer-aided technology linked to mammographic images, a radiologist or surgeon views the irregularity while guiding the needle to precisely target the suspicious area. Six to twelve tissue samples are removed through the needle with the help of a vacuum device. The procedure takes about twenty to forty minutes.

Afterward, pressure and possibly ice are applied to minimize bruising. The skin seals over the tiny cut within a few days. No stitches are required. Core needle biopsy may cause some temporary bruising but leaves only a tiny dot for a scar.

This biopsy technique may not be suitable for certain women, including those who have an irregularity close to the chest wall, nipple, or surface of the breast; those with a severe curvature of the spine that makes it impossible to lie flat on the table so that the breast can be properly positioned; those who cannot comfortably lie still for twenty to forty minutes; and those with very small breasts. In addition, calcifications that need magnification to be adequately seen may require an open surgical biopsy.

At experienced centers, 65 percent of women who have this procedure receive a benign diagnosis and can resume annual mammograms unless their doctors advise otherwise. Unfortunately, pathology reports for 25 percent will come back with a diagnosis of cancer. That leaves 10 percent of women whose results are inconclusive. Often, the next step for them is a surgical biopsy.

For example, if the pathology report suggests ADH (explained earlier), a surgical biopsy will help clarify whether that is the extent of the problem (true in 81 percent of cases) or if DCIS (13 percent) or an invasive cancer (6 percent) exists.

If the diagnosis is ALH (explained earlier), a surgical biopsy is usually not necessary. That's because, at worst, the abnormality might turn out to be the noncancerous condition LCIS.

Ultrasound-Guided Core Needle Biopsy

During this procedure, a woman lies on her back with her arm above her head. Ultrasound imaging precisely locates the mass in her breast for biopsy with the core needle. After numbing the skin and deeper breast tissue, the doctor makes a single puncture in the skin to extract three to six separate core needle tissue samples for analysis. A woman may feel pressure but usually no pain. The procedure takes only a few minutes.

Afterward, a bag of ice and pressure is placed on the site for fifteen to thirty minutes to minimize bruising. Usually, women can resume normal activity almost immediately, and the skin seals over within a day or two. No stitches are required.

Open Surgical Biopsy

During an open surgical biopsy, a surgeon makes an incision in the skin and removes all or part of the abnormal tissue for microscopic examination.

An *excisional biopsy* removes the entire area of concern. This is done when the area is small.

An *incisional biopsy* removes a portion of the abnormality. This technique is appropriate for larger lesions, to allow the surgeon to secure a diagnosis while minimizing the effect on the breast's appearance.

When a breast mass or calcifications cannot be felt, *wire localization* may be used to target the tissue to be removed later. After injecting a local anesthetic into the breast, the radiologist inserts a hollow needle into the breast and, while guided by mammography, locates the suspicious area. He or she then puts a thin wire with a hook on the end through the hollow needle and into the breast alongside the lesion. The radiologist removes the needle, leaving the wire in place to serve as a guide to help the surgeon locate the area of breast tissue to be removed.

When wire localization is used, there is a 2 percent chance that the surgeon will not remove the site in question. A miss necessitates a second surgery. Without wire localization, searching for an abnormality that cannot be felt is like looking for a needle in a haystack.

A surgical biopsy can be performed under local anesthesia, intravenous sedation, or general anesthesia, depending on your doctor's recommendation and your preference. The biopsy takes about an hour, with another several hours or less for the recovery period in the hospital. Unlike needle biopsies, a surgical biopsy leaves

GENETIC TESTS

Scientists estimate genetic inheritance underpins 5 to 10 percent of breast cancer cases. If you have been diagnosed with breast cancer, is there any reason to have a test for genetic mutations that raise the risk of developing this disease? For certain women the answer is a qualified yes. Women with a family history of breast cancer—particularly a mother, sister, daughter, or male relative who has had it at a young age, especially if it was diagnosed in both breasts—may have a genetic glitch that increases their odds of developing this disease and possibly has other health implications as well.

The BRCA1 and BRCA2 genes are two well-known sites where mutations that affect breast and ovarian cancer risk may arise. Because these genes are quite large, many different types of alterations in their structure are possible. These mutations may be handed down to children from either the mother or father, although this does not always happen. Certain BRCA1 and BRCA2 mutations occur more often among women of Eastern European Jewish, French Canadian, Mormon, Icelandic, Danish, Norwegian, Swedish, Finnish, Russian, and Hungarian ancestries amongst others. Other mutations are unique to a particular family.

The test for BRCA1 and BRCA2 mutations requires a blood sample. The test cannot tell whether any woman will definitely develop breast cancer, but those with a mutation of BRCA1 or BRCA2 have about a 36 to 85 percent lifetime chance of doing so. The comparable risk in the general population is about 13 percent. Likewise, the lifetime risk of developing ovarian cancer rises from roughly 1.5 percent to 16 to 60 percent among women with a BRCA1 or BRCA2 abnormality. Because ovarian cancer is difficult to detect early, when it is most curable, some women at higher risk opt to have their ovaries removed. This decision may be easier if you have already had all the children you desire.

Ask your doctor or a genetic counselor whether testing for gene abnormalities makes sense for you.

a visible scar and sometimes causes a noticeable change in breast shape. It's a good idea to discuss the placement and length of the incision with your surgeon beforehand. Also ask about scarring, which is discussed further in Chapter 8, and the possibility of changes in the size and shape of your breast.

One in five women is diagnosed with cancer after an open surgical biopsy. Most will need a second breast surgery to make sure all the cancer tissue has been removed along with a safe margin of healthy tissue.

Biopsy Results

The clock can tick very slowly while you are waiting for biopsy results. The pathologist may have findings to report to your doctor within the week, although it can take longer to obtain the results of certain tests.

Amanda waited out one long weekend before meeting with her doctor to go over biopsy results. Despite a suspicious ultrasound the previous week, she couldn't quite believe the news. "Hearing the big C word, cancer!" she recalled thinking, "I'm thirty-one. I'm healthy. I'm not supposed to have cancer. I feel great. Healthy people don't get cancer." As we all know, though, the truth is that they sometimes do.

UNDERSTANDING YOUR PATHOLOGY REPORT

How does a pathologist examine tissue samples and report the findings? Certain procedures are standard, but pathology reports may present the results differently. It's not unusual to have a series of reports because certain test results are available more quickly than others. When you speak with your doctor, he or she can help you glean the important information, including the following.

Tumor Evaluation

The first step after an initial laboratory evaluation identifies cancer cells is to determine whether the cancer is in situ (noninvasive—that is, still contained within the milk-producing gland) or invasive. The pathologist goes on to establish its size and, if it is invasive, looks for other characteristics that may suggest whether the cancer has spread beyond the breast. Size alone only crudely predicts an invasive tumor's potential to spread. Sometimes, tiny tumors spread beyond the breast to other organs and larger ones do not.

When classifying breast cancer, doctors consider the following:

- The size of the tumor

- What the tumor's *grade* is on a scale of one to three, which offers clues to how aggressive the cancer is

- Whether the tumor margins are cancer-free (*clean margins* or *negative margins*)

- Whether the tumor has invaded any blood or lymphatic vessels in the normal breast tissue surrounding the tumor (lymphatic-vascular invasion, abbreviated LVI)

- Whether tumor cells have receptors for estrogen and progesterone

- Whether the protein HER2/neu is present on the cancer cells

- Whether underarm (*axillary*) lymph nodes contain cancer cells (a surgeon must remove one or more of these nodes for examination, as explained in Chapter 3)

- Whether there are signs that the cancer cells have spread beyond the breast and nodes to other parts of the body (*metastatic* disease)

Tumor Staging

Staging is a uniform method used to describe a cancer. It helps your doctors determine your prognosis—how you might do with appropriate treatment—and how to treat the cancer.

When the pathologist examines the tissue, she or he assigns a series of letter and number codes that provide a standardized, shorthand description for three key factors: tumor size, whether lymph nodes are involved, and whether cancer cells have spread to other sites in the body. Recently, the staging system was refined to distinguish the size of the tumor cells found in the lymph nodes. Single cells or small clusters of cells called *micrometastases* are considered less serious than larger tumor deposits called *macrometastases*. Both refer to the lymph nodes and differ from *distant metastases*, which is cancer that has spread to other organs, such as the liver, lungs, or brain, or to the bones.

If the cancer is invasive, your doctor may request blood tests and a chest x-ray to evaluate whether cancer has spread to the bones, liver, or lungs. Usually, bone scans and CT scans are reserved for certain situations, such as more advanced tumors, checking on abnormalities seen in blood tests or x-rays, or following up on symptoms that suggest cancer may have spread. Along with the microscopic examination of cancerous tissue, information from such tests is used to determine the stage of the cancer.

The letter designations for tumor staging are:

- T, which stands for invasive **T**umor size

- N, which stands for extent of lymph **N**ode involvement (this includes micrometastases and macrometastases)

- M, which stands for extent of distant **M**etastases (bones, lungs, liver, brain, and, infrequently, other organs)

These designations are combined to determine a stage (Stages 0 to IV) according to the extent of the cancer. Stages appear in Roman numerals. Stage 0 is the earliest and is used to designate ductal carcinoma in situ without an invasive component. Stage IV is the most advanced and is used when metastatic disease is present. (See Table 1.1.) Consider staging a snapshot of your illness without a lot of fine detail. Even when the prognosis may seem very worrisome, life unfolds differently from woman to woman.

Because staging is so complex, doctors sometimes describe cancer in simpler terms that reflect just tumor size and the number of cancerous nodes. For example, a woman may be said to have a two-centimeter tumor with three positive nodes.

Tumor Margins

A chief goal for your surgeon is to remove the entire cancer plus a narrow margin of healthy—clean—tissue that has no cancer cells that can be seen microscopically.

UNDERSTANDING TUMOR GRADES
- Grade I (cells well differentiated): Score of 3 to 5 points. Cells are normal looking and do not appear to be growing rapidly. Such a low-grade tumor tends to grow and spread more slowly and has a better prognosis than more aggressive cancers.
- Grade II (cells moderately differentiated): Score of 6 to 7 points. Cell characteristics fall between Grades I and III.
- Grade III (cells poorly differentiated): Score of 8 to 9 points. Cells lack features of the tissue of origin and tend to grow more quickly and spread more aggressively.

Table 1.1 Breast Cancer Staging: Diagnosis by the Numbers

To determine your stage, find T, N, and M classifications from your pathology report on this list. For example, the pathology report might describe a tumor that is T1, N0, M0. That means the tumor is Stage I.

Stage Groupings	Stage 0	Stage I	Stage IIA	Stage IIB	Stage IIIA	Stage IIIB	Stage IIIC	Stage IV
T (Tumor)	Tis	T1*	T0 T1* T2	T2 T3	T0 T1* T2 T3 T3	T4 T4 T4	Any T	Any T
N (Nodes)	N0	N0	N1 N1 N0	N1 N0	N2 N2 N2 N1 N2	N0 N1 N2	N3	Any N
M (Metastases)	M0	M0	M0 M0 M0	M0 M0	M0 M0 M0 M0 M0	M0 M0 M0	M0	M1

*T1 includes T1 microinvasion

Understanding the T, N, M Classifications

T = Tumor

T0: no evidence of primary tumor

Tis: carcinoma in situ

    Tis (DCIS): ductal carcinoma in situ

    Tis (LCIS): lobular carcinoma in situ

    Tis (Paget's): Paget's disease of the nipple with no tumor

T1: tumor 2 cm or less in greatest dimension

    T1mic: microinvasion 0.1 cm or less (microinvasion is a small tumor within the breast only)

    T1a: tumor more than 0.1 cm but not more than 0.5 cm in greatest dimension

    T1b: tumor more than 0.5 cm but not more than 1 cm in greatest dimension

    T1c: tumor more than 1 cm but not more than 2 cm in greatest dimension

T2: tumor more than 2 cm but not more than 5 cm in greatest dimension

T3: tumor more than 5 cm in greatest dimension

T4: tumor of any size with direct extension to chest wall, skin, or both

T4a: extension to chest wall, not including pectoral muscle

T4b: edema or ulceration of the skin of the breast or scattered skin nodules confined to the same breast

N = Nodes

N0: no regional lymph node metastases

N1: metastases to 1–3 lymph nodes

N2: metastases to 4–9 axillary (underarm) lymph nodes or to internal mammary nodes (behind the breastbone) that are clinically apparent in the absence of axillary lymph node metastasis

N3: metastases to 10 or more axillary (underarm) lymph nodes or

- in infraclavicular lymph nodes (under the collarbone)
- in clinically apparent internal mammary nodes (behind the breastbone) with 1–3 positive axillary (underarm) nodes
- in supraclavicular lymph nodes (above the collarbone) on the same side as the breast cancer

M = Distant Metastases (Bones, Lungs, Liver, etc.)

M0: no distant metastases

M1: distant metastases present

MX: distant metastases cannot be assessed

Source: *American Joint Committee on Cancer, 2002*

A clean margin helps reduce the risk that cancer will recur in the breast. If the pathologist notes that the margins contain cancer cells or are indeterminate, another surgery may be required to secure clean margins.

Grading Invasive Cancer

Pathologists grade invasive cancer cells based on appearance, which helps indicate how wimpy or aggressive a cancer may be. The grading system considers how cells are arranged in relation to one another and the features of individual cells. Cells receive a certain number of points based on these characteristics and then a grade, as noted in "Understanding Tumor Grades." Recognizable cells that look a lot like the cells of the tissue in which they originated are well differentiated (usually Grade I). Cells that no longer resemble normal breast cells are considered poorly differentiated and receive a higher grade (usually Grade III). Generally, the higher the grade, the more aggressive the cancer.

Lymphatic–Vascular Invasion (LVI)

Tiny collections of cancer cells sometimes make their way into very fine blood vessels or lymphatic channels in the normal breast tissue. Called *lymphatic-vascular invasion* (LVI), this is somewhat worrisome because it suggests an increased risk of lymph node involvement and metastases. Some experts consider it the equivalent of a positive lymph node. One of the findings of my breast cancer, in fact, was lymphatic-vascular invasion. When weighing whether chemotherapy was needed, we took this into account.

Estrogen and Progesterone Receptors

Parked on the surface of cells are molecules known as *receptors* that recognize hormones circulating in the bloodstream. The hormones estrogen and progesterone influence breast maturation and sometimes encourage the development of breast cancer. Normal breast cells and some breast cancer cells have receptors that recognize these hormones.

When breast cancer cells are examined microscopically, the presence or absence of these receptors is revealed and noted in the pathology report. Estrogen-positive (ER+) cancer cells have the estrogen receptor; estrogen-negative (ER−) cancer cells do not. Progesterone-positive (PR+) cancer cells have the progesterone receptor; progesterone-negative (PR−) cells do not.

This is important information for two reasons. ER+ cancers tend to grow more slowly. Plus the growth of cancer cells with estrogen or progesterone receptors can be slowed or stopped by the use of *selective estrogen receptor modulator* (SERM) drugs, such as tamoxifen (Nolvadex). SERMs work by blocking access to estrogen receptors, which starves the cells of stronger estrogens that otherwise could speed tumor growth.

HER2/neu

Small amounts of a protein called *HER2/neu* are also found on the surface of healthy breast cells and some breast cancer cells. Roughly 25 to 30 percent of breast cancer cells have too much HER2/neu. Because this protein stimulates cancer cell growth, malignant cells that overproduce HER2/neu tend to spread more quickly than those with normal amounts of the protein. These cancer cells can often be destroyed by the drug trastuzumab (Herceptin).

2

ASSEMBLING YOUR CARE TEAM

◉

When I discovered my own breast cancer, I had several advantages not shared by many women. After more than a decade as a breast cancer surgeon, and seven years as director of the Comprehensive Breast Health Center at Brigham and Women's Hospital in Boston, the medical terms and statistics were completely familiar to me. Equally important, I knew many excellent doctors, nurses, and other health professionals. I could—and did—call upon them for help.

Trusting those who will treat and care for you is essential. Finding knowledgeable, caring health professionals can seem daunting. This chapter will guide you through assembling a cancer care team that will help you make the leap from hearing the news to taking the necessary action that may save your life. But this is just part of the help you need. Gathering emotional support, which is vital to your treatment and recovery, is discussed here, too, along with suggestions for friends and family who are ready to help.

BUILDING A STRONG TEAM

Most likely, you've already started to search out the medical professionals who will help guide your treatment. Perhaps a primary care doctor who confirmed your concern over a lump or the radiologist or surgeon who performed your biopsy set the wheels in motion with one or two referrals. But you'll probably need to muster a larger health care team to see you through treatment and recovery.

Team Members

Some of the professionals who will have a permanent or temporary place on your team are described under the following categories, which will help you understand what they do.

Breast Imaging and Certain Biopsies

One of the first team members you may meet is a *mammography technologist*, who is trained to take mammogram films, or an *ultrasonographer* or *ultrasound technologist*, who uses an ultrasound to view the internal structures of the breast. A *radiologist* interprets the results of these tests.

The radiologist—who might be called a mammographer, breast imager, or woman's imager—is a doctor trained in the uses and interpretation of a range of imaging tests, including mammogram, ultrasound, and magnetic resonance imaging (MRI). Radiologists also perform minimally invasive biopsies with guidance from imaging equipment, such as a core needle biopsy guided by ultrasound or mammogram, as well as wire localization to help guide a later surgical biopsy. (See Chapter 1.)

Surgery

A *surgical oncologist* is a surgeon who specializes in cancer surgery. A *general surgeon* may perform cancer surgeries, including breast procedures, in addition to noncancer surgeries, such as removal of the gallbladder and appendix. The term *breast surgeon* is applied to a surgeon whose practice focuses on women who have benign or cancerous breast conditions. A *plastic surgeon* is trained to perform breast reconstruction after mastectomy, as well as other types of plastic surgery.

Ideally, you'll want to choose a surgeon who focuses exclusively or mostly on breast cancer. A British study published in 2003 reviewed the cases of more than eleven thousand women with breast cancer. Five-year survival rates were significantly higher among patients whose surgeons performed more than fifty breast cancer surgeries yearly compared to surgeons who performed fewer than ten. Some states, such as New York, track the number of procedures a surgeon performs. Call your state department of health to see if it offers a way to obtain this information or ask the surgeon directly.

When choosing a plastic surgeon, find out what percentage of the practice is devoted to breast reconstruction and which types of reconstruction the surgeon prefers to do. Some plastic surgeons will not perform free flap surgery (see Chapter 7), for example, so if you wish to have this type of reconstruction, you need to find another surgeon.

Find out whether your surgeon's hospital is accredited by the Joint Commission on Accreditation of Healthcare Organizations (jcaho.org or 630-792-5000). If your surgery might be performed at an ambulatory (day surgery) center, check with the Accreditation Association for Ambulatory Health Care (aaahc.org or 847-853-6060). Accreditation helps ensure certain standards of care.

Pathology

A *pathologist* is a doctor who is trained to examine tissue and fluid samples for signs of cancer or other abnormalities and to test it for important characteristics, such as hormone receptors and proteins. Based on gross (visible to the naked eye) and microscopic evaluations plus a variety of laboratory tests, the pathologist determines the type of cancer and its stage as described in Chapter 1. It is worth knowing who looked at your tissue samples and slides because the pathology findings determine diagnosis and treatment. Ask about the pathologist's level of experience and what percentage of his or her time is spent on breast cancer. Your surgeon may recommend that your slides be forwarded to a breast pathologist for a second review.

Chemotherapy and Other Anticancer Medications

A *medical oncologist* is a doctor who has specialized training in chemotherapy, hormonal therapy, and other medications designed to combat cancer. Some medical oncologists focus mostly or exclusively on caring for women with breast cancer.

An *oncology nurse* has specialized training in administering chemotherapy and handling many other aspects of cancer care. While you probably will not have the opportunity to choose an oncology nurse, you will often be cared for by one who is part of a larger oncology practice.

Radiation

A *radiation oncologist* is a doctor trained to use a variety of radiation techniques to treat cancer. A medical *radiation physicist* and *dosimetrist* help plan the delivery and dose for radiation treatments. A *radiation technologist* positions you correctly at each session and administers daily treatments. A *radiation oncology nurse* cares for you over the course of treatment and will recommend ways to ease side effects.

Social and Psychological Services

An *oncology social worker* helps patients and their families handle social and psychological repercussions of cancer. For example, an oncology social worker might offer individual, family, or group counseling or help locate services to help make life run smoothly after surgery or during other treatments. Mental health professionals who offer therapy or counseling include *psychiatrists* (medical doctors trained in psychology who are licensed to prescribe medications) and *psychologists* (who have varied training). Preferably look for someone who has experience working with women who have breast cancer.

Nutrition

A *registered dietitian*, who has had course work and clinical training in nutrition and has passed qualifying exams, or a *licensed dietitian/nutritionist*, who has passed qualifying exams in nutrition, can advise you on a healthy diet or ways to sidestep certain side effects of treatment. (See Chapter 12 for more information.)

Physical Therapy

A *physical therapist* is trained to help people regain range of motion and strength after surgery or illness. Experience working with women recovering from surgery for breast cancer is preferable. (See Chapter 11 for more information.)

Comprehensive Center or Nearby Hospital?

Your local hospital may be convenient, but drive time shouldn't be the major factor in deciding where to get treatment if your health insurance allows some latitude. "I thought, why not go where the research is and the cutting edge is, where they're going to be talking to each other?" said one woman, summing up the reasons she decided on a well-regarded academic hospital that is a National Cancer Institute (NCI)–designated cancer center instead of obtaining care closer to home.

Comprehensive breast or cancer centers offer up-to-date treatments. Because they treat so many cancer patients, staff members tend to have well-honed skills. Their goal is to provide rapid, accurate diagnosis and a broad range of state-of-the-art treatment options. Close cooperation and communication is fostered among the health professionals that provide that care. Sometimes, complementary and alternative therapies are offered, too.

Ideally, consider a NCI-designated cancer center (a list is available at www.can cer.gov/cancercenters/centerslist.html). Not all states have these centers, so another option would be to select a comprehensive center affiliated with a medical school where staff is likely to have access to the latest information in the field. A third option is to seek a hospital offering a multidisciplinary team that convenes a weekly conference during which a variety of specialists discuss cases. A large institution might seem too impersonal, but usually you will be matched with one surgeon and one oncologist, and often one nurse practitioner. At each visit, you will see the same health care team, which allows you to build up rapport and trust.

If you live far from a comprehensive breast or cancer center, consider traveling to one for a consultation that can then be used to guide care locally. If you can make only one visit, the best time to do so would be when all your pathology tests are completed and you are ready to meet with a medical oncologist who can offer an opinion on chemotherapy, hormonal therapy, and immunotherapy. Slides, imaging tests, and pathology reports should all be reviewed then. Sometimes, laboratory tests or imaging studies will be repeated to clarify earlier results. At times this can affect a diagnosis or previously recommended treatment. Usually, the oncologist then writes a detailed report with his or her recommendations to local specialists who will care for you. Sometimes, the written report is supplemented with a phone call.

If you can make two visits, I recommend making the first one immediately after your breast cancer is diagnosed. At that time, imaging studies can be reviewed to make sure that the small possibility of another cancer in the breast has not been overlooked. At this meeting, you can also discuss whether you are a candidate for a lumpectomy and determine whether chemotherapy should be used to shrink the tumor before surgery. The second meeting would then come when all the information is available for the medical oncologist, as described in the previous paragraph.

GATHERING RECOMMENDATIONS AND ASSESSING SPECIALISTS

Sometimes, a cancer care team is put together for you, for example, if your health insurance plan restricts you to a specific list of doctors. A choice of several teams or networks that work well together might also be available through a comprehensive breast or cancer center or a multidisciplinary hospital program. When gathering recommendations and assessing cancer specialists, keep the following tips in mind.

Cast a Wide Net

Start by asking your primary care physician, gynecologist, and breast imager, as well as your breast surgeon if you already have one, for recommendations. Sometimes, the list is short due to insurance networks or locale. Be prepared to cast your own net to ensure that you know all your options for the best possible care. Contact the American Cancer Society for a list of specialists and cancer care centers in your region (cancer.org or 800-ACS-2345). Ask friends and have them ask their friends for recommendations. Speak with women who have had breast cancer about their experiences.

Check Certifications and Expertise

Doctors should be board-certified in their specialties (radiology, surgery, pathology, medical oncology, radiation oncology). Check by contacting the American Board of Medical Specialties (abms.org or 866-ASK-ABMS).

• Surgeons may also be a fellow of the American College of Surgeons (abbreviated after a doctor's name as F.A.C.S.; facs.org or 800-621-4111), which typically requires board certification plus a certain level of experience and competence as attested by peer recommendations. Some may be members of the Society of Surgical Oncology (surgonc.org or 847-427-1400), which requires that the majority of a surgeon's practice be devoted to caring for cancer patients. Plastic surgeons who are members of the American Society of Plastic Surgeons (plasticsurgery.org or 888-

475-2784) have been certified by the American Board of Plastic Surgery or the Royal College of Physicians and Surgeons of Canada.

- Oncologists of all types—medical, surgical, radiation—and other cancer care professionals may belong to the American Society of Clinical Oncology (ASCO; asco.org or 703-299-0150). ASCO membership presents opportunities for multi-disciplinary mingling and a way to keep abreast of rapid changes in breast cancer care. (An ASCO website called People Living with Cancer, plwc.org, offers information for patients.)

- Mental health professionals, including therapists and social workers, may belong to the American Psychosocial Oncology Society (apos-society.org or 866-APOS-4-HELP). Membership in the Association of Oncology Social Work (aosw.org or 215-599-6093) ensures master's degree social work training for those professionals and some expertise in working with people with cancer.

- Nutritionists and physical therapists should be licensed or certified in their own fields and preferably have experience and training in working with women who have breast cancer. The American Dietetic Association (eatright.org or 800-877-1600) and the American Physical Therapy Association (apta.org or 800-999-APTA) may help you locate professionals in your area.

Academic appointments at a university medical center, research affiliations, or a position at a teaching hospital suggest that a cancer care professional is likely to be apprised of new research as well as widely used therapies or techniques.

Bring Capable Support

"Bring somebody with you to every meeting," advised Greta, a lawyer, whose spouse fortunately could join her to listen, ask questions, and take notes. "I did not hear things. The only thing I was listening for in my little head was: Did they say I would die? Did they say there's a high likelihood I would die? Did they say what percentage likelihood I'm going to die? That's all I was hearing. I'm somebody who asks questions for a living and listens pretty well, but I could not listen at all. I was completely and utterly terrified."

Not everyone has a partner, of course, and those who do may not always find that that person is able to be helpful at this particular time. When choosing support, keep in mind that anyone who cries louder or worries more than you do may not be of much assistance. A caring friend or relative with a logical mind or background in health care might be especially helpful. Often, even when a partner, parent, or close friend can join you, it helps to use a tape recorder as well so that information given can be reviewed later. Ask before taping, of course.

Make It a Choice

Seeing more than one specialist is helpful. Not only will you get more than one perspective, but it allows you to consider how personality fits in. Skills, expertise, and up-to-date knowledge are obviously very important, yet this is likely to be a long-term relationship, especially where your surgeon and medical oncologist are concerned. Do you feel comfortable asking questions? Do you feel your case is being considered individually? Will you want to see this doctor year in and year out? Will he or she want to see you?

Keep Options Open

Whenever possible, do less initially. Waiting to take action until a breast surgeon and medical oncologist offer their opinions makes sense in certain circumstances and may expand your treatment options. For example, occasionally a woman who desires a lumpectomy rather than a mastectomy will have an invasive cancer that is relatively large with respect to the size of her breast. The surgery necessary to remove the cancer may have a negative effect on the way her breast will look. A core needle biopsy rather than a surgical biopsy preserves the opportunity for using chemotherapy prior to lumpectomy to attempt to shrink the tumor, which minimizes the amount of breast tissue that needs to be removed at the time of the lumpectomy.

Here is another example. A promising new breast cancer medication may be available through a clinical trial designed to test how well it works in women with early-stage cancer. While the medication may have proven helpful for women with advanced breast cancer, it wouldn't yet be available to women with earlier stages of cancer. A woman would only be a candidate for such trials before a surgical biopsy or other surgery was done to remove the tumor. Thus, diagnosis rendered after a core needle biopsy, rather than an open surgical biopsy, can give a woman more options in this situation.

Why Get a Second Opinion?

Sometimes, the decisions facing a woman diagnosed with breast cancer seem quite clear. However, even reasonable professionals may disagree over how treatment might best proceed based upon their interpretation of key studies. In my case, two excellent radiation oncologists offered me different advice on whether I should include radiation as part of my treatment. Ultimately, I felt comfortable forgoing radiation after considering the data on how women with breast cancers similar to mine fared with and without radiation.

Not every doctor trained to diagnose or treat breast cancer keeps up with the latest information and techniques. One woman, who lives in an area of the Northeast where several excellent cancer centers are within a few hours by car or train, first visited a local breast surgeon recommended by her gynecologist. He suggested doing a surgical biopsy quickly to evaluate a lump that looked suspicious during imaging tests. Get it over with, he urged. Why wait and worry? "If he had done that surgery, it would have limited my treatment and some of the other options I had, which he had never told me," she said. Fortunately, better advice prevailed, and she chose a more accomplished breast surgeon, who suggested having a radiologist perform a core needle biopsy. Later, when all the pathology information was available, the surgeon performed a lumpectomy and node evaluation during the initial and only surgery, thus sparing her from the need for two separate bouts with anesthesia.

Obtaining a second or even a third opinion from different breast specialists can be very important. Don't be too shy or feel too rushed to do so. This is common practice and no insult. If a doctor rushes you—perhaps by saying he or she can fit you into the surgery schedule very quickly—it may be wiser to continue your search for advice rather than giving in to fear or pressure. The cancerous cells in your breast have been there for several years, perhaps even a decade. Usually, it is safe and sensible to take a few weeks to thoroughly evaluate these very important decisions.

SHOULD YOU JOIN A CLINICAL TRIAL?

New treatments for breast cancer are routinely tested in clinical trials. Should you participate in one? If you do so, you will receive either standard therapy today considered most effective for your type of breast cancer or a therapy being tested to see if it offers advantages over the current standard, such as improved survival or fewer side effects.

Among the possible benefits listed by the National Cancer Institute is high-quality cancer care. If you do not receive the newer therapy being tested, you will receive the best standard treatment, which may be as good or better. If you do receive a new treatment that is proven to work, you may be among the first to benefit. And, of course, you are contributing to medical knowledge that may help others in the future.

There are possible drawbacks, too. New treatments do not always result in outcomes better than or as good as standard care. Or, sometimes, there are unexpected side effects or side effects that are worse than those of standard treatment. Health insurance does not always cover all patient care costs during a study.

Phase I trials (20 to 80 people) evaluate safety, establish safe dosages, and identify side effects. Phase II trials (100 to 300 people) consider effectiveness as well as safety. Phase III trials (1,000 to 3,000 people) further evaluate effectiveness, check side effects, make comparisons to standard treatments, and collect additional information to aid with safety.

Not all treatments—standard or new—work for everyone, but every woman who considers joining a clinical trial has certain rights and protections.

- Joining a study is entirely your decision. It may be only one of your treatment choices, so ask about all of your options.
- Throughout a study, doctors and nurses will follow your response to treatment carefully.
- If researchers learn that a treatment harms you, you will be taken off the study right away. You may then receive other treatment from your own doctor.
- You have the right to leave a study at any time.
- You have the right to be given all the facts about a study before deciding whether to participate (informed consent). Informed consent forms are long, so it's best to go over them with your physician and again at home, possibly with someone you trust, and then ask any questions that arise.

Your cancer care team can tell you about clinical trials you might be eligible to join or you can check clinicaltrials.gov (888-346-3656) for nationwide information on current clinical trials supported by federal and private funds.

JUMPING HURDLES

Choosing a great medical team is stressful for anyone, but some women may feel they have more hurdles to leap. Finding health-care providers and other women who understand their unique needs and concerns isn't always easy.

The Mautner Project, the national lesbian health organization, notes, for example, that lesbian women may be less likely to obtain regular health care because of concerns about coming out to health providers and the lack of a need for contraceptive services that forge health care links for heterosexual women. Worries about family support if sexual identity has caused rifts or has never been acknowledged and wondering whether partners will be welcome and included during consultations and treatment may ratchet up stress. That can interfere with early detection.

African American women are more likely than white women to die of breast cancer even though fewer will develop this disease after age forty-five (before that birthday, the risk of breast cancer is slightly higher in African American women). Exactly what accounts for the increased mortality rate is not known, but it may be traced partly to larger tumors and later stages of breast cancer at diagnosis. Latina and Hispanic women also may suffer from delays in diagnosis that contribute to lower survival rates despite the fact that their overall risk of breast cancer is less than that of white or African American women.

Cultural myths—that bruising a breast or touching it too often can trigger cancer, or that talking about cancer is unlucky—might play a role in getting less than optimal care, as could embarrassment that hobbles open discussion about breast cancer, concerns about prejudice, or worries about navigating the health-care system. Breast cancer only affects older women, right? Not true, but this persistent myth can impede diagnosis in young women, who may dismiss or not know the warning signs or may have to advocate strenuously to receive the appropriate tests.

Women who have little money or education tend to have fewer choices in medical care. Sometimes, language is the barrier and family members are serving as impromptu translators. That can be a problem if a relative is struggling to understand new medical terms and statistics, too. Some hospitals and cancer centers can provide a medical translator in addition to having family members attend visits whenever possible. Many of the larger breast cancer organizations offer an extensive range of publications in addition to help in Spanish and may be able to provide information in other languages as well (see Resources).

No one has a perfect solution to any of these dilemmas, but the following organizations may provide some help:

- The Mautner Project, the national lesbian health organization (mautnerproj ect.org or 202-332-5536, voice and TTY), or community organizations that focus on lesbians and bisexual women

- Sisters Network (sistersnetworkinc.org or 866-781-1808) for African American women

- National Alliance for Hispanic Health (hispanichealth.org or 202-387-5000)

- Young Survival Coalition (youngsurvival.org or 212-206-6610)

Local breast cancer organizations or chapters of the American Cancer Society may offer certain free or low-cost services, such as transportation, places to stay, wig banks, and sources of financial assistance. The Susan G. Komen Breast Cancer Foundation lists several resources for financial assistance, too (komen.org or 800-IM-AWARE).

WHEN TO LEAD, WHEN TO FOLLOW

With luck, you've assembled a wonderful cancer care team. Now who calls the shots? A collaborative effort is best. While these professionals certainly have medical expertise, you're the expert when it comes to your life. Do you want to know everything, or does delving into detail just make you more anxious? Does directing the action empower you, or do you feel comforted by having someone else take charge? One woman—a scientist, it is true—wanted to review her biopsy slides under the microscope and regularly discussed finer points of recent studies with her oncologist. Another woman made a beeline for a classic question when faced with four different options for treatment. "What would you tell your wife to do?" she asked her physician.

Your doctor should present what is known, tailor the information to your situation, and try to put the risks, benefits, and limits of current research in perspective. Often, the treatment choice that works best hinges on your tolerance for risk and your lifestyle rather than an obvious advantage that one path has over another.

When women have early-stage breast cancers, for example, survival rates are the same among those who choose mastectomy or lumpectomy plus radiation. Yet one woman may worry less if she has a mastectomy while another feels hugely relieved by the chance to have a lumpectomy.

Chemotherapy also can be viewed in different lights. Some women embrace its ability to crush cancerous cells, while others view its toxic actions with great anxiety. Ultimately, these feelings feed into decisions about whether a survival advantage offered by chemotherapy might outweigh its disadvantages.

Share your goals and concerns with your cancer care team. Knowing your priorities can help them supply the information you need to make the choices that are right for you.

GATHERING EMOTIONAL SUPPORT

Breast cancer is like a storm blowing in out of nowhere on a day that seemed sunny enough just moments before the rain sluiced down and jagged lightning flashed. Even if you had been sufficiently uneasy about a breast lump to see your doctor, it is shocking how quickly your life can change as vague worry gives way to certainty. As one woman noted, once the diagnosis sinks in, you cross an invisible bridge that separates you from even the most loving friends and family who haven't personally dealt with this illness.

Usually, anxiety and depression wax and wane and may spike at certain flash points. The moment you hear your diagnosis can be a terrible shock. It may even seem like a series of body blows as the results of imaging tests, biopsies, and laboratory tests are translated into pathology reports. Comforting a newly diagnosed friend, Juliana told her, "I promise you this is the worst part. It's hard to imagine that it's harder than chemo, harder than surgery, but it is. I remember I went to the grocery store, walked around in a circle, and went home. That shock, it's horrible. You think you're going to die. That is the hardest, hardest part."

Other times that are especially difficult are the stretch between diagnosis and starting treatment, treatment itself, and, perhaps more surprisingly, right after active treatment ends—a time most women might expect to celebrate. Distress is also natural around follow-up visits and, of course, if any recurrence or treatment failure occurs.

A report from the National Cancer Policy Board and the Institute of Medicine in 2004 underscored the importance of psychosocial services in alleviating some of the distress felt by women dealing with breast cancer. Crisis counseling, psychotherapy, support groups, sexual counseling, complementary therapies (such as yoga, acupuncture, and relaxation techniques), and workshops intended to buff a woman's self-image are all examples of psychosocial services.

Women who have access to these services generally enjoy a better quality of life and feel less distressed. Unfortunately, as few as one in ten breast cancer patients receive such services, possibly because they are not offered or paid for by many health insurance plans, because care is fragmented and nonmedical needs fall between the cracks, or because women are unaware that such help exists or feel too embarrassed to ask for it.

A bit of foresight and a few requests may do a good deal to improve your days as you move through treatment toward recovery. Gather sources of strength and healing that can complement your medical care. Vital support can flow from many quarters, including those described in the following sections.

Family, Friends, and the Merest Acquaintances

When people hear of your situation, a surprising number will step forward to offer their love, support, and help. Drink it in. One of the hardest tasks there is, especially if you are typically an independent, private person, is accepting help from others. I found this hard myself, despite feeling buoyed by the outpouring of affection and offers of assistance. I encourage my patients to learn to say yes to everyone. If you have all the help you need right now, ask people if you can call upon them later.

Katherine, who had worked for years as an oncology social worker before her own diagnosis of breast cancer, has seen the issue from both sides. She had watched family members wringing their hands over wanting to help but being rebuffed and women with breast cancer feeling conflicted over how to remain independent. "Are you independent by struggling along by yourself or by getting people to give you the help you need so that you can keep up your routine?" she wondered. When it was her turn, said Katherine, she felt no such conflict. "I've done a lot of good things for people in my life. Now it's my turn to need that and that's the natural order of things." She was happy to let people bring food or cook dinner while she rested, shovel her walk in the winter, and drive her to appointments. Telling people they are doing a good job is just as important as letting them know what you need, noted Katherine.

Other Women Who Have Had Breast Cancer

Very often, women who have been down this road themselves will try to smooth the path for you even if you barely know them or never knew of their breast cancer until you mentioned yours. This may happen informally as word gets around, or if it would be helpful, your medical team may provide visitors or callers from their own files or by drawing on Reach to Recovery, a service offered by the American Cancer Society. By talking with women who have been through similar experiences you can often gain information or insights into specific treatments, reconstructive surgery, and life after breast cancer not available to most doctors. Simply knowing that women resume active, meaningful, and joyful lives after treatment may make a difference, too.

Support Groups

Ask your medical team for suggestions or contact the American Cancer Society (cancer.org or 800-ACS-2345), the Wellness Community (wellness-community .org), or other organizations listed earlier in this chapter and under Resources. Also check local hospitals and community newspapers for listings. Some women prefer support groups that meet face-to-face. The mix of women in the group can make a big difference, so think about attending two meetings before considering another group if the first doesn't click.

Annette credited her support group with offering good advice on getting through treatment that her doctor hadn't mentioned. Sophie skipped her second group meeting after sizing up the fact that no one else was as young as she was or seemed to share her specific concerns. Juliana found she enjoyed forming her own support group, a handful of like-minded pals with breast cancer who meet up occasionally for a raucous lunch or dinner.

Can't get out of the house? Live in an isolated area? Practically every major cancer organization offers some variety of online support groups, bulletin boards where you can post messages and get responses, and chat rooms where you can type back and forth with respondents in real time. These are accessible to anyone with a computer and Internet hookup. While these resources are often quite helpful and are available around the clock, be aware that chat groups and bulletin boards sometimes spread questionable or frightening information. Before you get worried, check the information with a reliable source, such as your doctor or the National Cancer Institute (cancer.gov or 800-4-CANCER).

Psychiatrists, Psychologists, or Social Workers

Psychotherapy or counseling that focuses on treatment challenges, coping strategies, and locating specific assistance can be very helpful. Either can offer a supportive setting to acknowledge and mourn changes in body image and sexuality as well. Antidepressant or antianxiety medications also help enormously under certain circumstances. If possible, choose a therapist or social worker experienced in working with women with breast cancer. A cancer center may have helpful professionals on staff, or you can locate one through the American Psychosocial Oncology Society (apos-society.org or 866-APOS-4-HELP).

Religious or Spiritual Leaders

Even if you are not deeply religious or spiritual, you may find these connections comforting now. Seek support from your own religious or spiritual leader, or find someone empathetic to your situation at nearby places of worship, such as a church, a synagogue, a mosque, or another religious or spiritual center to which you feel drawn.

HANDLING DISTRESS, DEPRESSION, AND ANXIETY

When the demands or challenges you face outweigh perceived resources, you're likely to feel distressed. Each time you figure out how to cope with one set of circumstances, you may be pressed to take the next unfamiliar step. No wonder women dealing with breast cancer often swing between feeling very distressed and remarkably calm.

Depression and anxiety are reasonable responses to a difficult situation but should be transient feelings, not everyday moods. Typically, these feelings clamp down after the initial disbelief and shock over your diagnosis recedes, and then they ease as time goes by and you adapt yourself to a "new normal." New circumstances—surgery, your first chemotherapy treatment, or a worrisome symptom—may bring these feelings rushing back.

Despite what you might imagine, most women faced with breast cancer are not crushed by depression or anxiety. According to the National Cancer Institute, about 15 to 25 percent of people with all kinds of cancer can be considered clinically depressed, and while 44 percent of cancer patients report anxiety, only 23 percent experience significant anxiety. That said, prolonged depression or anxiety can make both daunting challenges and the simplest tasks seem insurmountable. Supportive therapy or counseling, possibly along with antidepressants or antianxiety medications, can do a great deal to help.

Talk with your doctor or contact a mental health professional if prolonged bouts with symptoms of depression interfere with your daily life. Suicidal thoughts or feelings are reason to seek help immediately. The following are common signs of depression:

- Sadness, inappropriate guilt, or feelings of worthlessness

- Loss of interest or pleasure in many activities

- Difficulty concentrating

- Marked slowness or agitation

- Insomnia

- Fatigue (this may have many causes related to your cancer treatment, however, and a recent, randomized trial showed relieving depression did not affect fatigue in cancer patients, so speak with your medical team about this symptom)

- Significant changes in appetite, such as eating constantly or eating very little

- Frequent intrusive thoughts about illness and death

Likewise, talk with your doctor or a mental health professional if symptoms of anxiety, such as those that follow, interfere with your daily life:

- Jitteriness or nervousness

- Feelings of tension, fear, or apprehension

- Unexplained sweating or trembling

- Panic attack (racing heartbeat, trouble breathing, sweating, sense of impending doom, which may sometimes seem like symptoms of a heart attack)

- Being afraid to close your eyes at night lest you never wake up again

PARTNERS, FAMILY, AND FRIENDS

An entire cast of people in addition to your health care team will play pivotal and cameo roles in the coming months. Your diagnosis has shaken them up, too. Some will step forward to help immediately, while others may retreat in a way that proves painful all around. Often, partners, family, and friends—the very people who give your world shape and joy—want desperately to help but feel unsure and scared themselves.

Helping Hands, Loving Words

If someone you love has been diagnosed with cancer, you may wonder how you can help. Laura decided to jump in with both feet and act as a manager for Sloan, a very close friend. That way, said Laura, Sloan could pour her energy into making medical decisions and getting well. Laura made a list of the phone numbers and e-mails of everyone who had offered help and contacted others who might wish to join in once they heard the news. She asked these people how they wished to assist and talked to Sloan and her husband about what was needed. "Food was at the top of the list because they had two young children," said Laura. She organized a schedule so that abundant home-cooked meals were delivered every few days for months on end. When transportation, company, or child care was desired, it was easy enough to round up willing souls by referring to the master list of helpers.

Not everyone has managerial skills, but most of us can cook or buy a healthy meal, shop for groceries or run errands, pick up children, run a vacuum, provide occasional taxi service, and so on. No job is too small. Even waiting for deliveries or offering to supervise repairmen or contractors can be a huge help when a woman is feeling overwhelmed or exhausted. If you have more specialized skills—a knack for doing minor home repairs, perhaps, or gathering information—you may find that these are welcome, too. Ask what is needed and make specific suggestions of your own, or offer to take on any task necessary during a given time slot on specific days each week.

Listening well is a great trait in friends and family, but cracking a joke or two or sending a silly card rarely comes amiss if your relationship was lighthearted in the past. It's hard to be solemn all the time even when breast cancer looms. Your friend may long for comic relief, not just a shoulder to cry on. Greta fondly remembered that a pal who had been treated for breast cancer herself played "Chemo Fairy" by making sure goodies awaited Greta each time she went for chemotherapy. On one occasion, it was a beautiful baby pillow so that time spent in the infusion chair would be more comfortable; on another day, it was a big homemade chocolate chip cookie to munch. "One time she brought me two T-shirts. One said, 'Stick 'Em Up, Sister,' and the other one, for my husband, said, 'It's All About Me,' which he didn't get at all." It lightened the atmosphere for others undergoing chemotherapy sessions on the same days, noted Greta. "Everyone in the room was waiting for me to arrive to open the Chemo Fairy's package. It was a really great idea."

Perhaps you can't offer help or make these gestures because you're still tongue-tied about what to say. Plenty of people worry so much about saying the right thing that they fail to say anything. Silence can be hurtful, so try to break the ice. "When you're worried about what to say, you're focused on yourself. Focus on the other person," advised Sloan. "Try something. If you blow it, you're still trying to connect with me and I will know. How could you make it worse? I think I'm going to die and I'm afraid and I'm feeling alone because no one will talk to me about it."

While overly pointed questions, unsolicited advice, or frightening stories understandably might be rebuffed, genuine feeling and warm wishes rarely go wrong. Even a few simple words make a fine start. "Don't ignore people," said Annette, who endured her share of averted eyes. "I taught my kids to just say to people, 'I hope this is a good day for you' or 'I hope you're having a nice day.'"

Don't underestimate the power of a letter or card. I have saved every single letter I received. Some are so beautifully written, so inspiring, so thoughtful and poetic that I read them time and again. While e-mail exchanges and phone calls help you stay in touch, more old-fashioned snail mail is very special. The time you spend putting pen to paper, looking up an address, and finding a stamp will truly be appreciated.

Giving Help, Getting Help

The sonic boom that trails a breast cancer diagnosis rocks many worlds. Family members and close friends often find they could use some help themselves.

Children benefit when a parent can simply and directly explain breast cancer and treatment plans. Deciding what to explain, when, and how can be tricky, though. Some women choose to break the news right away. Some wait until they have a handle on their own emotions and a good sense of how treatment will proceed. Still others ask their partner or a trusted relative or friend to say the first few words.

Understanding, questions, and fears will vary depending on a child's age and personality. Generally, children have three very basic questions: Are you going to die? Who is going to care for me? How will this affect my life? Breast cancer treatments can certainly prompt a fourth: Why do you have to have treatments that make you tired and sick? If you are at a loss about how to start or proceed with the conversation, an oncologist, an oncology social worker, or your child's pediatrician may be able to suggest ways to explain the illness and address worrisome issues. The American Cancer Society also has information on talking to children about breast cancer. Cancer care centers, hospitals, or local organizations may offer support groups for children as well. A few books for children are listed in the Resources section.

Remember, children want to help, too, so give them opportunities to express their love and concern, or brainstorm with them over a few simple ways they might do so.

Partners, spouses, and close friends who are caregivers frequently need both hands-on help and emotional support. While wrestling with abundant fears they may be more likely to squelch than share, those closest to you often scramble to become impromptu nurses, medical experts, and all-around assistants. It is totally appropriate to focus on the woman who is struggling with a breast cancer diagnosis and certainly natural to ask how the children are holding up. Often, a partner or spouse is pretty well ignored, though, and might certainly appreciate kind words of support or inquiries.

My husband, Bill, recalled how surprised and appreciative he felt when, several months into my treatment, a friend and colleague asked him how he was coping with our situation. "The challenges of breast cancer have a ripple effect on the whole family," he notes. "What's normal doesn't exist anymore." The entire landscape shifts as uncertainty reigns and priorities that once felt so important recede compared to what truly matters.

Understanding friends can certainly help care for the caregiver by checking in regularly and offering to assist with specific tasks. Support groups available through many of the organizations listed earlier in this chapter or under Resources can help, too. Yet it is also important to go a little easy on yourself when someone you love is being treated for breast cancer. Be mindful of your needs as well as hers. Spouses and partners may find the book *Breast Cancer Husband: How to Help Your Wife (and Yourself) Through Diagnosis, Treatment, and Beyond* helpful (see Resources). Consider counseling to help air and ease your own anxieties. Try to carve out time to decompress and attend to your mental, physical, and spiritual well-being. It is not a sign of weakness or selfishness and can help you to be a source of strength.

3

MAKING DECISIONS
ABOUT SURGERY

⊙

More than many other illnesses, breast cancer demands that you take an active role in your care. Two different treatments may offer the same chance for controlling the cancer while affecting your daily life in different ways. Often, the final decision hinges on quality of life and personal preferences. This chapter details different types of surgery, including lymph node surgery. It also discusses lymphedema, a swelling and discomfort in the arm that is sometimes a side effect of lymph node surgery.

MAKING YOUR FIRST
TREATMENT DECISIONS

In most cases, breast cancer surgery can be performed several weeks after the diagnosis. Before making a decision, you can take the time to learn about all of your treatment options and how they are likely to affect the way you will look and feel. It's not necessary to decide about surgery while you're still in shock over your diagnosis. You may choose to seek a second opinion, preferably from a breast cancer specialist at another breast center, hospital, or medical school. The more informed you are, the more likely it is that you will find a treatment appropriate for your cancer and your needs and be satisfied with that choice.

Most breast cancers are treated with a combination of *local therapies*, designed to eliminate cancer cells in the breast and minimize the chance of the cancer return-

---

Some of the material in this chapter also appears in the *Brigham and Women's Hospital Breast Surgery Guide*, developed by staff of the Comprehensive Breast Health Center at Brigham and Women's.

ing in this primary (original) site, and *systemic* treatments, which send drugs through the bloodstream to reach and destroy cancer cells that may have spread to other parts of the body. Breast surgery and radiation therapy are the most common treatments for the local control of breast cancer. Systemic treatments include chemotherapy, hormonal therapy with drugs such as tamoxifen (Nolvadex), and other agents such as trastuzumab (Herceptin), a monoclonal antibody designed to target specific cells.

Originally, doctors believed that cancer simply grew larger and outward. However, research and experience have demonstrated that even in the early stages of the disease, cancer cells can separate from the primary tumor and spread through the bloodstream and lymphatic system to start new tumors in other organs or bones. It is the spread of cancer cells to other parts of the body (metastatic disease) that is life threatening, so systemic treatment plus local treatment is often necessary.

Overview: Lumpectomy Versus Mastectomy

Is *lumpectomy* (breast-conserving surgery) or *mastectomy* (full removal of the breast) the best choice for you? This is a difficult decision, yet you can make it with your surgeon's help. An additional good source for information is the National Cancer Institute booklet *Surgery Choices for Women with Early-Stage Breast Cancer* (see Resources).

Six clinical studies with follow-up information spanning more than two decades show that long-term survival is equivalent between women who have a lumpectomy plus radiation and those who have a mastectomy. In 1990 such compelling data persuaded the National Institutes of Health to recommend lumpectomy rather than mastectomy as an effective way to treat the primary cancer among most women with Stage I or II disease. Five years later, an analysis of all randomized studies showed that long-term survival rates were equal for mastectomy and lumpectomy in early-stage breast cancers. Thus, when weighing choices, you and your doctor can consider rates of local recurrence in the breast or chest area and cosmetic and lifestyle concerns.

Tumors Grow Slowly

Given what we know about breast cancer growth rates, it makes sense biologically that both procedures offer the same chances for survival. Most often, breast cancer cells form relatively slow-growing tumors. It can take about one hundred days—more than three months—for just one cancer cell to divide into two. After another hundred days, those two cells would divide into four and so on. By the time a mass of cells is big enough to detect on mammography or feel during a breast exam, it has been present for several years or longer.

If those cancer cells were biologically capable of gaining access to the lymphatic channels or bloodstream, they did so long before the day of your planned surgery. So whether your surgeon excises the cancer plus a small rim of surrounding normal breast tissue (a lumpectomy) or excises the cancer plus a larger rim of normal breast tissue (a mastectomy) has no bearing on the cells that may have already scooted into the general circulation. Cancer cells that are not biologically capable of migrating from the breast can be safely removed with either lumpectomy or mastectomy.

Treatment Influences Later Options

After either surgery, there is still a chance cancer might recur in the remaining tissue. The risk is slightly higher with lumpectomy than with mastectomy. The implications of a local recurrence differ.

When a woman has a lumpectomy, the radiation dose she is given falls just short of the maximum amount tolerable for the skin and underlying tissue. Usually, when a recurrence occurs, it is found during a mammogram or can be felt during a breast exam. If cancer recurs, it would not be safe to apply a full course of radiation treatment a second time. Thus, a mastectomy would be recommended at that point. It's worth noting, however, that local recurrence of breast cancer following a breast-conserving surgery does not appear to raise the risk for metastatic disease.

That's not the case if a woman has had a mastectomy. Here, a recurrence may look like a red, raised skin lesion, often lying on or close to the scar, an area where the blood supply is weakest and possibly beyond the reach of cancer-fighting immune cells. Alternatively, the recurrence might be a painless lump in the pectoral muscle, which lies under the chest wall skin. When the original cancer was present, some of its cells moved up into the skin or down into the chest wall muscle via local lymph channels or blood vessels.

Sometimes, these cells can set up shop, generate their own blood supplies, and grow large enough to be detected clinically. Knowing that cancer cells did this in the chest wall after a mastectomy raises suspicion that similar tumor clusters have spread through the same lymph channels or blood vessels and may lurk elsewhere in the body. Laboratory blood work and imaging studies to evaluate the lungs, liver, and bones, common sites of metastases, will be performed to evaluate this. In some women, a chest wall recurrence after a mastectomy is the first sign of metastatic disease that is too small and limited to detect elsewhere but may blossom at a later time. Thus, the woman is monitored very closely by her physician.

BREAST-CONSERVING SURGERY

Breast-conserving surgery aims to fully excise a cancer plus a slender rim of surrounding healthy tissue (*clean margin*) (Figure 3.1). The terms *lumpectomy, wide local excision, partial mastectomy, quadrantectomy,* and *tylectomy* interchangeably describe surgeries in which this is done. Usually, general anesthesia, a spinal block, or intravenous sedation with local anesthesia is used during the surgery.

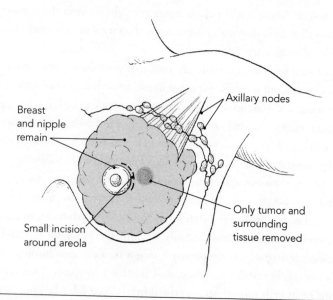

Figure 3.1 Lumpectomy. In this breast-conserving procedure, the surgeon removes only the cancer and a margin of normal surrounding tissue. The nipple and the areola are left intact. For central cancers, the surgeon may place the incision on the border of the areola in order to obtain the best cosmetic effect and to allow the woman to wear a bathing suit or low-cut dress without a scar showing. If the tumor is invasive, lymph nodes under the arm may be removed for analysis.

SHRINKING THE TUMOR

Neoadjuvant chemotherapy, which shrinks a tumor before surgery, is becoming increasingly common, particularly for T2 and T3 breast cancers. (See Table 1.1, "Breast Cancer Staging: Diagnosis by the Numbers," in Chapter 1.) Sometimes, it helps make a lumpectomy rather than a mastectomy possible. It also minimizes the tissue that needs to be removed, thus ensuring less of a change in breast appearance.

Nowadays, many breast cancers are identified during a mammogram as a density or cluster of calcifications or a combination. Before a lumpectomy, a mammographer will use magnification views to more accurately assess the extent of calcifications. If the area is fairly small, a single wire is placed to help guide the surgeon in removing the cancerous tissue. If calcifications are more widespread, several wires may be placed to bracket the area.

The surgeon excises the specimen and inks it with six different colors (one for each side) so that it will be possible to tell which edge corresponds with a given edge within the surgical cavity. A second—or even third—surgery, called a *reexcision*, can be performed if one or more of the edges of the specimen have positive margins. This is not unusual. When it happens, the six-color inking allows the surgeon to excise selective additional tissue from the appropriate area. Importantly, this technique minimizes the amount of tissue removed while helping to ensure safe, clean margins. When less tissue is removed, it is more likely that the breast will look much like it originally did. As more tissue is removed, a smaller breast and change in contour become more likely.

The inked specimen is sent to mammography. There, an x-ray confirms that the calcifications or density is contained in the specimen and assesses how close the mammographic finding is to the specimen's edge. If the lesion is close to an edge, the mammographer can match the image with the edge ink color and relay this information to the operating room. The surgeon can then remove a slender rim of tissue from the corresponding spot in the cavity with the hope that a second, later surgery will not be required.

Cancer cells, especially ductal carcinoma in situ (DCIS), are difficult or impossible to see or feel in the operating room. A pathologist will microscopically assess the removed tissue, or *specimen*, for clean margins. *Negative margins* mean no cancer cells were found near the edge of the specimen; *positive margins* indicate that cancer cells were at the edge.

Sometimes, further surgery is needed. If the original mammogram showed calcifications, or calcifications with a mass, another mammogram will be performed after the surgical site has healed. If calcifications are still present, residual disease may be present as well. At that point, a reexcision with wire localization to guide the surgeon would be performed.

After a Lumpectomy

As you heal, it may take several weeks for the initial discomfort to ease. However, lumpectomy does not affect the underlying pectoral muscles, so after the discomfort subsides, you won't notice any impact on physical activity or have any exercise restrictions.

If surgery creates a noticeable difference in size between your two breasts, you may wish to consider wearing a breast form in your bra to plump up volume, having a *reduction mammoplasty* (surgery to reduce the other breast), or having a mastectomy and breast reconstruction.

MASTECTOMY

During a mastectomy, the entire breast, nipple, and areola (dark circle of skin around the nipple) are removed. The incision usually leaves a horizontal or gently sloping scar. Several variations of mastectomy remove different degrees of surrounding lymph nodes and muscle. The operations are performed under general anesthesia or with an epidural block plus intravenous sedation.

Simple (or Total) Mastectomy

The surgeon removes the entire breast, nipple, and areola but not the lymph nodes or muscles underneath. Women who have in situ cancer or invasive cancer with a negative sentinel node biopsy frequently have this operation.

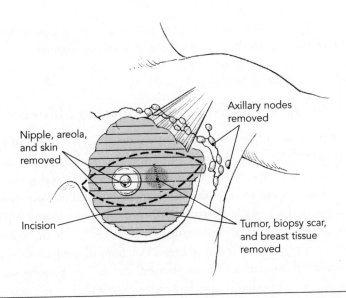

Nipple, areola, and skin removed

Axillary nodes removed

Incision

Tumor, biopsy scar, and breast tissue removed

Figure 3.2 During a modified radical mastectomy, the surgeon makes an incision and removes the breast tissue plus the nipple and areola as well as axillary lymph nodes. If breast reconstruction is not planned, the surgeon removes much of the skin of the breast as well.

Modified Radical Mastectomy

The surgeon removes the entire breast, nipple, areola, and pocket of fat containing lymph nodes in the underarm (axillary nodes) (Figure 3.2). Women who have invasive breast cancer that has spread to the lymph nodes commonly have this operation, as do women with invasive breast cancer who are not candidates for sentinel node biopsy.

Radical Mastectomy

Rarely performed today, this extensive operation removes the entire breast, the pectoral muscles beneath it, and all the axillary lymph nodes up to the collarbone. Lymphedema, swelling and tenderness of the arm that is described later in this chapter, is a common side effect. Overall, modified radical mastectomy has proven equally effective with fewer side effects and few women are diagnosed with such advanced local disease that this extensive surgery would be required.

Skin-Sparing Versus Non-Skin-Sparing Mastectomy

If a woman plans to have immediate breast reconstruction, at the time of mastectomy the surgeon removes the nipple, areola, and recent incisions due to breast cancer biopsies while sparing as much of the native skin of the breast as possible. The skin serves as an envelope to cover the reconstruction. Called *skin-sparing mastectomy* (Figure 3.3), this procedure is particularly helpful when a muscle flap reconstruction is chosen because it allows the surgeon to use less skin from the abdomen or back, which may make the reshaped breast look more pleasing cosmetically.

If immediate reconstruction is not planned, the surgeon removes sufficient breast skin to achieve a smooth, flat surface on the chest wall. This *non-skin-sparing*

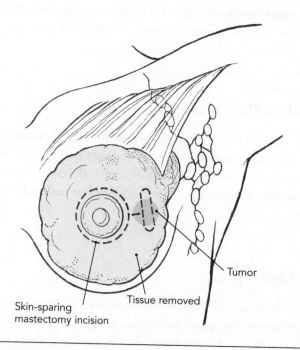

Figure 3.3 The surgical technique for a skin-sparing mastectomy is illustrated above. You can compare this with the modified radical mastectomy illustrated in Figure 3.2.

mastectomy enables a woman to more comfortably wear a breast form, if she chooses to do so.

Subcutaneous Mastectomy

During this uncommon operation, the surgeon removes breast gland tissue but leaves the skin, nipple, and areola intact in an effort to provide a better cosmetic result. However, research has shown that breast gland tissue comes very close to the undersurface of the areola. Surgeons cannot leave a viable flap of areolar skin without also leaving behind breast tissue at risk for developing into cancer. Sparing the nipple raises the same risk since glandular tissue courses through it. Usually, when the nipple and areola are left behind, they feel quite numb, but some women actually develop bothersome pain (*dysesthesia*). Given all of these points, subcutaneous mastectomy is rarely performed.

After a Mastectomy

Generally, surgeons allow women to start a formal exercise rehabilitation program three to six weeks after surgery. Because surgery typically spares the pectoral muscles, there are no activity restrictions. Because of initial postoperative pain, some women will not have moved their shoulder much for several weeks.

That can contract and shorten the pectoral muscles, limiting shoulder range of motion. Scar tissue at the mastectomy site and possibly where lymph nodes were removed may also affect comfortable movement. Rehabilitation initially involves stretching exercises that help you regain full range of motion in the affected shoulder. Direct massage of scar tissue by a physical therapist is often beneficial and complements stretching.

When a Lumpectomy Isn't an Option

Sometimes, lumpectomy isn't an option even if that is a woman's preference. My journey through the early weeks of breast cancer is certainly proof of this. At first, I thought the tiny skin retraction in my breast that I had noticed was just a flaw in the mirror. You know, like a fun house mirror: move in one direction, you're skinny, but move in the other direction, you're not. No matter where I moved, this tiny, tiny dimple didn't go away. Ultimately, it proved to be a sign of breast cancer.

With that knowledge, I set forth in a steadfast effort toward breast conservation (lumpectomy to the laywoman). One surgery was followed by another and yet another as my surgeon tried valiantly to get clean margins. Eventually, I learned there was not one cancer in my breast, but rather three. I couldn't choose between having a lumpectomy or a mastectomy but required a mastectomy. At the time, my health seemed very much out of my control, yet in the end, I found the surgery and recovery easier, physically and emotionally, than I had imagined.

Unfortunately, circumstances sometimes dictate situations where the choice between lumpectomy and mastectomy evaporates and physicians on your team will be steadfast in recommending mastectomy. In my case, two factors played into this: multicentric disease and an extensive intraductal component, as described in the following sections.

Multicentric Disease

A lumpectomy excises a single tumor with a rim of surrounding normal tissue. Occasionally, two very closely aligned tumors (*multifocal disease*) can be excised in a single specimen. This is usually followed by six weeks of radiation treatments to minimize the chance of a local recurrence in that breast.

Two or more cancers existing in separate areas of the breast are called *multi-centric disease*. In this case, only rarely does removing the two separate cancerous regions followed by radiation therapy offer an acceptably low risk of recurrence. One reason is that the separate tumors harbor a cluster of genetic mutations in the tissue between the tumors. These cells may be almost ready to evolve into cancerous cells themselves. Another reason is that removing two separate areas of the breast, then using radiation treatment, can cause more extensive scarring. That may make any recurrence of the cancer harder to identify.

Extensive Disease in the Duct

Usually, when a woman has DCIS (cancer contained within the milk duct) only a small portion of the milk-producing gland is affected and it is possible to remove it with a rim of normal tissue. However, sometimes cancerous cells course through the length of most of the duct or maybe even several ducts. This is called an *extensive intraductal component* (EIC). So much of the breast might need to be removed that what remains would no longer look pleasing to a woman. Sometimes, closely aligned clusters of calcifications apparent in a good deal of the breast on a mammogram signal this condition. At other times, the mammogram may appear normal and the extent of hidden (*occult*) DCIS is found only when the pathologist reviews the tissue under the microscope. Often, multiple surgeries are performed, as in my case, in hopes of achieving clean margins. After my mastectomy, the pathologist found that DCIS occupied more than half of my breast.

Appearance

Sometimes, the efforts to excise a tumor and secure clean margins would make a woman's breast look unacceptable cosmetically, so she might opt for a mastectomy and possibly reconstruction afterward. Some women prefer to wear a breast form, and still others choose to leave their bodies unadorned (see Chapters 6 and 7).

Radiation

Not every woman can undergo radiation treatment. Radiation is not an option if, for example, a woman is pregnant or has previously had substantial amounts of radiation to the chest perhaps because of previous breast-conserving surgery, Hodgkin's disease, or non-Hodgkin's lymphoma. Usually, a specific site on the body can receive radiation treatments only once. Too much radiation can cause even healthy tissue to die. When radiation therapy is not an option, a mastectomy will lower the risk of local recurrence more than lumpectomy alone.

Some other conditions, such as scleroderma and lupus, can also make a woman a poor candidate for radiation.

Personal Preference

Personal preference plays into this decision, too. A woman may not feel strongly about preserving her breast for a number of reasons. She might want to reduce anxiety she may otherwise feel over follow-up mammography and breast exams if she has a lumpectomy. She might live hours away from the nearest radiation facility and it could be impractical for her to move to another town for six weeks. The extent of her tumor may be such that she would prefer the way her body looked clothed after a mastectomy coupled with reconstruction or a breast form or left as is.

Lymph Node Surgery

Illness-causing bacteria and viruses and even cancer cells are frequently caught and destroyed through the work of the lymphatic system. Lymph channels throughout the body carry a thin, milky fluid, which is filtered through the soft, bean-shaped *lymph nodes* and ultimately drains into the bloodstream. The nodes also produce infection-fighting white blood cells. Unlike blood, which the heart pumps around the body, only pressure from your circulatory system and the massaging action of your muscles keep lymph flowing along.

Axillary Nodes

The lymph nodes in the underarm area (*axillary nodes*) are the major drainage sites for the lymphatic system in the breast. They are divided into three levels based on their relationship to the pectoralis minor muscle on the chest wall. This muscle fans across the chest from the shoulder to the breastbone. Level I nodes can readily be found in the lower underarm by placing your hand there and pressing the fat pad against the ribs. They may be difficult to feel because they can blend into the fat pad. Level II nodes rest high in the underarm directly beneath the pectoralis minor. Level III nodes are found between the top border of the muscle and the collarbone. These nodes are hard to feel even on a slender woman with thin chest wall muscles. (See Figure 3.4 on page 63.)

During surgery for an invasive breast cancer, the surgeon usually removes one or more lymph nodes. A pathologist examines these under a microscope to see if cancer cells are present. Generally, the fewer nodes containing cancer (*positive nodes*), the earlier the stage of the cancer. (For more on staging, see Table 1.1, "Breast Cancer Staging: Diagnosis by the Numbers," in Chapter 1.) Any positive lymph node means the odds that the cancer has spread, or metastasized, are greater than if the lymph nodes are negative. Although cancer may potentially spread through the blood vessels, negative nodes mean metastases are less likely.

Even in the early stages of the disease, cancer cells can separate from the primary tumor and spread through the bloodstream and lymphatic system to start new tumors—*metastatic disease*—in other organs or bones. In the era before screening mammography, women with breast cancer were often diagnosed only after they had developed more advanced disease in the breast. At that time, doctors believed that the cancer simply grew larger and outward and that performing a radical mastectomy, which removes the breast, pectoral muscles of the chest wall, and all the axillary lymph nodes up to the collarbone, would afford a woman her best chance of surviving the disease.

Although this turned out to be untrue, this operation removed the axillary fat pad with all three levels of lymph nodes. Many women suffered side effects, including loss of underarm sensation and limited shoulder range of motion. The surgery also disrupted the vessels that drain lymphatic fluid from the arm back into the general circulation. The fluid would back up in the arm, creating permanent swelling termed *lymphedema*. Interestingly, a distinct, though small, group of women never developed this condition. They had an extra-wide lymphatic channel or channels that coursed around the back of the shoulder. This anatomic variation was able to accommodate all of the lymph fluid draining from the arm.

Axillary Dissection

An *axillary dissection* is removal of the underarm lymph nodes. Researchers have found that if a breast cancer is to spread to the axillary nodes, positive nodes will first be confined to the Level I region. It is unusual for the cancer to skip Level I and go to Level II and very unusual for the cancer cells to skip Levels I and II and be found in Level III. Knowing this and hoping to leave undisrupted lymphatic channels behind to minimize the chance of lymphedema, surgeons began leaving Level III nodes alone. Instead, they removed only the fat pad containing the ten to twenty nodes in the Level I and II regions.

Sentinel Node Biopsy

Up to 25 percent of women who undergo axillary dissection develop lymphedema even when Level III nodes are left intact. Yet no evidence of cancer is found in the nodes of as many as two-thirds of the women who have this surgery. Now node-negative women can be identified through a less invasive procedure, a *sentinel node biopsy*. During this surgery, only the first node to receive lymphatic drainage from the site of the primary tumor—the sentinel node—is removed and analyzed. The remaining nodes and lymph channels are left intact, thus minimizing the chance of lymphedema.

How Sentinel Node Biopsy Is Performed

A dye injected around a known breast cancer is taken up by lymphatic channels and carried to the first draining underarm node (Figure 3.4). This sentinel node (and possibly one or two other closely aligned nodes) is removed. It will be examined twice, first by the pathologist during surgery and a second time in more detail afterward. If the sentinel node is cancer-free, the other nodes downstream in the lymphatic basin are also presumed to be negative, and you can be spared further underarm surgery. Thus, most of the lymphatic channels are preserved and your risk of lymphedema is minimized.

If the sentinel node contains cancer cells, a fifty-fifty chance exists that other nodes under the arm may as well. At that point, several options emerge:

• **Traditional axillary dissection:** Along with the underarm fat pad, the remaining Level I and II nodes can be removed to evaluate the extent of disease. If you are having a mastectomy, this information can help determine whether chest wall radiation afterward is required. If you are having a lumpectomy, knowing how many lymph nodes are positive for cancer helps in planning the extent of the radi-

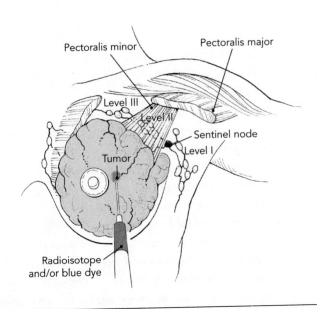

Figure 3.4 To help determine the stage of an invasive cancer, the axillary (underarm) lymph nodes are examined under the microscope for cancer cells. In conventional lymph node surgery, the surgeon removes Level I and II nodes. But removal of these nodes disrupts lymph channels and may injure nerves. In sentinel node biopsy, the surgeon locates the first node into which the tumor drains (the sentinel node) and examines it for the presence of cancer cells. To identify the sentinel node, the surgeon injects the tumor with a radioisotope and/or blue dye, which travels through the breast lymph channels to the first node in the underarm chain. This sentinel node is removed and examined microscopically for signs of cancer.

ation field, and particularly whether Level III nodes around the collarbone should be irradiated.

• **Radiation therapy to the nodes:** Leaving the nodes in place and using radiation therapy is most applicable if you are having a lumpectomy and there is only a very small amount of cancer in the sentinel node; that is, it is not congested with or replaced by cancer cells. Then the radiation oncologist can extend the breast radiation field to encompass the axillary nodes. Preliminary research suggests that this may lessen the odds of lymphedema developing, and multiple clinical trials

Locating the Sentinel Node

When mapping the sentinel node, the doctor first injects a small amount of either a radioisotope or blue dye near the tumor.

The radioisotope technetium is administered several hours to one day before the breast surgery. After the injection, a scan evaluates if it is draining into the axilla. Rarely, the first site of drainage is to the internal mammary lymph nodes, which lie behind the breastbone in the center of the chest. Before making any incision, the surgeon scans the armpit with a gamma probe, a device like a Geiger counter. This relays an audible signal—a beep—over the radioactive sentinel node, indicating precisely where to make the incision.

If the technetium does not locate the node, the surgeon may inject isosulfan blue dye around the tumor immediately before the operation. It drains through the lymphatic system. After the skin incision is made, the axillary fat pad is carefully inspected to visually identify the blue, draining lymphatic channel leading to the blue sentinel node. Unlike technetium, the blue dye carries a slim risk of provoking an allergic reaction. On rare occasions, this can be severe and life threatening. The blue dye also may permanently stain the surrounding breast skin a pale blue. For these reasons, many surgeons prefer technetium and reserve blue dye as a backup if the technetium fails to identify the sentinel node.

to further evaluate this are under way. Whether this approach fully treats the site so that cancer will not recur is still under investigation. Initial results seem promising.

• **Observation only:** Sometimes, a woman and her doctors choose no further treatment. Instead, her physicians will closely monitor the underarm nodes with periodic, careful physical examinations.

False Negative Results with Sentinel Node Biopsy

The major concern with sentinel node biopsy is the possibility of *false negative* results, in which the sentinel node is thought to be cancer-free and a cancerous node is left behind. Research estimates that the false negative rate ranges from 1 percent to as high as 11 percent. The most experienced centers and surgeons have the lowest false negative rates. To be certified by the American College of Surgeons

SENTINEL NODE WHEN A WOMAN HAS DCIS

By definition, *ductal carcinoma in situ* (*DCIS*) is breast cancer cells sealed within an intact duct without access to the lymphatic or circulatory systems. However, when axillary node dissection is performed during a mastectomy for DCIS, positive nodes are identified in 0 to 4 percent of cases. So how did the cancer cells reach the lymph nodes?

In fact, a small number of cancer cells broke through the gland wall and invaded surrounding tissue in what is called a *microinvasion*. The gland wall has been breached by an invasive ductal breast cancer measuring less than two millimeters. That's smaller than a pinhead.

If DCIS was diagnosed by core needle biopsy and you plan to have a mastectomy, your surgeon may recommend a sentinel node biopsy. Sometimes, an unsuspected invasive cancer is found during mastectomy, as it was in Natalie's case. Her surgeon had urged her to do a sentinel node biopsy just as "insurance" and was surprised herself when the pathologist found evidence that cancer had reached that lymph node.

In a 2000 study from Brigham and Women's Hospital, researchers looked at women who had an 11-gage-G-DVA (directed vacuum-assisted) core needle biopsy that diagnosed DCIS. After breast surgery was performed and the pathologist microscopically reviewed slides from the lesion, an invasive cancer was identified in 12 percent of the cases.

A 1989 study from the University of California at San Francisco highlights the fact that sometimes an invasive cancer is present but may not be visualized using standard pathology evaluation methods. The researchers evaluated 115 mastectomy specimens thought to contain only DCIS. Each specimen was sectioned, as if slicing a loaf of bread, and each slice was x-rayed. Any calcifications or other irregularities were thoroughly evaluated microscopically with multiple slides.

The odds of microinvasion varied with the size of the specimen. It was 0 percent in specimens measuring forty-five millimeters or less, 17 percent in specimens measuring forty-six to fifty-five millimeters, and 48 percent in specimens measuring fifty-six millimeters or larger. No patients with DCIS specimens measuring fifty-five millimeters or less had cancer cells in the axillary nodes. Among the twenty-five patients whose specimens measured fifty-six millimeters or more, twelve (48 percent) had microinvasion; two of these patients (17 percent) had positive axillary nodes.

When extensive DCIS is suspected and a woman will be having a mastectomy, this research suggests reasons to consider sentinel node biopsy. Because the breast must be intact to map the node, both procedures must be performed during the same operation. If a lumpectomy is planned, there is no rush to evaluate lymph nodes at the same time. Usually, no invasive cancer will be identified. If one is, sentinel node biopsy can be performed as a second surgery.

to perform this type of node biopsy, a surgeon must reliably identify the cancer status of sentinel nodes in at least thirty consecutive operations.

RECOVERY AFTER SURGERY

Recovery differs from woman to woman and depends partly on the extent of the surgery. Discuss with your surgeon the following issues and any concerns that you have.

Discomfort

Pain is very subjective. Some women find they need little or no pain medication after surgery. Natalie was uncomfortable after her initial lumpectomy and more so after a reexcision that included a sentinel node biopsy. She found node biopsy the most painful. When she had a mastectomy, she was surprised to feel very little pain at all and was happy to turn down narcotic pain medication. Other women experience considerable pain or discomfort with either operation and really need narcotic pain medication.

I tell my patients this is the time to be comfortable, not stoic. Pain makes healing and activity difficult. Gradually increasing appropriate activity, such as walking and stretching exercises permitted by your surgeon, can actually help you recover faster and more completely.

When you are discharged from the hospital, you will be given a prescription for narcotic pain medication, such as Tylenol (acetaminophen) combined with codeine or Percocet (acetaminophen with oxycodone). Take it as directed for pain relief without worrying about addiction. Waiting too long to quell pain makes it harder to relieve. To minimize nausea, take pain medications after eating.

If the prescribed medication doesn't work or you experience nausea, vomiting, or dizziness, call your surgeon. An alternative that causes you fewer side effects can be prescribed.

Narcotics often cause constipation. To help prevent this, add fruits and vegetables and bran muffins or cereal to your meals. Drink plenty of fluids and take an over-the-counter stool softener, such as docusate sodium (Colace), starting on the very first day you take a narcotic.

Narcotics can make you sleepy. If you need to remain alert while on pain medications, discuss the options with your nurse or surgeon.

Driving

Do not drive after taking narcotics. Depending on your surgery, you may be asked to wait several weeks to drive anyway because you must be able to move freely to observe oncoming traffic and react quickly without being limited by pain or weakness.

Incision Care

After surgery, your incision will be covered with a dry sterile dressing. The skin around it may feel thickened or firm. These changes are normal. In about three weeks, the incision will be mostly healed and you can massage the area with vitamin E or an over-the-counter cream, such as Mederma, to help minimize scarring (see Chapter 8). Within a few weeks to several months, the scar will begin to soften.

Drain Care

A drain to siphon off lymphatic fluid is usually placed at the time of a mastectomy or axillary dissection and removed a week or two later. (No drain is necessary after a lumpectomy or sentinel node biopsy.) After leaving the hospital, you need to empty the drain whenever it fills one-third of the way and record the amount of fluid. Do this in the morning and before you go to bed. Check your drains periodically to make sure they do not become too full. If the bulb becomes full during the day, you will need to empty it more often.

A little bit of leakage around the drain site is normal. If a blockage occurs, drainage may stop suddenly and noticeable leaking may occur. Try milking the

EMPTYING AND CLEANING THE DRAIN

Follow these guidelines:

1. Gather all supplies, including a measuring cup.
2. Wash and dry your hands.
3. Take the stopper out of the bulb and empty the fluid into the measuring cup.
4. Grasp the entire bulb in your hand and squeeze it tightly. Then reinsert the stopper.
5. Record the amount of fluid collected.
6. Flush the fluid down the toilet.
7. Wash and dry the measuring cup and place it with the drain output record sheet.

drain tube if this happens. Hold the tubing tightly near your skin with one hand. Then pinch the tubing with the other hand and slide your fingers down toward the bulb. Gripping the tube with a small alcohol pad makes this easier. This should help dislodge blockages. Do this at least twice a day until the drain is removed. Call your surgeon's office if there is still no drainage.

Gradually, the amount of fluid collected in twenty-four hours will decrease and the liquid may change from cherry red to reddish yellow to a straw color. When the total collection over the course of a day is less than an ounce (30cc)—about half of a Dixie cup—the drain can be removed. Call your surgeon for an appointment to do this.

After the drain is removed, the hole will be covered with a small gauze dressing for a day or two. You can remove this once the small hole seals itself.

Possible Complications and Side Effects of Surgery

Breast surgeries may cause complications, such as the following:

• An infection at the incision site (reddened skin, swelling, and discomfort). This should be treated with antibiotics. Infrequently, it requires a return trip to the operating room to wash out the surgical cavity.

- A *hematoma* (an accumulation of blood in the surgical cavity), which can be painful and cause striking bruising. Although unusual, this may occur immediately after surgery while a woman is in the recovery room or several days later. Generally, hematomas are caused by a small blood vessel called an *arteriole*. The wall of the arteriole has muscle fibers that can constrict and close off the vessel during the surgical procedure. Hours after the surgery, when the muscle fibers begin to relax, the divided end of the arteriole reopens and bleeding begins. A large hematoma requires follow-up surgery during which the surgeon removes it and seals off the source of the bleeding.

- A *seroma* (an accumulation of lymph fluid in the surgical cavity), which may cause swelling and discomfort without bruising. If this keeps you awake or interferes with daily activities, your surgeon can drain it through a needle. This is done in the surgeon's office.

Nerves

Sensory nerves in the breast arise from between the ribs, course through the breast, and mushroom onto the skin. During a mastectomy, many of these nerves will be cut, causing permanent loss of sensation on that side of the chest. You probably will regain some sensation around the edges, but the scar area almost always remains numb. During axillary surgery, sensory nerves (intercostobrachial nerves) that exit from between the ribs and supply feeling to the underarm and back of the upper arm are often divided, leaving these areas numb.

Rarely, the long thoracic nerve (LTN) or thoracodorsal nerve (TDN) is cut. The LTN brings branches to the serratus anterior muscle responsible for keeping the scapula (wing bone) flat against your back. Dividing the LTN causes the scapula to poke out somewhat, a cosmetic deformity that has little impact on shoulder strength. The TDN branches into the latissimus dorsi muscle, which allows the shoulder to rotate and the arm to pull inward toward the body. Losing this function can make it challenging to push upward out of a car seat or the bathtub, close the trunk of a car, or perform a lat pull-down at the gym.

Asymmetry

If you are very large-breasted, losing one breast may cause an imbalance severe enough to pull your spine out of alignment. Back discomfort and pain result. If you choose not to have breast reconstruction, you might consider making the remaining breast smaller (*reduction mammoplasty*) to improve your balance.

LYMPHEDEMA

Lymph vessels carry *lymph*, a protein-rich fluid containing water, fat, bacteria, and fragments of old blood cells from the arm to larger channels in the underarm and, ultimately, to the main circulatory system. When surgery or radiation alters these channels, there may not be enough remaining channels to drain all the lymph fluid from the arm. Those remaining around the shoulder will dilate due to increased lymphatic pressure as they take over the work of those channels lost to surgery. Sometimes, this doesn't work well. Fluid then backs up and accumulates in the arm.

The result is *lymphedema*, a swelling of the arm and hand that affects 10 to 25 percent of women after an axillary dissection. It ranges from barely noticeable to a very obvious, uncomfortable enlargement that may disable the arm. Lymphedema may appear soon after breast surgery or even months or years later. While lymphedema can be short-lived, more commonly it is a permanent condition that may wax and wane somewhat. For Sophie, lymphedema occurred transiently after packing and lifting many boxes while moving to a new home. Otherwise, it rarely bothers her. Repeated, severe episodes during which swelling overwhelms the arm and hand may cause tissue inflammation, produce rough, leathery, thickened skin, and harden underlying fat tissue. Greater numbers of lymph nodes excised and underarm radiation therapy raise the risk of lymphedema. Obesity is believed to do so, too.

Minimizing Risks

Typically, the risk of lymphedema is minimal after sentinel node biopsy, so most surgeons do not suggest restricting the use of the arm. Check with your surgeon, however.

If you had an axillary dissection, the following steps may help prevent lymphedema. For more information, contact the National Lymphedema Network (lymphnet.org or 800-541-3259).

Avoid High Heat and Burns

Limit sun exposure and wear sunscreen when in the sun. Likewise, avoid extreme heat from the sun and while bathing or washing dishes. Do not use a sauna or hot tub. These steps minimize extra lymph production.

Take Care of Skin

Try to avoid injuries because attendant infections can cause scarring and narrowing of lymphatic vessels. Bathe with an antibacterial soap, such as Dial or Lever 2000. Apply a hypoallergenic moisturizer on the arm and hand to keep the skin moist (twice daily in dry winter months). Wear protective gloves while washing dishes or gardening. Avoid pet scratches and bites, especially with kittens, which can carry cat-scratch disease. Wear long sleeves and insect repellent when outside during insect season. Use an electric shaver, wax, or laser hair removal if you wish to remove underarm hair. If you do use a razor blade, stand in front of a mirror and take great care to avoid nicking the skin. Try not to cut cuticles during a manicure or pedicure. Avoid having blood drawn or an IV or injections in that arm.

Take care of cuts, burns, or scrapes right away. Cleanse the area well with antibacterial soap. Apply an antibiotic ointment, such as bacitracin or Neosporin, and cover it with a bandage. If signs of infection develop, such as redness, warmth, or swelling, call your doctor. You may need an antibiotic to help treat the infection.

Keep Lymph Channels Open

Lymph channels can collapse if too much pressure is applied. Use the unaffected arm for blood pressure measurements. Avoid tight clothing, jewelry, and accessories on the shoulder, arm, or hand. Examples include pocketbooks slung over the shoulder, narrow bra straps that cut into the skin, tight elastic sleeves, and tight bracelets, watches, and rings.

Avoid Muscle Strain

Stretching and strengthening exercises are important after breast cancer surgery but must be done especially judiciously when a woman has had an axillary dissection. The goal is to promote dilation of collateral lymph channels in the shoulder while tempering increased lymph flow to the arm so that channels there do not become overtaxed. Vigorous exercise and arm movements that increase blood flow and lymph production may overwhelm remaining lymph channels, creating fluid backup and starting the lymphedema cycle. Speak to your surgeon before starting any exercise program.

Generally, use your arm normally, not excessively, and minimize heavy lifting. Warm up muscles before exercise. Avoid long spans of repetitive, vigorous movement against resistance, such as scrubbing, pushing, or pulling. Start new exercise gradually and limit sports with forceful, repetitive arm strokes.

Reduce stress on the arm due to exercise. Wear a compression sleeve. If you are strength training, alternately work on the arms and other parts of the body to allow time for the arms to rest and additional lymph to clear. Start with no or very little weight, limit repetitions to ten, and increase weights very slowly. See Chapter 11 for more specific exercise tips.

If your arm begins to ache, lie down and elevate it.

Maintain a Healthy Weight

Obesity is believed to increase lymphedema risk, too. Thus, a program encouraging a woman to attain and maintain weight in a healthy range may help lessen her risk for lymphedema. Chapters 11 and 12 give tips on exercise and nutrition.

Additional Tips

Consider buying a Lymphedema Alert™ bracelet, which warns medical personnel not to put needles or blood pressure cuffs around that arm. On a plane, you may need to wear a compression sleeve because cabin-pressure changes may cause lymphedema. The sleeve needs to be refitted if it is worn often or your weight changes.

Treating Lymphedema

Tell your surgeon or primary care provider about even the slightest swelling, tightness, or feeling of heaviness in the arm after lymph node surgery. If lymphedema develops, continue to take meticulous care of your skin to keep it supple and minimize infections. Wear a compression sleeve to provide external support for the lymph system, especially if you plan to exercise, work hard physically, or travel by plane.

Schedule regular lymphatic drainage sessions with a trained therapist, who can direct fluid toward functioning lymph channels using a technique called *manual lymphatic drainage*. She or he will also show you how to properly apply a compression bandage.

4

RADIATION THERAPY

◉

When Luz was diagnosed with breast cancer, she decided to have a lumpectomy. She needed chemotherapy, too, and not long after, she embarked on a standard course of radiation therapy. At the suggestion of her doctors, she chose to do this at a hospital close to her home. Five days a week for roughly six weeks, carefully calibrated radiation beams targeted breast tissue, including the area where her tumor had been removed. Except for feeling walloped by fatigue as the weeks went by, Luz had few side effects. The treatments didn't hurt and the sessions were quite short. The hardest part, she said, was lying awake and very still for the brief treatments and just trusting that her radiation team—which certainly was quite experienced—really knew their jobs.

Just like Luz, many women who have breast cancer surgery go on to have other treatments collectively known as *adjuvant therapy*—treatments given after surgery to kill any remaining cancer cells. Radiation therapy, which is discussed in this chapter, and anticancer drugs, detailed in Chapter 5, are both forms of adjuvant therapy.

Local therapy is defined as treatment to the breast and/or chest wall to reduce the risk of cancer returning in that area. Both surgery and radiation therapy are considered local therapy. Surgery removes as many cancer cells as possible in the breast. Radiation, typically delivered after surgery, works best when directed at minimal remaining cancer cells and may be given to the breast, the chest wall, and sometimes the nearby lymph nodes. Eradicating cancer cells in this way helps reduce the possibility that some residual cells could multiply in the breast or chest wall. This is called a *local recurrence*.

MAKING DECISIONS ABOUT RADIATION THERAPY

During standard radiation therapy, high-energy x-ray beams are delivered to the region considered at risk for local recurrence in order to kill any cancer cells lurking after surgery. These beams come from a radiation machine called a *linear accelerator*.

Working with a Radiation Oncologist

A *radiation oncologist* is a medical doctor trained to use a variety of radiation techniques to treat cancer. She or he heads a larger team responsible for deciding the type of radiation, the dose, and the area to be treated. Their goal is to include the tissues at risk for recurrence, while minimizing radiation to normal tissues, such as the heart and lungs.

Before making a recommendation, the radiation oncologist reviews your records, including mammograms and your pathology report. During this consultation, she or he will discuss the findings, examine you, make a treatment recommendation, and, if radiation therapy is indicated, review the details of the proposed therapy, including possible side effects. The radiation oncologist may also discuss the overall treatment plan with the other physicians involved, such as the breast surgeon and medical oncologist.

The next step is to schedule a radiation planning appointment, or *simulation session*, during which the radiation oncologist decides how best to target the areas being treated while minimizing radiation to normal tissues.

The radiation team also includes a *medical radiation physicist* and *dosimetrist*, who help plan the delivery and dose; *radiation therapists*, who position you correctly at each session and administer the treatments under supervision; and a *radiation oncology nurse*, who cares for you over the course of treatment and will recommend ways to help handle any side effects.

Here are a few important questions to consider asking the radiation oncologist:

- What course of treatment is recommended and why?

- Are radiation treatments likely to offer a survival advantage? Will they help decrease the chance of the cancer returning in the treatment area and, if so, by how much?

- Are any clinical trials relevant to your situation? If so, what are the potential advantages and possible disadvantages of joining one?

- Is it possible to have radiation treatments closer to home or work if your facility is too far away to reach easily? If you need to choose among facilities, try to find out more about each one. How many breast cancer patients are treated each year? What type of radiation equipment would be used? What is the training or expertise of the people who take measurements of the area that will be targeted and calculate the dose? And of the radiation therapists who deliver it?

You should feel comfortable asking these and other questions of the radiation oncologist who will be treating you.

Briefly, Who Gets Radiation Therapy?

Nowadays, radiation is routinely paired with the breast-conserving surgery known as lumpectomy, an option available to many women with early-stage breast cancers. Extensive research with twenty years of follow-up has found that this potent combination nets women with Stage I and Stage II breast cancers the same long-term survival rate as mastectomy does.

Six large randomized trials have demonstrated equivalent survival with these two approaches for appropriately selected patients. In one study comparing lumpectomy plus radiation to lumpectomy alone, after twenty years of follow-up, standard radiation treatments lowered the risk of cancer recurring in the same breast from 39 to 14 percent. In addition, when recurrences did happen, 40 percent of these events occurred within the first five years after treatment in the radiation group compared to 73 percent in the group that did not receive radiation. Thus, radiation decreases and delays local recurrences of breast cancer. Postoperative radiation is routinely recommended for women who undergo lumpectomy for invasive breast cancer; given the clear benefit of radiation therapy, the option of lumpectomy alone is not considered a standard treatment choice.

While many patients who undergo mastectomy do not need radiation, some will. Radiation therapy after a mastectomy benefits women at higher risk of recurrence, such as those with four or more positive lymph nodes; positive margins (cancer cells at the edge of the mastectomy specimen); large tumors; or a breast cancer that has infiltrated the lymphatic channels of the surrounding skin (inflammatory breast cancer). Radiation after mastectomy for a woman with one to three positive nodes is controversial; discuss potential benefits with your radiation oncologist.

Radiation treatments are not recommended for certain women, including the following:

- Women who are pregnant

- Women who previously had substantial doses of radiation to the breast, chest, or chest wall, either for breast cancer or another reason, such as Hodgkin's disease, a cancer that affects the lymphatic system

- Women who have a connective tissue disease, such as scleroderma or lupus; because radiation affects the skin, women with these conditions may not tolerate this treatment well

TUMOR MARGINS

Tumor margins are the most important variable that a radiation oncologist considers when deciding whether a woman is a good candidate for lumpectomy plus radiation or whether she may require a mastectomy. No uniform definitions exist, however, so the three main subcategory labels that follow can vary in meaning depending on where you get your care.

- **Positive:** Cancer cells directly on the surface of the inked tumor specimen. This can be further subdivided into *focally positive* (a touch of tumor cells approaching an inked edge) or more than focally positive.

- **Close:** Cancer cells within one, two, or three millimeters of the inked surface of the specimen.

- **Negative:** At minimum, no cancer cells directly on the inked surface of the specimen.

Experience from the Joint Center for Radiation Therapy reported in the *Journal of Clinical Oncology* in 2000 shows that margins make a difference in recurrence. During eight years following lumpectomy and radiation, local recurrence rates were 7 percent in those with negative and close (one millimeter) margins, 14 percent in those with focally positive margins, and 27 percent in those with more than focally positive margins.

If your tumor margins are positive or seem unclear, the radiation oncologist may consult directly with the pathologist and breast surgeon. If concern remains, another surgery to secure adequate margins may be necessary.

- Women who did not have clean margins after breast-conserving surgery even after reexcision; standard treatment in these instances is a mastectomy rather than lumpectomy plus radiation

Other conditions may dictate against using radiation as well, but these are the most common ones. For more information that takes your specific situation into account, talk with your radiation oncologist.

Standard Therapy: External Beam Radiation

External beam radiation is the radiation therapy technique most commonly used to treat breast cancer. As you might guess, it employs equipment outside the body to send the radiation beams to the targeted tissue. The beams are aligned to provide even and precise coverage of the area to be treated and, depending on the parameters of the tumor, can encompass several areas:

- Tissue surrounding the spot where the tumor lay (called the *lumpectomy cavity* or *tumor bed*)

- The rest of the breast, if you had a lumpectomy (whole-breast radiation)

- The chest wall

- Lymph nodes under the arm (*axillary nodes*) in some cases, depending on whether they harbored cancer cells and the extent of surgery in this area

- Lymph nodes around the collarbone (*supraclavicular nodes*) that may contain cancer cells

During the planning session or simulation, careful measurements are taken to determine the best angles for aligning the beams on the target area while avoiding the normal tissue nearby, including the lung and heart (if the left side is being treated since the heart is positioned under the left rib cage). Special x-ray equipment and sometimes CT scans or other imaging studies are used to most accurately arrange the beams. The targeted region is known as the *treatment port* or *field*. You need to lie very still on an x-ray table during simulation, which typically takes about an hour.

Radiation therapists work with you to adjust your position and make the measurements. Part of your body may be placed in a device designed to help reproduce your position accurately; the type of device varies depending on the facility. After looking at several possible beam arrangements, the radiation oncologist approves the final radiation fields chosen. Finally, the radiation therapist makes permanent pinhead-sized tattoos on your skin that will aid in accurately reproducing the treatment field at each session.

After the correct target for the radiation beams has been identified, the dose of radiation must be prescribed. The goal is to use enough radiation to quash abnormal cells, while minimizing side effects of treatment. The total dose is divided into a series of many small doses. While gradually weakening and killing off vulnerable abnormal cells, the small doses help protect normal tissues and produce a better long-term cosmetic result.

A standard course of external beam radiation is delivered to the whole breast (if you had a lumpectomy), chest wall, and, if necessary, the region encompassing key lymph nodes. (See Figure 4.1.) Treatment sessions usually take about ten to fifteen minutes, although you probably will be told to set aside thirty to forty-five minutes to allow for the time it takes to check in, get undressed, be positioned, and get dressed again. Typically, women receive treatments five days a week, for five to seven weeks. Although receiving the radiation isn't painful—that is, unless it hurts to hold your body in position with your arm above your head—this time commitment can be hard for some women.

At the start of your treatment session, the radiation therapists will help you into position. They will set up the radiation beams and check to see that everything is accurately aligned before leaving the room during the actual treatments. Don't worry—the room is set up with a monitor and intercom so you can communicate during the session. Your radiation oncology nurse also will be available when you come for your daily sessions and can check your skin and talk with you about any side effects you might be experiencing.

Getting a Boost

During the first several weeks of radiation treatments, the whole breast or chest wall and sometimes adjacent lymph node areas are treated. Then a "boost" of radi-

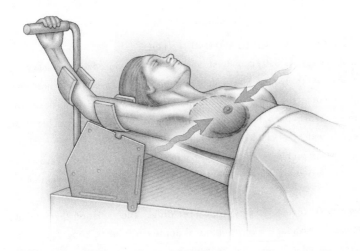

Figure 4.1 In external beam radiation therapy, one beam is positioned to be roughly level with the breast and another is angled down from above on the opposite side of the body. The two beams meet at the designated treatment area. The radiation equipment is positioned in a very spacious, open way and does not feel confining.

ation is given, targeting the smaller area of the tumor bed within an intact breast or sometimes the mastectomy scar. These are the spots where a recurrence is most likely to happen.

A 2001 *New England Journal of Medicine* study explored the value of adding an eight-day radiation boost following five weeks of whole-breast radiation in more than five thousand women with Stage I and II breast cancers who had undergone lumpectomy and lymph node removal. After five years of follow-up, the boost was found to reduce the risk of a local recurrence by 40 percent—4.3 percent of those in the boost group had a local recurrence compared with 7.3 percent in the non-boost group.

Younger women benefited most. Those who were forty or younger experienced a 10.2 percent rate of local recurrence with the boost and a 19.5 percent recurrence rate without the boost. Among women aged forty-one to fifty, the local recurrence rate was 5.8 percent with a boost and 9.5 percent without. Rates of metastases and overall survival were comparable in the two groups.

Nowadays, adding a boost to whole-breast radiation is standard treatment for women undergoing lumpectomy for Stage I and II breast cancers.

RADIATION: HELPFUL FOR OLDER WOMEN, TOO?

Life can be sweet at any age, as Betty can attest. She was first diagnosed with breast cancer in 1969, when she was just thirty-nine. She made it through fairly harrowing old-school treatments employing chemotherapy with few of the supportive drugs used today and heavy-duty radiation that burned her skin badly. Five years later, she fought off a recurrence of her breast cancer and went on to watch her children have children and to enjoy life with her husband. Despite subsequent health problems, she's simply not ready to give up on life. "I have a good husband. I appreciate everything. I appreciate the sun every day. And I'm thankful that I'm here."

Since Betty was first treated, surgery, anticancer drugs, and radiation therapy have advanced enormously. Nowadays, a more minimal approach is often sought. Recently, researchers have considered whether certain older women with breast cancer who are at very low risk for local recurrence might forgo radiation.

One prospective study of more than six hundred women aged seventy and older published in the *New England Journal of Medicine* in 2004 suggests forgoing radiation may be safe for some older women at low risk for local recurrence. All had had a lumpectomy to remove Stage I, ER+ tumors. Half received tamoxifen (Nolvadex) alone, and half received tamoxifen plus radiation therapy.

After an average of five years of follow-up, disease-free survival and overall survival was similar in both groups. A recurrence in the breast or axillary nodes was experienced in 4 percent of the tamoxifen-only group and in 1 percent of the group that also received radiation. While this difference of three percentage points was statistically significant, it may or may not be compelling to a woman contemplating treatment.

During the initial years after treatment, women and their doctors agreed that radiation had a detrimental effect on breast appearance, but by the fourth year differences between the groups had leveled out. Breast pain and shoulder function were rated worse by the women in the radiation group, even after four years of follow-up.

Experimenting with a Shorter Course of Treatment

Shortening the course of external beam radiation would be a real boon to many women. Right now, though, this is considered experimental rather than a proven therapy. Some experts are concerned that more intensive doses delivered during accelerated treatment schedules might negatively affect skin and underlying breast tissue over the long term. And it's still not known definitively whether an abbreviated schedule of radiation would deliver the same benefits as time-tested standard therapy in five years, ten years, or two decades hence. In a 2002 Canadian study, women with early-stage, node-negative breast cancer who had lumpectomy all received the same total radiation dose: half received it over the standard thirty-five-day schedule and half over an abbreviated twenty-two-day schedule. While the early data are promising, further studies are necessary before larger numbers of women try this approach.

HANDLING POSSIBLE SIDE EFFECTS

It's difficult to predict who will sail through radiation and who will run up against significant side effects. Fatigue, which often grows as treatments continue, affects many women. Some women experience what amounts to a mild sunburn, while others have more significant skin reactions. It is possible, though, to take steps to minimize side effects and ease this phase of treatment. More information on this is contained in Chapter 8, and your radiation oncologist and radiation oncology nurse can also help.

Possible Side Effects

Side effects from radiation can be short-term, occurring during radiation and resolving within a few months of completing therapy, or long-term, beginning during or years after radiation. Long-term effects also may fully resolve or may linger. While no one can predict which side effects, if any, you will have, it may help to know that a 2003 study of 265 women that evaluated the cosmetic outcomes of lumpectomy plus radiation found that nearly half of the women participating experienced excellent results with no skin changes and very minor, or no, differences in size between their breasts at the six-month mark. That said, common and less common side effects include the following.

Skin

Sunburnlike skin irritation and redness, peeling, skin thickening (*fibrosis*), swelling or shrinkage of breast tissue, and discoloration are all possible skin side effects of radiation. Incisions and injuries after radiation may heal more slowly than usual because small blood vessels beneath the skin and other factors important to healing are affected by radiation.

Fatigue

By the time you finish radiation therapy, fatigue can be quite noticeable. This is not unusual: your body is working overtime to heal tissues and repair normal cells. Try to get the rest you need, rather than continuing to push yourself. According to the National Cancer Institute, fatigue commonly lasts four to six weeks after radiation treatments end. Some women report feeling this way for quite a bit longer, especially if they have had chemotherapy, too. Because there can be many reasons for persistent fatigue—including anemia, depression, and insomnia—you should discuss this and possible solutions with your cancer care team.

Bones and Cartilage

Radiation beams typically include the ribs underlying the breast. This affects the *fascia* (the thin covering over the ribs) and cartilage that connects the breastbone to each rib, which can cause inflammation and pain that may wax and wane. This condition is called *costochondritis*. It is most noticeable when firmly touching the area or during a cough or sneeze. Treatment includes an over-the-counter nonsteroidal anti-inflammatory medication, such as Motrin or Aleve. Rarely, radiation to the ribs can weaken them, making fractures more likely to occur.

Heart and Lungs

Harm to the lungs or the heart, which lies mainly on the left side of the body, due to radiation is rare. The likelihood depends partly on the anatomy of your body, which breast was affected by cancer, and the extent of the radiation fields necessary. When calculating the target area, your radiation team does everything possible to avoid these organs.

Occasionally, the outer lining of the lungs becomes inflamed, a condition called *pneumonitis*. While rare, it is more likely to occur in women who need to have nodes near the collarbone irradiated and those who have radiation plus chemotherapy at the same time. The symptoms, which usually become noticeable six months to a year and a half after radiation treatment, are a dry cough, shortness of breath, and a low fever. Pneumonitis may resolve on its own or with a course of steroids, such as prednisone.

Easing Treatments and Side Effects

While you should ask your radiation oncology nurse for specific recommendations, the National Cancer Institute and other sources suggest the following advice for easing treatment and side effects (also see Chapter 8).

Clothes

Dress for treatment in loose clothes you can slip off and on easily. Scratchy or synthetic fabrics and a tight bra—or even your regular bra—may be quite uncomfortable during the course of radiation treatments. Try wearing soft, lightweight garments, such as a camisole or an old cotton T-shirt (especially handy because creams used to ease skin discomfort can stain clothes). If your skin is too tender for a bra, stop wearing one temporarily.

Skin Care

Before using skin products on areas that will receive treatment, check with your nurse or doctor. Skin creams, soaps, talcum powder, and deodorants sometimes contain ingredients that may increase skin irritation during radiation. Your radiation team can best advise you about which products to avoid entirely, such as deodorants with metallic ingredients like aluminum chlorohydrate, and which will help ease discomfort, such as creams and salves like Aquaphor and Lubriderm, provided you don't apply them right before radiation treatments.

During the initial weeks of radiation, breast skin may look and feel like you have a minor sunburn. Some women find that's as bad as it gets; others may find the burn worsens as time goes on, especially in skin folds and on the underside of heavier breasts. Sometimes, peeling and even blistering occurs. Report any burns or peeling, however minor, to your radiation team. Usually, daily use of a salve is recommended to soothe redness and peeling. No products have proven better than others. Some examples include aloe vera, Aquaphor, Lubriderm, or Biafine. Gel pads or sheets may also be suggested to help cool the burn. Your radiation oncology nurse can make specific recommendations.

Blistering or peeling skin requires extra care. Usually, gentle cleansing is recommended. Your radiation nurse might suggest a thin layer of a burn ointment and a nonstick covering that blocks bacteria and water while allowing air to circulate.

Coverings and gel pads should be held in place lightly by a bra or camisole or with paper tape applied only outside the affected area. Using adhesive tape can further hurt skin. Likewise, hot or cold packs can damage skin, too, and generally should be avoided.

Washing Skin and Shaving Underarms

Cool or lukewarm water is best for the entire area that is being treated. Unless your nurse or doctor advises otherwise, shaving with an electric razor is fine during treatment as long as skin is not too irritated. Do not use a safety razor or depilatory products because these can cause further irritation.

Sunscreen

Irradiated skin is very sensitive to sun during treatment and even for years afterward. It's best to keep the treated area covered with clothing when possible. Otherwise, be sure to limit time spent in the sun and use a broad-spectrum sunscreen of SPF 30 or higher.

Nutrition and Complementary Treatments

Healthy eating, described in Chapter 12, is important to help your body heal during radiation treatments. A basic multivitamin and calcium and vitamin D supplements are probably fine. Antioxidant supplements might potentially interfere with the ability of radiation beams to harm cancerous cells, so avoid them. Discuss other types of complementary or alternative treatments with your radiation team.

PROMISING, NOT PROVEN: PARTIAL-BREAST RADIATION

Can radiation treatments be compressed into a few days or otherwise downsized safely in women who have had lumpectomies? Perhaps one day, although at this writing, studies are still preliminary and it's simply not clear how women who undergo these techniques will fare over extended periods of time, whereas years of solid data back the benefits of standard radiation therapy.

What makes such largely unproven techniques enticing? Part of their promise lies in the fact that they expose less tissue to radiation and thus, to unwanted side effects. Research shows most, though not all, recurrences in the breast after lumpectomy appear near the tumor bed whether or not radiation therapy is performed. Just as important to many women, these approaches cut treatment time from several weeks to a few days.

Nonetheless, it's a long road from "promising" studies to accepted clinical practice. Right now no long-term data assessing the safety and efficacy of these techniques compared to whole-breast radiation exist. Key questions must be answered through long-term, randomized clinical trials that compare newer approaches to standard therapy. How high a total dose of radiation is necessary to equal the effects of whole-breast radiation? What impact do different techniques have upon long-term recurrence and survival rates? Might some of these techniques create "hot spots" of radiation in the breast that can do more damage to normal tissue and underlying structures than a better dispersed dose of radiation? Until more data are available, the American Society of Breast Surgeons suggests that partial-breast radiation be performed only as part of a medical center protocol or multi-institutional trial and limited to certain women.

Tiny Tubes: Multiple-Catheter Brachytherapy

Brachytherapy employs a small radioactive source that emits radiation from within the affected breast. In one type of brachytherapy, ten to twenty tiny tubes called *catheters* hold the source. They may be placed in the breast at the time of the lumpectomy or after the incision has healed and are held in place by buttons that lie flush with the skin. (See Figure 4.2.)

While you are under general anesthesia or after the skin is numbed with a local anesthetic, a radiation oncologist carefully positions the catheters in a grid encompassing the lumpectomy site. The catheters remain in the breast with their ends protruding through the skin for the duration of the radiation treatment. Their ends are wrapped and taped up after each session.

Twice a day for five days, a computer-controlled device feeds radioactive pellets into the catheters, one by one. Dividing a daily dose into two smaller doses, usually separated by four to six hours, is called *hyperfractionated radiation therapy*. The

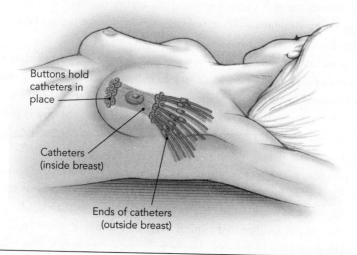

Figure 4.2 Multiple-catheter brachytherapy. Catheters are threaded through the breast tissue surrounding the lumpectomy site. During treatment, a machine feeds a radioactive source into each catheter.

pellets remain in place for a specified time. The sessions take about fifteen minutes each and generally require no overnight hospital stay.

During low-dose brachytherapy, which is less common, the radioactive source remains in the breast for the entire five-day treatment period. This procedure requires hospitalization and several days of isolation.

Balloon Brachytherapy: MammoSite

Placing catheters in a grid around the breast requires a good deal of expertise. Instead, the MammoSite Radiation Therapy System employs a catheter tipped with a single balloon that is placed in the lumpectomy cavity of the breast. This can be done at the time of surgery or shortly afterward. The balloon at the end of the catheter is then inflated to fit the site. (See Figure 4.3.)

During treatment, a computer-controlled loader feeds a single radioactive source into the balloon. Once it has emitted the prescribed dose of radiation, the source is removed. After two sessions a day for five days, the balloon is deflated and the catheter is removed.

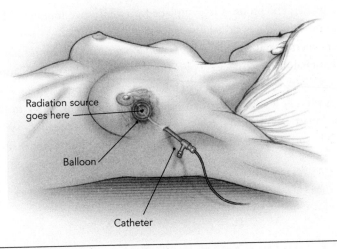

Radiation source
goes here

Balloon

Catheter

Figure 4.3 Balloon brachytherapy. In the MammoSite procedure, a radioactive source is fed through a catheter to a balloon inflated in the lumpectomy cavity.

At this writing, there are no published reports on the effectiveness of this technique, which was approved by the U.S. Food and Drug Administration in 2002 on the basis of a small study considering only safety. It is easier to use and less invasive than other forms of brachytherapy, so many medical centers around the country offer it. The amount of radiation delivered may vary from center to center, which worries some experts.

At Dana-Farber Cancer Institute and Brigham and Women's Hospital, as at many other institutions, this procedure is offered only under a protocol with strict guidelines that govern which breast cancer patients can receive this particular therapy and standardization of treatment techniques. Radiation oncologists also make it clear that this procedure is experimental, the risk of recurrence is unknown as yet, and the standard of care is still whole-breast radiation.

Other Experimental Approaches

Intra-operative radiotherapy, a single dose of radiation to the lumpectomy site at the time of surgery, is another approach. One such technique being tested in Europe requires a surgeon to place a probe tipped with an x-ray source in the tumor bed. The surgeon then gathers the surrounding tissue up around it with a suture like a drawstring purse. The probe is left in place for twenty-five minutes. Then it is removed and the incision is closed.

Another experimental technique is *3D conformal external beam therapy*. It uses three-dimensional scans to precisely plot and shape the delivery of radiation from the outside. As with brachytherapy, two treatment sessions per day take place over five days. Although less invasive than other techniques, it is tricky to perform because the breast can move and may not line up in exactly the same way for each session, and in some cases it may be difficult to define the lumpectomy site.

5

BLOCKING CANCER WITH CHEMOTHERAPY, HORMONAL THERAPY, AND MORE

◉

Today, slightly more than two million women living in the United States have undergone treatment for breast cancer, according to the American Cancer Society. As new life-saving drugs and therapies emerge, many with fewer side effects, that number will continue to grow. In the past, when breast surgery was used alone, roughly one in three women whose cancers had not spread to the lymph nodes, and three out of four women whose cancers had reached the lymph nodes, experienced recurrences and died. The outlook brightened after chemotherapy regimens became widely used and grew better still once newer drugs were added. *Adjuvant treatment*, a range of anticancer therapies that follow breast surgery, has helped many thousands of women become breast cancer survivors.

What are the medications used to fight breast cancer? How are they given and how do they work? What drives the decision to choose certain drugs over others? Which side effects may occur and what can be done to ease them? Before answering these questions, this chapter explains a bit about how cancer cells find a firm foothold in the breast and in some cases spread beyond it. As researchers learn more about this complex process, they are able to use that knowledge to craft drugs that slow cancer or bring it to a grinding halt by exploiting a wide range of vulnerabilities.

Because breast cancer research and drug development evolve so quickly, new information is likely to be available by the time you read this. Always check with your oncologist or another reliable source, such as the National Cancer Institute (cancer.gov or 800-4-CANCER), to see what new developments have turned up. You also may find it helpful to check treatment guidelines for patients published by the National Comprehensive Cancer Network (nccn.org or 888-909-6226).

The Basics: How Breast Cancers Grow

If you carefully cut a square of white paper in half and then cut the two halves in half, you'll end up with four small squares that look much like the original. Normal cell division, which happens at a rapid clip during fetal development and childhood and continues throughout life as a way to replace worn-out cells, proceeds in much the same way. Normal cells, though, are programmed to die, making room for others to replace them. Cancerous cells are immortal. They have genetic glitches that enable them to multiply almost endlessly, eventually clumping together to form a *primary tumor*.

Even cancer cells stick to a set of instructions, however. Research shows that not just one, but rather a combination of critical genetic changes occurs before a cell begins to multiply as a cancer cell. An *oncogene* (cancer gene) that tells cells to multiply can be switched on. A tumor-suppressor gene that normally puts the brakes on cell division (such as p53) can be switched off or disabled. Some genes (such as BRCA1 and BRCA2) are important because they help to repair mutations that arise spontaneously during the course of normal cell division or due to exposure to certain cancer-causing agents in the environment.

The immune system regularly identifies and kills off abnormal cells before they get a strong foothold. Even if that fails to happen, cancer cells need fuel to grow and will die off without it. Breast cancer tumors rely on tiny blood vessels for oxygen and nutrients.

The growth of breast cancer cells can be modulated by hormones in the blood circulation and by receptors on the cell's surface. Some breast cancer cells feed on estrogen or express an overabundance of proteins like HER2/neu, which encourage some tumors to continue to grow. Scientists are likely to discover additional conditions that encourage growth.

How Breast Cancer Spreads

The tiny clump of cancerous cells that forms the start of a primary tumor squeezes against normal cells. If unchecked, the cancerous clump eventually can drill a pathway between the normal cells. This is called *invasion*. If invading cells find their way to a blood vessel or lymph vessel, some of these cells may be able to break loose from the boundary of the clump and travel to other sites in the body. Usually, cells in the body adhere to one another like firmly interlocked stones. What allows cancerous cells to make this leap has long been a mystery, and research on this question continues.

Fortunately, most cancer cells that do break loose from a primary tumor will not survive a punishing trip through the bloodstream or will be destroyed by immune cells in the lymph system. Among the small number of cancerous cells that do successfully spread to a new site, or *metastasize*, many will simply fail to grow once there. However, in some women, a few of these tiny tumor cell deposits, called *micrometastases*, or "micromets," may start to multiply and grow into a *secondary tumor*. The lymph nodes, bones, lungs, liver, or brain are the usual sites for this.

It's confusing but true that these straying cells remain breast cancer cells no matter where they move in the body. So although a secondary tumor may appear in the bones, for example, it is not bone cancer because the cells retain the essential characteristics and vulnerabilities of breast cancer. It is metastatic breast cancer in the bones.

Although women fear metastases for good reason—metastatic breast cancer is generally incurable—there are therapies available to try to control advanced-stage cancer. Some women successfully use these drugs for years, often switching over to a new medication when one stops working and another is needed.

OVERVIEW: ANTICANCER MEDICATIONS

The complex processes that encourage cancerous cells to develop, grow, and spread are not well understood yet. But what we do know thus far has permitted the development of drugs that can block cancer by many different means. Doctors once had just a handful of medications to treat breast cancer. Now there is an ever-lengthening list of drugs designed to destroy cancer cells outright or slow their growth. Chemotherapy drugs travel the body to trounce fast-replicating cells. The stalwarts of chemotherapy, such as doxorubicin (Adriamycin) and cyclophosphamide (Cytoxan), continue to be widely and successfully used. Hormonal approaches target estrogen so that breast cancer cells in women whose tumors are hormone receptor–positive will not be stimulated by this hormone. The drug trastuzumab (Herceptin) is a protein antibody that blocks the effects of HER2/neu in women whose tumors are stimulated to grow by this protein.

Briefly, Who Gets Anticancer Medications?

Anticancer drugs, such as chemotherapy and hormonal therapy, work *systemically*; that is, they fan out via the bloodstream throughout the body to destroy any cancer cells that may have spread beyond the breast.

When a woman has early-stage breast cancer, the benefits of systemic therapy depend on the risk that the cancer will metastasize. It is important to minimize that risk, because once this happens, it is generally impossible to completely eliminate the disease. Thus, the higher your risk, the greater the need for treatment and the bigger the benefit you can reap from the treatment. At the same time, when making treatment decisions, potential side effects should be part of this equation. The possibility of experiencing side effects remains the same no matter what your risk is from the cancer. The higher the risk of your disease, the more likely the potential side effects will seem worth that risk in order to gain the benefits from the treatment. Conversely, the lower the risk of your disease, the lower the benefit you might gain from the treatment, so risking certain side effects may not be worthwhile.

One major factor in estimating risk and thus choosing medications is whether a woman has breast cancer that is node-negative or node-positive. *Node-negative* indicates there are no signs of cancer in the lymph nodes evaluated. The cancerous cells appear localized in the breast. *Node-positive* indicates that cancer cells are seen microscopically in the lymph nodes. While positive nodes increase a woman's risk of developing metastases, even node-negative cancers can metastasize, most likely through the bloodstream. Other important considerations are whether the cancer cells are fueled by the hormones estrogen (ER+) or progesterone (PR+) or the HER2/neu protein.

"Weighing the risks and benefits of treatment can be difficult," says Eric P. Winer, M.D., associate professor of medicine at Harvard Medical School and director of the Breast Oncology Center at Dana-Farber Cancer Institute. "A given treatment— let's say chemotherapy for a woman who has a node-negative, estrogen receptor– positive cancer—may only improve her chance of being cured by 1 to 2 percent in some cases. If she already has a very good prognosis, perhaps a 95 percent chance of being alive in ten years, then the extra benefit may not be worth the side effects and inconvenience of treatment. She needs to carefully consider the benefit in light of the fact that some of the more intensive forms of chemotherapy treatments can cause leukemia in as many as one in two hundred women along with other temporary side effects like hair loss, nausea, and menstrual irregularities. On the other hand, there are many other situations where the benefits clearly outweigh risks. For a woman who has an estrogen receptor–negative cancer, particularly if underarm lymph nodes are involved, the benefits from chemotherapy can be very substantial."

Oncologists also take into account the size of the invasive tumor, whether there is any evidence of cancer in breast blood vessels or lymph vessels near the tumor (*lymphatic-vascular invasion*), the apparent aggressiveness of the tumor (*tumor grade*), and a woman's age, menopausal status, and general health. Because an oncologist weighs a multitude of factors when selecting treatments, the following information on early-stage breast cancer is merely offered as examples. Discuss your specific situation with your cancer care team.

Early-Stage, Node-Negative Cancer

If a woman has a tumor that is one centimeter or smaller, and there is no evidence of breast cancer in the lymph nodes and no sign of lymphatic-vascular invasion in the breast tissue surrounding the tumor, she probably will not receive chemotherapy because the expected benefits are minimal compared to the potential risks. If the tumor is larger or there is evidence of lymphatic-vascular invasion, she may be offered chemotherapy. In these instances, women who have hormone receptor–positive tumors also will be offered a hormonal therapy, such as tamoxifen (Nolvadex), to help ward off recurrence and new cancers. In general, hormonal therapy often is more effective than chemotherapy for reducing risk in women with ER+/PR+ cancers.

Early-Stage, Node-Positive Cancer

Usually, women with early-stage breast cancers that are node-positive receive chemotherapy. If the breast cancer is hormone receptor–positive, hormonal therapy afterward may add substantial benefit. Although not yet considered standard therapy, when a tumor is HER2/neu-positive, increasingly the drug Herceptin also may be offered through a clinical trial.

CHEMOTHERAPY

Chemotherapy drugs travel through the bloodstream to reach rapidly dividing cancer cells almost anywhere in the body. Depending on the circumstances, the same

Understanding Research Trial Results: Relative Risk and Absolute Risk

Relative risk and absolute risk are the two most common ways to describe risk when discussing the results of research trials. It's important to understand the difference so that study results aren't blown out of proportion in your mind. As an example, women who have already undergone a full course of chemotherapy followed by five years of tamoxifen may have a very small risk of breast cancer relapse over the next five years, say 5 percent. A promising new medication becomes available to take following chemotherapy and tamoxifen. This new medication reduces relapse by 40 percent, a seemingly impressive *relative risk* reduction. However, this translates into a decrease in *absolute risk* from 5 to 3 percent. Here's the math: 5 percent × 0.40 = 3 percent. So, yes, it's a 40 percent decrease in relative risk, but overall it ends up providing a small absolute benefit of two percentage points. Thus, relative risk reductions may appear to overstate the benefits of a given treatment when the absolute benefit is actually quite small. Furthermore, if the side effect profile of the new medication is significant, it may overshadow the absolute benefits of further treatment. When you talk to your cancer care team, ask them to help put risks in perspective for you, considering your circumstances.

drugs may be used differently—given more frequently, perhaps, as in dose-dense therapy or in various combinations as explained in the following sections.

Early-Stage Breast Cancer: Combinations

Usually, chemotherapy drugs for early-stage breast cancer are given in combinations, which offer a better chance of stopping breast cancer. By combining two or three drugs, your oncologist can attack cancer cells at several key points in their growth cycle. Plus certain cancer cells may resist some drugs while succumbing to others.

Certain combinations deliver very similar results in terms of risk of recurrence and survival rates, but one combination may offer certain risks in exchange for certain benefits. AC (see Table 5.1), for example, which carries a very slight risk of heart damage and virtually guarantees hair loss, usually takes three months to administer. CMF (see Table 5.1) usually takes six months to administer, but there is no additional risk of heart problems and only half of the women who take this combination with Cytoxan in pill form lose their hair. When you and your oncologist discuss treatment plans, you'll want to consider these factors and other issues relevant to your specific situation.

Table 5.1 Common Chemotherapy Combinations for Early-Stage Breast Cancer

Generic	Brand Name
AC (doxorubicin, cyclophosphamide)	Adriamycin, Cytoxan
A-CMF (doxorubicin followed by cyclophosphamide, methotrexate, 5-fluorouracil*)	Adriamycin followed by Cytoxan, Mexate, Adrucil
AC-T (doxorubicin and cyclophosphamide followed by paclitaxel)	Adriamycin and Cytoxan followed by Taxol
CEF/FEC (cyclophosphamide, epirubicin, 5-fluorouracil*)	Cytoxan, Ellence, Adrucil (CEF/FEC designates somewhat different drug doses and schedules)
CMF (cyclophosphamide, methotrexate, 5-fluorouracil*)	Cytoxan, Mexate, Adrucil
EC (epirubicin, cyclophosphamide)	Ellence, Cytoxan
FAC/CAF (5-fluorouracil*, doxorubicin, cyclophosphamide)	Adrucil, Adriamycin, Cytoxan (FAC/CAF designates somewhat different drug doses and schedules)
TAC (docetaxel, doxorubicin, cyclophosphamide)	Taxotere, Adriamycin, Cytoxan

*5-fluorouracil, abbreviated 5-FU
Adapted from the National Comprehensive Cancer Network

Late-Stage Breast Cancer: Combinations or Single Agents

In some parts of the country, chemotherapy combinations, rather than single agents, are also given for metastatic breast cancer. Current research suggests that combination therapy offers a slightly longer delay in progression during late-stage breast cancer but provides no clear improvement in length of survival and may exact considerable cost in terms of quality of life. For this reason, many oncologists have a strong preference for using chemotherapy drugs one at a time. (See Table 5.2.)

At Dana-Farber Cancer Institute, medical oncologists typically use chemotherapy combinations either as part of a clinical trial or in crisis situations, such as if a cancer appears to be growing very rapidly and interfering with organ function—"a now or never situation," explained Ann H. Partridge, M.D., M.P.H., a medical oncologist at Dana-Farber Cancer Institute specializing in breast cancer.

Otherwise, she and her colleagues tend to rely on single chemotherapy drugs, or a single agent paired with the medication Herceptin if the cancer is HER2/neu-positive. When advanced breast cancer stops responding to a particular medication, that drug is usually discontinued and another one is started. This strategy can work to stem further growth of the cancer and possibly shrink existing tumors while minimizing side effects.

Treatment for late-stage cancer may be daily, weekly, or every three to four weeks, depending on the drug or drugs selected and a woman's tolerance for any side effects. Usually, the medication that has a reasonable chance of working with the fewest side effects is used first, although drug selection will differ from woman to woman because the response is individual. We know continuing treatment delays

TIMING OF CHEMOTHERAPY: BEFORE SURGERY OR AFTER

Generally, women start adjuvant chemotherapy about two to six weeks after surgery. This allows the body time to heal without giving any remaining cancer cells much time to grow. Sometimes, *neoadjuvant chemotherapy*, or preoperative chemotherapy, is given before any surgery takes place. This approach might be a good choice if your oncologist is hoping to shrink the tumor enough to allow you to have a lumpectomy rather than a mastectomy or if a tumor is so extensive that a surgeon would have trouble removing all of the cancerous tissue even if a mastectomy was performed.

Table 5.2 Anticancer Medications for Breast Cancer

Generic Name (Brand Name)	Description	Some Possible Side Effects
Common Chemotherapy Drugs		
Often, certain anticancer medications are called by their generic names (such as tamoxifen and methotrexate), while others are usually referred to by their brand names (such as Cytoxan and Taxol). We present both the generic and the brand name for a medication the first time it appears and afterward refer to it by the name cancer care professionals most commonly use.		
cyclophosphamide (Cytoxan)	Used for early-stage and advanced cancer	Hair loss, nausea and vomiting, drop in blood cell count; may affect fertility
doxorubicin (Adriamycin)	Used for early-stage and advanced cancer	Hair loss, fatigue, nausea and vomiting, drop in blood cell count; may affect fertility; rarely, heart damage
methotrexate (Mexate)	Used for early-stage and advanced cancer	Fatigue, drop in blood cell count, nausea and vomiting, mouth sores, rash
5-fluorouracil (Adrucil) (abbreviated 5-FU)	Used for early-stage and advanced cancer	Fatigue, drop in blood cell count, rash, diarrhea, mouth or lip sores
epirubicin (Ellence)	Used for early-stage and advanced cancer	Hair loss, fatigue, nausea and vomiting, drop in blood cell count; rarely, heart damage

(continued)

Table 5.2 *(continued)*

Generic Name (Brand Name)	Description	Some Possible Side Effects
Chemotherapy Drugs: Taxanes		
docetaxel (Taxotere)	Used for early-stage and advanced cancer	Hair loss, fatigue, fluid retention, drop in blood cell count; neuropathy (numbness and tingling in the hands and feet), usually after long-term use
paclitaxel (Taxol)	Used for early-stage and advanced cancer	Hair loss, fatigue, drop in blood cell count; neuropathy (numbness and tingling in the hands and feet), usually after long-term use
Chemotherapy Drugs: Advanced Cancer		
capecitabine (Xeloda)	Used mainly for advanced cancer	Fatigue, diarrhea, mouth sores, hand-foot syndrome, drop in blood cell count
gemcitabine (Gemzar)	Used for advanced cancer	Fever, rash, hair loss, drop in blood cell count
vinorelbine (Navelbine)	Used for advanced cancer	Hair loss, fatigue, nausea and vomiting, muscle and bone aches, neuropathy (numbness and tingling in the hands and feet)
Hormonal Medications		
anastrozole (Arimidex)	Used for early-stage and advanced hormone receptor–positive cancers in postmenopausal women	Hot flashes, mild nausea, rashes, bone loss, pain in joints or muscles

Drug	Usage	Side effects
exemestane (Aromasin)	Used for advanced hormone receptor–positive cancers in postmenopausal women	Hot flashes, mild nausea, fatigue, bone loss, joint pain
goserelin (Zoladex)	Sometimes used to treat hormone receptor–positive cancer in premenopausal women and women approaching menopause (perimenopausal)	Menopausal symptoms (hot flashes, vaginal dryness, reduced libido)
letrozole (Femara)	Used for early-stage and advanced hormone receptor–positive cancers in postmenopausal women	Hot flashes; bone loss; pain in back, joints, or muscles; hair loss
leuprolide (Lupron)	Sometimes used to treat hormone receptor–positive cancer in pre- and perimenopausal women	Menopausal symptoms (hot flashes, vaginal dryness, reduced libido)
megestrol (Megace)	Used for advanced hormone receptor–positive cancers	Weight gain, increased appetite, shortness of breath
tamoxifen (Nolvadex)	Used for early-stage and advanced cancer	Hot flashes, vaginal discharge, fatigue, nausea, headaches; less often, blood clots (deep venous thrombosis), blood clots traveling to the lungs (pulmonary emboli), possibly stroke, uterine cancer, cataracts
fulvestrant (Faslodex)	Used for advanced hormone receptor–positive cancers in postmenopausal women	Hot flashes, vomiting, nausea, constipation, diarrhea, headache, sore throat
Targeted Therapy		
trastuzumab (Herceptin)	Used for advanced cancers with high levels of HER2; used in clinical trials for early-stage cancer	Early, temporary allergic reaction that may include shortness of breath, fever, and chills; rarely, serious side effects include allergic shock, respiratory distress, and damage to the heart

progression of the disease. However, this delay does not necessarily lead to increased life expectancy, and treatment may have negative side effects. Therefore, the decision of how long to continue a given treatment and when to switch to another is based on a woman's response to the therapy and its toxicity.

Standard-Dose Chemotherapy Versus Dose-Dense Chemotherapy

Chemotherapy may be given in a variety of ways, including as standard-dose or dose-dense chemotherapy.

Standard-Dose Chemotherapy

Usually, women receive chemotherapy drugs in cycles. Each treatment period is followed by a rest period to allow the body to recover. White blood cells rise to safe levels again so they can fend off infection. Red blood cells suppressed by chemotherapy need to rise, too. Otherwise, fatigue tied to anemia can occur because the oxygen-carrying red blood cells are suppressed. Possibly, more bleeding or bruising than is normal after minor injuries might happen, too, because there are fewer available platelets (cell fragments that help blood clot).

The combination AC is typically given in four cycles. Each cycle is separated by a three-week rest period and both medications are given on day one of the cycle. The combination CMF is generally given in six cycles of four weeks each, with Cytoxan taken by mouth daily during the first two weeks of the cycle and methotrexate (Mexate) and 5-fluorouracil (Adrucil, abbreviated as 5-FU) given through IV infusion on days one and eight of the cycle. The rest periods are long enough for blood cells to rebound, but hopefully not long enough for cancerous cells to do the same.

Dose-Dense Chemotherapy

Dose-dense chemotherapy came into use when researchers trying to ensure that stray cancer cells are thoroughly trounced decided to give patients the same dose of anticancer medications as usual but cut the rest period down to two weeks. For dose-dense chemotherapy to be safely used, drugs such as filgrastim (Neupogen) or pegfilgrastim (Neulasta) are given to boost white blood cells responsible for quelling infections that might otherwise seriously threaten health. Neupogen is a short-acting agent, so injections are given on days three through ten of each cycle. Neulasta is longer-acting, so a single shot is given on day two of each cycle.

In one dose-dense versus standard-dose study, approximately two thousand women with node-positive breast cancer were treated with Adriamycin, paclitaxel (Taxol), and Cytoxan. Over an average of three years the overall survival rate for dose-dense therapies was 92 percent versus 90 percent for the standard-dose therapies. An estimated 82 percent of those who took dose-dense therapies stayed disease-free for four years compared to 75 percent of those who took standard-dose therapies. The two dose-dense groups, who were given Neulasta, experienced less severe suppression of white blood cells. Otherwise, side effects among the groups were similar. However, side effects were somewhat easier to handle for women who were given the drugs sequentially (one after another) rather than in combination.

More research needs to be done on dose-dense therapy, especially where long-term side effects and the use of other combinations or sequences of medications are concerned. Thus far, though, this is an approach that looks promising, and many patients are receiving these more compressed therapies.

Lowering Doses

Cutting down doses of chemotherapy or falling short of the standard number of treatment cycles to help reduce side effects can compromise survival. Nonetheless, it may happen a lot more often than we think. Researchers at the University of Rochester cautioned against such practices after their 2003 study of twenty thousand women found that more than half did not receive the full recommended schedule of chemotherapy. Reducing the dose or the schedule of treatment may put women at risk of the disease recurring or worsening, the researchers noted.

It can be hard for women to keep this in mind while handling side effects. After her lumpectomy was followed by three cycles of AC, Greta, on the night before the fourth treatment was scheduled, flatly refused to go back. "What's the difference?" she asked her husband. "One treatment. They've done enough, I'm sure they've killed everything." Only her husband's alarmed appeal persuaded her to return. Another woman remembers swearing up and down that she wasn't going back for her last treatment either. Her spouse, although worried, simply told her to do whatever she felt was best. Having vented her feelings, she did indeed show up for her final treatment.

Boosting Doses: High-Dose Chemotherapy

At the opposite end of the spectrum are regimens that boost rather than lower the standard dose. So-called *high-dose chemotherapy* regimens have been used against advanced or aggressive breast cancers in the hope that more intensive chemotherapy would more effectively kill cancer cells.

Bone marrow transplant is an example of this. Bone marrow produces red blood cells, platelets, and many white blood cells, which are central players in the immune system. During a bone marrow transplant, a woman is treated with very high doses of chemotherapy intended to entirely wipe out cancer cells in her body. In the process, the cells of the bone marrow are wiped out, too. To rebuild her immune system, she then receives an infusion of cells from her own bone marrow that were harvested before she was given the high-dose chemotherapy.

This aggressive treatment has been successful with other types of cancer. Although it initially looked quite promising for women with advanced breast cancer, more definitive, randomized studies show that there is no survival benefit when compared to standard-dose chemotherapy and there are serious, sometimes long-term side effects sparked by administering high doses of chemotherapy drugs, as well as higher medical insurance costs.

KINDER, GENTLER CHEMOTHERAPY FOR OLDER WOMEN?

For several reasons, chemotherapy is used less often in older women than in younger women. In premenopausal women, it seems to offer more benefit, probably partly because certain chemotherapies cause the ovaries to shut down and stop producing the estrogen that feeds some cancers. Plus older women are more likely to have health conditions that make chemotherapy drugs riskier, especially if the potential benefit for an individual woman is small.

At this writing, a new study sponsored by the National Cancer Institute is looking at using capecitabine (Xeloda) tablets in women aged sixty-five and older. The drug has proven quite successful for women with metastatic cancer and is now being tested in women with early-stage cancers. The idea, said Dr. Partridge, is to see if the therapy works better than standard chemotherapy in this population or at least works just as well while minimizing side effects.

How Are Chemotherapy Drugs Given?

Chemotherapy drugs are usually given as pills or *intravenously*—that is, by threading a needle attached to a thin plastic tube called a *catheter* into a vein. The catheter is linked to a plastic bag containing the medication, which drips down at a measured rate. A course of treatment might take one to three hours, or occasionally longer. Less often, a syringe is used to inject chemotherapy drugs, such as Adriamycin, into a vein.

Because a few chemotherapy medications may damage veins, and some women may have veins that are fragile or difficult to locate or place an IV into, a *port* is sometimes surgically placed beneath the skin of the chest or arm. The port allows blood to be drawn for lab tests and medications to be injected directly into it. It must be kept scrupulously clean so that infection does not occur. If an infection arises, the port is removed, the infection is given time to clear, and a new port may be placed, if necessary.

The experts—that is, the women who have had chemotherapy as well as other sources of expertise—offer the following advice for easing treatments:

- Have a light meal or snack beforehand (some women suggest avoiding favorite foods, though, lest they forever after hold unfortunate associations).

- Bring a large water bottle or beverages to drink so you stay well hydrated. Popsicles or ice chips can help with fluids, too. Experts disagree over whether sucking on medicated Popsicles or ice chips for thirty minutes starting five minutes before certain chemotherapy regimens helps prevent mouth sores. Ask your doctor or nurse about this.

- Take a small pillow and soft blanket or sweater to help you feel more comfortable and ward off chills.

- Bring a headset to listen to soothing (or raucous) music or to relaxation or guided imagery recordings, plus juicy new books or magazines to while away the time.

- Ask a reliable, thoughtful partner, friend, or relative to come along for support, as well as to do the driving, especially the first time. Choose carefully. Sophie noted that, while she loves her family, she felt more relaxed if they didn't accompany her to treatments. "My sister, the first time she went during my chemo, she broke down. The second time, my mother was here and she was so nervous, she drove me nuts. She's not usually like that. I said, 'I'm doing this *alone* from now on.'"

VISUALIZATION

Military images pop up repeatedly in books on cancer. Cancer cells are battled, fought, and destroyed. Arsenals of drugs are employed to annihilate or eradicate tumors. Even visualization or guided imagery—a relaxation technique that helps you focus on an outcome you desire—often means picturing cancer cells being zapped or vaporized by drugs or radiation beams. Not surprisingly, some women find these words and images off-putting.

Luz, a schoolteacher who discovered her breast cancer at age fifty-three, chose a different route. Before her surgery, she visualized golden hands scooping out any tissue that needed to go. Healing light poured down upon her breast. These images were suggested by a healer she had visited. Luz also created other images for chemotherapy and radiation that centered on "the cancer dissipating and just being sort of flushed out or blown out or seeping out of my body," she said. She ventured into yoga, Reiki, and acupuncture and found joy in simply being mindful—"just stopping to listen, just stopping to breathe." Along with the visualizations, these measures helped her feel that her body was in balance and her spirit unafraid.

- Try stress relief techniques, such as deep breathing or visualization.

- Be prepared to wait: blood tests and treatments can take more time than you expect. Keep a cell phone handy and have backup plans (such as for picking up children at school or asking a coworker to take notes at a meeting).

Thinking About Side Effects

Several decades ago, chemotherapy had a well-deserved reputation for debilitating side effects. Now supportive medications and therapies have made quite a difference.

Reading any list of potential side effects can be alarming to many women, but truly the possibilities must be weighed against the very real benefits of the medications. When compared to a longer period of no recurrence or an extended survival benefit, even potentially serious side effects may pale. It's easy enough for your oncologist to see this but may be far harder for you, especially if your breast cancer diagnosis is quite recent and you feel reasonably healthy. After all, a month or so ago, you weren't expecting to lose your hair or even entertaining the possibility of mouth sores.

Always tell your treatment team about any side effects you do experience, no matter how minor. Often, there are ways to avert or ease problems. Review potential red flags with them, too, so you will know what warning signs are especially important to heed and report. Even a low fever, for example, could signal the start of an infection, while shortness of breath may be a sign of a serious allergy or other problems.

Allergic Reactions

Just as with any drug, an allergic reaction that may range from mild to quite severe can occur in some people. Flushing on the face, itching, a rash, or shortness of breath may all be signs of allergy. Report any of these symptoms promptly. Changing the regimen or adding a drug to block an allergic reaction can help minimize the possibility of a future allergic reaction.

Infusion Site Reactions

A few chemotherapy drugs, such as Adriamycin, can seriously irritate or harm skin if they escape from the vein. This is unusual but happens occasionally. Tell your nurse about any skin discomfort, burning, tingling, itching, or pain during chemotherapy, as well as any signs that crop up days or weeks later, such as injection site swelling, redness, pain, dark discoloration, peeling, or blistering. When caught while the IV is still running, this problem is easier to treat.

Temporary Effects

The short-term effects of chemotherapy depend on the drug, the dosage, the length of treatment, and individual chemistry. These effects typically resolve within months of completing therapy. Talk with your cancer care team about what to expect based on your circumstances. Most commonly, possible temporary effects include the following:

• **Nausea and vomiting:** Within hours after the drug is given or after a few days when antinausea medications are tapered, nausea (usually mild) and vomiting may occur. Symptoms can last for up to a week.

- **Loss of appetite:** Nausea or changes in taste and smell triggered by chemotherapy may dampen appetite.

- **Hair loss:** Depending on the drug or combination used, you may experience hair loss. For example, while hair loss happens to virtually 100 percent of women given the combination AC, it occurs in just 50 percent of women taking CMF. Often, hair starts to grow back within a month after you complete chemotherapy (although fuzz may begin to grow back between cycles).

- **Diarrhea or constipation:** During the days following treatment, diarrhea or constipation may occur. This varies depending on the type of chemotherapy and one's constitution.

- **Dips in blood components:** As bone marrow growth is suppressed, usually between seven and fourteen days after treatment, platelets or red or white blood cells can decline. This differs by drug. A decrease in white blood cells may make you more susceptible to infections, such as colds or other viruses and food-borne illnesses. A shortage of red blood cells leads to anemia, which contributes to deep fatigue. Having fewer platelets, which help blood clot, may mean more bruising or bleeding after fairly minor injuries.

- **Mouth sores:** These usually start as small ulcerations between the fifth and eighth day after a treatment and last a week or two before healing.

Longer-Lasting Effects

Usually, breast cancer treatments slip into jumbled memories as time passes. Yet sometimes, the very treatments that work so well against breast cancer leave reminders in their wake. Fatigue is common. Osteoporosis, fertility problems, or a condition called peripheral neuropathy are possibilities. Far more rarely, heart problems or another cancer may occur. Following are descriptions of some of the longer-lasting effects you might experience:

- **Fatigue:** Between each chemotherapy cycle, fatigue may ease somewhat as your red blood cell count rises. However, fatigue frequently snowballs as treatment proceeds, so it may be quite a while before your energy returns. Try to be patient if you find you recover in fits and starts. One day you may feel energized, the next day you might not. Even a year after treatment, some women say they are not quite as energetic as they used to be; others find they feel like themselves again within months. Helpful tips on how to combat fatigue can be found in Chapter 13.

- **Premature menopause:** A common consequence of adjuvant chemotherapy in premenopausal women is the loss of ovarian function. The chance of going through menopause prematurely as a result of chemotherapy is more common in women over the age of forty and more commonly seen with certain chemotherapeutic agents and at higher total administered doses. The consequences of early menopause may include symptoms like hot flashes and frequent urinary tract infections, osteoporosis, infertility, and possibly emotional and sexual difficulties.

- **Weight gain:** Studies show weight gain occurs in 50 to 96 percent of women receiving chemotherapy. Usually, gains range from five to fifteen pounds, but greater gains are not uncommon. Factors that make weight gain more likely include longer chemotherapy regimens, the steroid prednisone, receiving chemotherapy through pills rather than IV infusion, and being premenopausal or experiencing premature menopause. Weight gain is discussed further in the chapters on exercise, nutrition, and handling menopause (Chapters 11, 12, and 14, respectively).

- **Osteoporosis:** After menopause, bone thinning that can set the stage for fractures accelerates. When chemotherapy causes a woman's periods to cease, bone loss may be rapid, too. A healthy diet, calcium and vitamin D supplements, and weight-bearing exercises such as strength training, walking, or running help fend off bone loss. In some cases, bone-saving medications are necessary, too. See Chapter 11, which covers exercise, and Chapter 12, which covers nutrition, for more information, and talk with your cancer care team about what strategies would be best for you.

- **Fertility:** Chemotherapy can affect fertility, a subject explained more thoroughly in Chapter 15. Menstrual cycles may become irregular or cease temporarily or permanently. A woman's age, the drug, and the dosage all influence this. It's also possible that a woman may *feel* menopausal—she might, for example, temporarily stop having periods or experience hot flashes or vaginal dryness—without actually being menopausal. For that reason, sexually active heterosexual women are advised to use nonhormonal birth control, such as condoms, diaphragms, or a nonhormonal IUD, to avoid an unexpected pregnancy.

- **Peripheral neuropathy:** Tingling, numbness, or discomfort in feet or hands called *peripheral neuropathy* can occur with certain chemotherapy drugs, such as the taxanes Taxol and docetaxel (Taxotere). It may go away when the drug is stopped, but it can also be permanent. Report these symptoms to your cancer care team.

- **Cognitive changes:** As detailed in Chapter 13, some women experience changes in mental sharpness and abilities during or after chemotherapy treatments. Difficulty recalling words or memories; trouble multitasking, learning new information, or interpreting patterns; and problems with coordination and comprehension are some examples of this. These problems may ease up fairly quickly or last for years.

- **Heart problems:** Rarely, the chemotherapy medications Adriamycin or epirubicin (Ellence) can damage the heart muscle so that it cannot pump blood as efficiently as usual, resulting in a condition called *congestive heart failure.* The risk is slim—less than 1 percent at the most commonly used dosages. It rises to 2 to 7 percent at higher cumulative (lifetime) doses, which the majority of women would never reach. It is a bit more common in elderly women and those with a history of heart disease. Even less frequently, heart damage may occur with epirubicin or with a drug used in metastatic cancer called mitoxantrone (Novantrone).

- **Other cancers:** Another rare side effect of chemotherapy is the later development of leukemia or myelodysplastic syndromes (MDSs), cancers that originate in the blood cells of the bone marrow. These disorders typically occur six months to seven years after treatment. With standard-dose AC, the risk is between 0.1 and 0.2 percent (approximately one to two in one thousand people). Some high-dose regimens and adjuvant radiation increase this risk.

Supportive Medications and Therapies

The only cells your oncologist wants to wipe out are the ones responsible for breast cancer. Yet medications designed to zero in on rapidly dividing cells hit unintended targets, such as white blood cells, hair follicles, and cells lining the mouth, stomach, and intestines, which also tend to divide quickly. Resultant side effects or complications include dips in blood cell counts, hair loss, mouth sores, and nausea. Sometimes, ingredients in medications can prompt mild or serious allergic reactions. Chemotherapy and hormonal medications also may set off hot flashes and trigger other menopausal symptoms.

To minimize these side effects or ameliorate them, you may be given supportive drugs before a treatment or afterward, as necessary, including the following:

• Blood cell boosters, such as filgrastim (Neupogen) and pegfilgrastim (Neulasta) for the white blood cells and erythropoietin (Procrit) for the red blood cells.

• Antinausea medications, such as prednisone, ondansetron hydrochloride (Zofran), dexamethasone (Decadron), and prochlorperazine (Compazine). These work in a variety of ways that may make them a better match for certain chemotherapy drugs than for others. Two new medications approved in 2003 were aprepitant (Emend), which acts on a brain pathway affecting nausea that previous drugs were not able to single out, and palonosetron (Aloxi), which helps with moderate nausea.

• Medications to help prevent or quash allergic reactions, including H2-blockers such as diphenhydramine (Benadryl) and ranitidine (Zantac) and steroids such as dexamethasone or methylprednisolone sodium succinate (Solu-Medrol).

• Medications and products for menopausal symptoms, such as hot flashes, vaginal changes, and insomnia. Hot flashes, for example, may be lessened by the antidepressants fluoxetine (Prozac) and venlafaxine (Effexor), antiseizure medication gabapentin (Neurontin), hormone modulators such as medroxyprogesterone (Depo-Provera), and vitamin E. Personal lubricants and moisturizers like Astroglide or Replens can help ease vaginal dryness. Estring, a flexible ring placed at the top of the vagina that delivers a very low dose of estrogen locally, can help with dryness and other vaginal changes. These medications and products are more fully described in Chapter 14.

• Complementary therapies. Acupuncture, for example, has been shown to reduce nausea and vomiting. Relaxation techniques may cool hot flashes somewhat and ease insomnia. Biofeedback can help relieve pain. Guided imagery may boost immune response and help ease nausea. It is important to tell your physician if there are any herbs or remedies you are considering, because some choices can adversely affect chemotherapy or radiation treatments and other choices have not been adequately tested in the context of a breast cancer diagnosis. If you are interested in learning more about complementary therapies, you can gather information through the National Center for Complementary and Alternative Medicine (http://nccam .nih.gov or 888-644-6226) or ask your medical team.

Additional information on handling side effects can be found in other chapters.

HORMONAL THERAPY

While hormonal medications are also systemic, they are better targeted than chemotherapy drugs. They do their work by cutting the fuel supply lines for cancer cells that depend upon the hormones estrogen or progesterone to grow. Cancer cells that have estrogen or progesterone receptors are abbreviated ER+ or PR+, respectively. At this writing, no hormonal therapy specifically targets progesterone, but women whose breast cancers are PR+ may respond to therapies that focus on reducing available estrogen. This works best when the cancerous cells are ER+, too. Data from a retrospective study (which is not as strong as a prospective, randomized trial) of almost fourteen thousand women with early-stage breast cancer found that tamoxifen cut the risk of recurrence by 25 percent in women whose tumors were ER−/PR+ compared to 53 percent in ER+/PR+ patients.

Typically, hormonal therapies are used after breast cancer surgery and often after chemotherapy or radiation if these treatments were also used. Tamoxifen is also used in women at high risk for breast cancer to help decrease their risk.

Shutting Off the Estrogen Supply

Before menopause, the ovaries produce most of the estrogen in a woman's body. Fat cells also produce small quantities of estrogen. The adrenal glands, which ride atop the bean-shaped kidneys, manufacture *androstenedione*. This is primarily a male steroid hormone that women have in lesser amounts. An enzyme called *aromatase* converts androstenedione to estrogen.

After menopause, the ovaries shut off estrogen production. Now the main source of estrogen supplies in the body stem from fat cells and the two-step production process launched by the adrenal glands and aromatase.

Hormonal therapies employ a variety of strategies to reduce the supply of estrogen. They may compete with estrogen, as tamoxifen does. Or they may block a source of estrogen, which is how medications called *aromatase inhibitors* and a range of therapies that affect the ovaries, such as leuprolide (Lupron), work.

Competing for Hormone Receptors: Tamoxifen

Cells throughout the body have hormone receptors. Think of them as signal towers on the cell designed to receive instructions issued by chemical messengers. In this case, the messenger is the hormone estrogen, which circulates in the bloodstream. When estrogen binds to a hormone receptor on a breast cancer cell, it tells the cell to grow and multiply. If large numbers of cells in the breast have these receptors, the message is dangerously amplified and cancer cells have an opportunity to divide.

A group of medications called *selective estrogen receptor modulators* (SERMs) are clever mimics of estrogen that seek out and bind to estrogen receptors on cells throughout the body. Tamoxifen is the best-studied SERM. The ideal SERM would truly be selective, retaining the positive effects of estrogen in some organs (acting as an *agonist*), such as the skeletal system to maintain bone density, and preventing the adverse effects of estrogen in other organs (acting as an *antagonist*), such as the effect of estrogen in contributing to breast and endometrial cancers.

Tamoxifen is an excellent SERM in the breast, where it functions as an antagonist both to prevent a first breast cancer from occurring in high-risk women and to decrease the chance of recurrent breast cancer. While it blocks the action of estrogen in breast cells, it acts like estrogen in bones. That means it actually can help counter osteoporosis, which may reduce the risk of fractures, particularly in the hips. Likewise, it lowers cholesterol, which can lessen the likelihood of heart disease. Unfortunately, it also acts like estrogen in the uterus and circulatory system, increasing the risks of uterine cancer and blood clots.

Over the last twenty-five years, a number of large, long-term studies have proven how effective tamoxifen can be and chronicled its side effects. A 2004 analysis of multiple studies showed that women with ER+ cancers who take tamoxifen for five years annually experience a 40 to 50 percent reduction in recurrence and a bit more than a 30 percent reduction in deaths. What's more, these benefits appear strong in younger, premenopausal women—who have higher amounts of estrogen in their bodies—as well as in older, postmenopausal women. Among women younger than forty, recurrences were cut by 44 percent and deaths from all causes plummeted 37 percent when tamoxifen was compared to a placebo (sugar pill). Furthermore, in women whose breast cancer is estrogen receptor–positive, a five-year course of tamoxifen reduces the risk of developing a second, new cancer in the other breast by 50 percent.

Taking tamoxifen for five years provides a greater survival improvement than taking it for a shorter duration. Taking tamoxifen longer than five years does not appear to yield additional benefits and may merely lengthen a woman's exposure to possible side effects and adverse events. Its positive influence on recurrence and survival continues for years even after women stop taking it. One question that awaits further study is whether tamoxifen is just as effective as chemotherapy for younger women, whether used alone or if combined with a therapy that suppresses the

PREVENTING BREAST CANCER IN HIGH-RISK WOMEN

A woman may be at increased risk of developing breast cancer because of a strong family history of the condition, a known genetic mutation, atypical microscopic findings observed in a biopsy specimen, or other factors. Women at very high risk have three options: very close surveillance with breast-imaging studies including mammography and MRIs coupled with periodic clinical breast exams; taking medications to reduce the risk of developing breast cancer (*chemoprevention*); or surgically removing both breasts (*prophylactic mastectomy*) or both ovaries (*prophylactic oophorectomy*).

The National Surgical Adjuvant Breast and Bowel Project mounted a chemoprevention trial to test tamoxifen in more than thirteen thousand high-risk women. The women were randomly divided into two groups that received either tamoxifen or a placebo. During the five-year follow-up period, women taking tamoxifen cut in half their risk of developing breast cancer. Specifically, the chance of developing invasive breast cancer was forty-three per one thousand women in the placebo group versus twenty-two per one thousand women in the tamoxifen group—overall, that's a 49 percent decrease. The chance of developing an ER+ breast cancer was reduced by almost 70 percent. There was no reduction in risk for ER− tumors. Tamoxifen also decreased the risk of ductal carcinoma in situ by 50 percent and was highly effective for women with atypical cells found during a biopsy.

Prophylactic mastectomy has been found to reduce breast cancer risk by 90 percent (see Chapter 3). A 2002 *New England Journal of Medicine* study found that decreasing estrogen levels by surgically removing the ovaries in women with BRCA1 and BRCA2 mutations also cut the chance of breast cancer in half, from 42 percent to 21 percent, at eight years of follow-up. The risk of ovarian cancer was also decreased from roughly 20 percent to 1 percent.

Again, it bears saying that women at highest risk stand to gain the greatest absolute benefits. Check with your physician about what that might mean in your case.

ovaries. Another question—one which researchers are addressing in postmenopausal women—is whether a woman should stay on tamoxifen for five years or switch to another drug partway through that time period. This is discussed later in this chapter.

Side Effects

Hot flashes and vaginal discharge are common. Irregular periods, vaginal itching or irritation, fatigue, headaches, nausea, and skin rashes have also been reported.

Uncommon side effects of tamoxifen include a slightly increased risk of endometrial cancer in postmenopausal women (an average annual risk of roughly 0.2 percent with tamoxifen versus 0.1 percent with a placebo), blood clots (deep venous thrombosis), clots traveling to the lungs (pulmonary embolism), cataracts, and cancer of the uterus muscle (very rare).

Be assured that not every woman has these symptoms, however. Researchers have also noted that some of the symptoms may be traced to changes around menopause and aging, rather than the drug, in some women. Data from a large study of women at high risk for cancer who were given tamoxifen show no apparent differences in weight gain or depression among women given the drug compared to those who received a placebo. That said, women on tamoxifen not infrequently cite weight gain as a concern to their physicians. Often, there are the compounding factors of less physical activity as they recover from surgery or are being treated with chemotherapy or metabolic changes that may occur when abruptly entering menopause.

Shutting Off the Ovaries: Ovarian Suppression and Ablation

Remember, the ovaries pump out significant supplies of estrogen in women who are still having periods. Some experts believe part of chemotherapy's benefit on these premenopausal women stems from shutting down estrogen production in the ovaries, even temporarily.

Several studies strongly suggest that purposefully quieting the ovaries, which can be accomplished with medications (*ovarian suppression*) or through surgically removing the ovaries (*ovarian ablation*), can improve survival in women with early-stage, hormone receptor–positive breast cancer. Definitive studies have not yet been done, although some are under way and should help answer many important questions. For example, might ovarian suppression substitute for modern chemotherapy treatments, providing equal or superior benefits while sparking fewer side effects? Might ovarian suppression added to tamoxifen be superior to tamoxifen alone? Might alternatives to tamoxifen, such as an aromatase inhibitor, provide superior results?

Right now, European and American researchers believe that ovarian suppression can be a very important tool in treating ER+ breast cancer in premenopausal women. Several international trials are under way, though it will take years to complete them and answer these questions. It is particularly difficult to mount randomized trials to test the effects of surgery on the ovaries, to say the least.

Ovarian Suppression with Medications

Medications called *luteinizing hormone-releasing hormone (LHRH) agonists*—quite a mouthful—are sometimes used to suppress the ovaries. The drugs, which include goserelin (Zoladex), Lupron, and triptorelin (Trelstar Depot), keep the ovaries from manufacturing hormones. Zoladex and Lupron are approved by the U.S. Food and Drug Administration (FDA) for use in pre- and perimenopausal women with hormone receptor–positive cancer. Triptorelin is presently being used in two European trials but will not be available in the United States until its efficacy and side effects are established by the FDA.

One advantage to choosing drugs alone rather than ovarian ablation via surgery is their temporary nature. A woman can essentially test-drive the drug to see whether the benefits outweigh any side effects she experiences. As with surgically removing the ovaries, the drugs cause menopausal symptoms, such as hot flashes, a crimp in sex drive, and vaginal dryness.

With Lupron, some women report that the shot itself—which is given monthly or every three months in the gluteal (buttocks) muscle—can be surprisingly painful, though this doesn't last long. Treating the injection site beforehand with a numbing agent cuts the sting. There is some concern that medication to suppress the ovaries may not lower estrogen levels as well as ovarian ablation through surgery. Whether or not this is so, and if it is, what effect that has in treating breast cancer is currently unknown.

Ovarian Ablation with Surgery

Ovarian ablation can be accomplished in a premenopausal woman by surgically removing her ovaries. This technique is permanent, however, and triggers an abrupt menopause. The symptoms that may accompany this—hot flashes, night sweats, vaginal dryness, loss of sex drive, bone loss due to lack of estrogen, and other menopausal issues—may be difficult to handle. Estrogen replacement therapy, which works well to counter these problems, is considered quite controversial for women who have had breast cancer and is not recommended. Other remedies (see Chapter 14) are available but often imperfect.

Tampering with Aromatase

A few of the newer anticancer medications exert influence over the enzyme aromatase. Aromatase helps convert the hormone androstenedione, which is produced by the adrenal glands, to estrogen. This is a significant source of estrogen in older women whose ovaries are no longer active. Thus, these drugs, called *aromatase inhibitors*, reduce blood levels of estrogen and are used in postmenopausal women with ER+ breast cancers.

New information about these drugs is expanding treatment choices for many women. According to a status report from the American Society of Clinical Oncology, published in the *Journal of Clinical Oncology* in 2005, aromatase inhibitors now may be chosen as a first-line therapy for postmenopausal women who have contraindications to tamoxifen. For postmenopausal women who don't have contraindications to tamoxifen, sequential therapy can be considered. In this case, women may take tamoxifen for two, three, or five years before switching to an aromatase inhibitor for two, three, or five years.

In premenopausal women, ovarian estrogen production overwhelms estrogen production from other sites in the body. Because aromatase inhibitors do not suppress the ovaries, they are not effective for premenopausal women and should not be administered. If an aromatase inhibitor were to be used and have an effect, the ovaries would need to be suppressed also. First, though, researchers would need to determine how aromatase inhibitors in premenopausal women stack up compared to standard therapies—are they better, as effective, or worse?

Options for aromatase inhibitors currently include the following:

• **Anastrozole (Arimidex):** This drug is approved for treating early-stage and late-stage cancers. Currently, it has the distinction of being the only aromatase inhibitor tested directly against tamoxifen as first-line adjuvant hormonal therapy. According to a large trial dubbed ATAC (anastrozole and tamoxifen alone or in combination), 86.9 percent of the women who took anastrozole avoided a relapse compared to 84.5 percent of those who took tamoxifen after an average of four years. To date, there is no survival advantage. Side effects of the two hormonal therapies differ, which might be a reason to choose one drug over another. Women who took anastrozole less frequently experienced endometrial cancers, strokes, blood clots, vaginal bleeding and discharge, and hot flashes; those who took tamoxifen less frequently experienced fractures and musculoskeletal disorders.

- **Letrozole (Femara):** In postmenopausal women with hormone receptor–positive disease who had completed a five-year course of tamoxifen, the addition of letrozole increased the proportion of women who were cancer-free from 87 percent to 93 percent when compared to placebo, according to an updated analysis of an international drug trial presented at the 2004 American Society of Clinical Oncology meeting. In the fall of 2004, the FDA approved letrozole for extended treatment of early-stage breast cancer after a woman has taken five years of tamoxifen. Currently, more data are needed to better understand long-term outcomes beyond the median of twenty-nine months reported in the initial trial.

- **Exemestane (Aromasin):** This drug, which is approved for postmenopausal women with metastatic breast cancer, is now being studied in women with early-stage breast cancer. An international study published in 2003 in the *New England Journal of Medicine* showed that postmenopausal women who switched from tamoxifen to exemestane after two or three years reaped more benefits at the five-year mark. Among those who switched, 93.9 percent avoided a relapse, cancer in the other breast, or death; among those who stayed the course with tamoxifen, 86.8 percent avoided a relapse, cancer in the other breast, or death. No significant difference in overall survival was found. The study—which, at this time, only provides an average of two and a half years of follow-up—currently cannot be considered definitive.

Based on such promising information, aromatase inhibitors are likely to be used more often in postmenopausal women with ER+ cancers either early in treatment or after some period of tamoxifen therapy, depending on prognosis, other health problems, and other evolving factors.

Side Effects

In general, the side effects of aromatase inhibitors include an increased risk of osteoporosis, muscle and bone aches, gastrointestinal symptoms, and hot flashes. The National Cancer Institute notes that, unlike tamoxifen, aromatase inhibitors do not increase the risks of endometrial cancer or blood clots. However, their long-term effects are not well studied, especially when compared to tamoxifen, which has been in use for a quarter century.

Aromatase inhibitors are known to speed bone loss and raise the risk of fractures. That is why strategies to minimize bone loss—regular weight-bearing exercise, a healthy diet paired with calcium and vitamin D supplements, and bone-saving medications, if necessary—are crucial.

A Targeted Therapy: Herceptin

One of the tumor characteristics oncologists use to guide therapy is the presence of cancer cells that produce high levels of a protein called HER2/neu. This protein exists in small amounts on the surface of healthy breast cells and on some breast cancer cells. However, about 20 to 25 percent of women with breast cancer have too much HER2 on the cancer cells. Cancer cells that overexpress (produce too much) HER2 tend to spread more aggressively.

Monoclonal antibodies are drugs designed to target specific proteins. The monoclonal antibody Herceptin targets the HER2/neu protein receptors on the cancer cells. The drug can block HER2/neu from stimulating cell growth and appears to encourage the immune system to attack cancers more effectively.

Right now, Herceptin is mostly used in women with metastatic cancer, although trials of it in women with early-stage cancer are under way. The drug is often used with chemotherapy, forming a combination that is more effective than chemotherapy alone. Herceptin is given intravenously, generally every week. Studies also show that it can be given every three weeks.

Side Effects

Although serious side effects are rare, 30 to 40 percent of women have mild to moderate reactions, such as fever, chills, shortness of breath, or blood pressure changes, the first time they receive the drug. Most of the time, these are easily controlled by slowing the Herceptin infusion rate or by giving a supportive medication to counteract the symptom. Nausea, weakness, pain, vomiting, diarrhea, headaches, and rashes also have been reported. Occasionally, the drug can damage the heart muscle, especially if combined with Adriamycin, or can affect the lungs.

Part II

Preserving Your Sense of Self: Responding to Treatment Challenges

6

A CHANGE IN LOOKS: BREAST APPEARANCE

◉

Unless your surgery was truly minimal, your confidence in how you look may be shaken. No one can tell you exactly how you'll respond. You may choose to do all you can to reshape your body or decide you are comfortable with it as is. Your new appearance may be profoundly unsettling or it may affect you less than you or anyone in your circle expects. Often, your initial reaction softens over time.

Beneath the skin, where your heart still beats and healing starts, remember, you are essentially the same person. Cancer takes away certain choices but leaves others in its wake. Whether you've always been the wild one, utterly demure, a mother to all, or someone else entirely, you can still choose the look that you want to project to the world after your surgery as well as how you wish to see yourself.

One myth about cancer is that it forever separates mundane concerns from deeper priorities. While wrestling with fear and difficult treatments may give you hard-won insight into what truly counts in your life, don't feel compelled to snub less lofty issues. If how you look affects the way you feel, spending some time on your appearance will probably make you feel much better. And that counts, too.

This chapter explains how your appearance may change after a lumpectomy or mastectomy and touches on whether reconstructive surgery, a breast form, or accepting your body unadorned will suit you best. It details options in breast forms, lingerie, activewear, and dressing for many occasions that can ease you back into the stream of your life.

WHAT WILL I LOOK LIKE?

One key question my patients ask is, "What will I look like afterward?" Your surgeon will explain how your body will change and may show you photos of women who have had similar operations, if you like. The following is a general description of what to expect after a lumpectomy or a mastectomy.

After a Lumpectomy

When you look at your breasts after a lumpectomy, your eye may focus on the differences. When your surgeon removed the cancerous tissue, usually as a small ball or a wedge, she or he also took out a margin of normal tissue. Initially, you may notice swelling at the surgical site, which may even make the breast on which the surgery was performed seem larger than your other breast. The swelling occurs as fluid from the divided lymphatic channels collects within the breast (*seroma*). Your body will naturally reabsorb this lymphatic fluid during the weeks following surgery. (See Figure 6.1.)

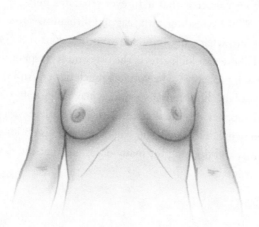

Figure 6.1 After removal of a small lump, the surgical site may look puckered or scooped out.

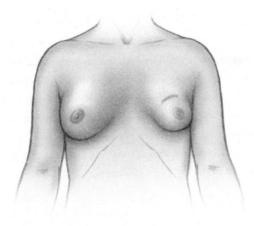

Figure 6.2 If a larger amount of tissue is removed, the breast may look noticeably smaller than its mate and the position of the nipple and areola may shift as well.

If the lump removed was small, you may have hardly any visual token of your surgery. If the lump was larger or if your breast is small, you may notice dissimilarity between your breasts. No woman's breasts look exactly the same, of course. But now there may be an obvious pucker or a spot that looks scooped out. Or the breast may be a smaller size and shaped differently. (See Figure 6.2.) The areola and nipple, too, may have moved off-center or been changed by surgery.

While removing cancerous cells is their paramount concern, surgeons also try to minimize scarring. Usually, the incision is closed with stitches placed under the skin. These will dissolve on their own in six weeks or so. These absorbable stitches are covered either with adhesive strips called Steri-Strips or surgical glue. Less commonly, the surgeon may use visible, external stitches that require removal in the office one to two weeks after the procedure.

The scar left by a lumpectomy may be lighter or darker than your skin tone and will blend in more over time as the body replaces skin cells. If the incision was placed along the border of your areola, no scar will show when you wear a bathing suit or revealing clothes. Otherwise, the scar may be apparent.

Before your surgery, talk with your surgeon about the placement and length of the surgical incision, the type of closure to be used, and what dressing will be

VISUALIZING THE CHANGE

As a breast cancer surgeon, I was well aware of how my body would change after surgery. Yet a picture can be worth a thousand words. Some women find it relieves their worries to get a better idea of what to expect from their surgeries, either through photos that their doctors can show them or other sources. You may not always like what you see, but at least your mind won't work overtime imagining the worst. One website that offers a closer look is breast cancer.org. Another option is the book *Show Me: A Photo Collection of Breast Cancer Survivors' Lumpectomies, Mastectomies, Breast Reconstructions, and Thoughts on Body Image*. (See Resources.)

applied. Waterproof dressings will enable you to shower while the incision is healing. One such dressing is Tegaderm, which looks like a piece of plastic wrap that is sticky on the skin side like a bandage and smooth on the outside like plastic wrap.

Initially, there may be bruising at the incision site if a small amount of blood leaks into the skin when the final stitches are placed. This will disappear as your body reabsorbs this blood. If the bruising extends beyond the boundaries of the surgical dressing and there is a firm swelling at the surgical site, you might have a *hematoma*, a collection of blood inside the biopsy cavity from a bleeding vessel that has reopened. Although uncommon, hematomas can occur immediately after surgery while a woman is in the recovery room or several days later. A possible hematoma requires evaluation by your surgeon. A second operation may be necessary to remove the blood and seal off the bleeding vessel.

If axillary (underarm) lymph nodes were removed, you will notice an incision toward the bottom of your underarm where the hairline ends. Usually, it will not be visible if your arm is down at your side. However, if you are wearing a sleeveless shirt and waving exuberantly to someone with your arm up over your head, the scar can be seen. Generally, the contour of the underarm area is unchanged. The lymph nodes that were removed lie beneath the underarm fat pad directly below the skin. If there is a hollow in the underarm area, some of the fat between the skin and lymph node basin was probably taken out, too.

After a Mastectomy

No matter how well prepared you were for the surgery, your first look at yourself after a mastectomy is likely to be a shock. Your body looks profoundly different than your memory of it. A few women shrug this off stoically. Most need time to grieve the loss of their breast and adjust slowly to the change in body image.

Breast tissue slopes downward from the collarbone, gathering fullness along the way, and wraps around beneath the armpit. During a mastectomy, skin, the entire underlying breast tissue, and the nipple and areola are removed. Infrequently, muscles are taken out, too. How much skin is taken depends on whether you are going to have breast reconstruction at the time of the mastectomy. If you are planning to do so, the surgeon will try to leave more skin intact. (See Chapter 3.)

At the time of the mastectomy, one or two soft plastic drains are placed to siphon off excess lymphatic fluid that might otherwise hamper healing. The drains extend through small holes in the skin in the outer part of the chest wall, where they are secured with a nylon suture. When the drains collect less than 30cc of fluid over the course of twenty-four hours (about half of a Dixie cup), they are ready to be removed (typically one to two weeks after surgery).

As with a lumpectomy, swelling and bruising will disappear first. The incision site scar will fade more gradually over time. The scar itself may be horizontal or vertical or it may arc diagonally from the midline to the outside of your chest.

Once it heals, slender women may find their chest wall looks relatively smooth, with a few dips and rises of the ribs. Heavier women may notice an uneven intersection where the newly flattened chest wall meets a roll of flesh beneath the arm, in the center of the chest at the breastbone, or at the level of the collarbone. Closing the skin too tightly could cut off blood supply, compromising healing and perhaps even damaging skin. Thus, the surgeon will close the incision with some laxity of the skin to optimize blood flow to the skin edges. Because you are lying flat during surgery, it is hard for even the most experienced breast cancer surgeon to visualize exactly how your healed chest will look as you stand or move around.

Consider Your Choices

Should you choose reconstructive surgery? Wear a breast form? Go au naturel? Only you can decide what would make you feel most comfortable. Gather information on your choices and try to talk with women who have faced them before you. If you wish, the American Cancer Society, Y-ME, or other helpful organizations have volunteers who can share their experiences. (See Resources.)

Reconstructive Surgery

Without reconstructive surgery, it's reasonably simple to accomplish a natural look while clothed, but surgery goes much further, of course. Reconstructive surgery, although not for every woman, is chosen by thousands each year who hope to make their bodies look and feel as natural as possible. If you enjoy water sports, running, or other vigorous activities, as I do, you may be much more comfortable with a reconstructed breast that moves when you do. While the surgery cannot make you look exactly as you once did, it may help you feel more confident and attractive sexually as well. Unfortunately, reconstruction cannot restore sensation lost or muted due to nerves that were cut during the original breast surgery.

Chapter 7 discusses the options for reconstruction more fully. In a nutshell, though, the first decision is whether to have the procedure in tandem with your cancer surgery or later after other treatments, such as chemotherapy or radiation. A plastic surgeon can help you evaluate when to have the surgery and which of these operations would suit your wishes and body:

- A saline or silicone breast implant placed under the chest muscle (usually a tissue expander is inserted first to gradually stretch the muscle before an implant is placed)

- A flap procedure that reconstructs the breast with skin, fat, and sometimes muscle taken from another area of your body

- Reduction surgery to the other breast, if, for example, a lumpectomy made one breast significantly smaller or if there is a size discrepancy between the breast not treated for cancer and the reconstructed breast

Breast Forms

Wearing a breast form (or *prosthesis*, if you prefer the medical term) falls between reconstructive surgery and leaving your body as it is. Often, women who postpone reconstructive surgery will use a breast form, or even a variety of these forms, during the interim period. Some women who don't intend to have reconstructive surgery find this a good long-term choice.

Breasts come in many shapes and sizes. So do breast forms, which may be fashioned after pears, hearts, triangles, ovals, circles, or teardrops. Contours vary, too, depending on the extent of the surgery. The range of choices may seem startling or even overwhelming. But it also may be comforting to know that with a little effort you can find a form that more closely approximates your shape.

Until your breast or chest wall heals, any breast form that you wear is likely to be lightweight foam or polyester fluff. You can leave the hospital with one tucked into a pocket in a bra designed to hold a form (see "Bras and Camisoles" later in the chapter) or wait until your chest wall or breast feels less tender. Later you can choose from the breast forms described next or new options that become available. Some breast forms—sometimes called *box forms*—are mass-produced. Others are custom-made.

Choosing Among Breast Forms

When you buy a breast form, a fitter can select the right size and shape for you (see the sidebar "The Right Fit" a little later in the chapter). Handle the merchandise so that you know how it will feel and move. Ask to see, touch, and try on as many forms as possible. If this seems embarrassing, remember that you are the customer and you need to know what you are buying. Here are some options to consider:

• Puffs are typically inexpensive, light foam or fluffy polyester filling with a fabric covering. (See Figure 6.3.) Some have a central, vertical seam that may show through clothing, while others are smooth. Extra filling can be added in some cases, which is helpful because padding becomes more compact with wear. Because puffs have virtually no heft, they tend to ride up unless pinned securely into a bra pocket or shelf bra of a camisole. These don't have the "give" of a breast either but can be a good choice right after surgery when much weight against the chest would be uncomfortable. These forms are fine to wear while swimming if you choose not to buy a separate swim form (just bring a dry form to change into).

• Standard forms are closer to the weight of the remaining breast. When filled with silicone or gel, they tend to look natural and feel that way, too, when someone hugs you. These forms move as you do and may even be designed to flatten

Figure 6.3 Puffs use a lightweight material (foam or polyester). This type of breast form is likely to be the most comfortable right after surgery and as you heal. These come both with and without seams.

out somewhat when you lie down, just as a breast normally does. Alternatively, latex may be used as a covering for foam or as material for the whole form. Such forms are inexpensive and not quite as natural looking. Latex allergies make them a poor choice for certain women.

• Lightweight forms can be a boon for certain women, especially those with larger breasts or concerns about lymphedema. Some women simply find them easier to wear, particularly if the chest wall remains uncomfortable after the surgical site has healed. Blended or whipped silicone or latex may be used in these lighter versions, or the form may be scooped out or designed to incorporate more air.

• Swim forms are durable and waterproof. They may be hollowed out or made with light materials. Some have tiny pores throughout the form that allow water to flow through them. Such forms then can be gently squeezed out when you emerge from swimming.

- Asymmetrical forms are designed to help fill out certain areas of the breast or underarm removed during surgery. They may cover much of the breast or just a portion of it to achieve the right balance for a woman after lumpectomy.

- Lumpectomy pads, shapers, balancers, or filler pads can plump out small areas of the breast that need a bit extra after surgery.

- Shells are thin, concave forms designed to smooth out or enlarge the look of the breast. They may be firm or filled with gel. Breast form manufacturers and some lingerie stores carry these.

- Uplifts, boosters, or enhancers push breasts upward to enhance cleavage. They are regularly sold in lingerie stores. If a breast form makes one side look fuller or project more than the other, tucking an enhancer beneath the natural breast can even this out. These can also be used to fill out scooped-out areas in the same way as lumpectomy pads.

- Hybrid forms mix materials, such as a gel breast form with a pocket for polyester fluff. This form can be helpful in matching breast size and shape more closely or possibly when an expander is being used during reconstructive surgery before the permanent implant is placed.

Be aware that terms vary. One manufacturer's "lumpectomy pads" may be called "shapers" by another company.

Backing and Color Choices

Backing materials differ. Some are soft fibers, such as a cotton blend or polyester knit fabric or a microfiber designed to absorb perspiration. Others employ materials that shape themselves to the body, such as a gel. Still other breast form backings may be sculpted or textured for a comfortable fit against the chest wall or are slightly sticky so that they adhere well (see "How Do Breast Forms Stay Put?" a little later in the chapter).

Commercial breast forms may be offered in a choice of just a few colors: very light skin, medium light skin, and tawny, for example. Women of color often find very few options in darker skin shades. Custom forms can offer more than twenty colors to choose from, which makes it much more likely that you will find one that comes closer to matching your skin tone. Thus far, no manufacturer, custom or commercial, offers to match your skin tone exactly.

Nipples

Some breast forms come with nipples on them and others do not. "After having a mastectomy, I felt like I was walking around with one headlight on and one headlight off," Antonia wryly reported. Women who decide to wear breast forms also note the same problem. The nipple on your natural breast responds to cold or touch, but the nipple on a reconstructed breast or breast form clearly does not. One headlight on, one headlight off, indeed.

Custom breast forms allow you to match your own nipple or choose from a few styles that vary slightly in projection—that is, how relaxed or aroused the nipple appears. You can also buy latex nipples that attach to the skin or breast form. These are sold by some breast form companies, like Amoena and Airway, and, sometimes, at lingerie shops. Often, they can be found at hospital appearance boutiques as well.

How Do Breast Forms Stay Put?

Breast forms may be tucked into a pocket in a bra or clothing or pinned securely if made from foam or fluff. Some are designed to adhere to the chest wall with a roll-on adhesive (Figure 6.4) or stick-on Velcro pads (Figure 6.5). Sometimes, a system of adhesive disks and magnets (Figure 6.6), adhesive patches, or backing material that has a sticky quality is employed. There are skin solvents available to remove the adhesive material that may remain on the skin after the form is removed.

How well a form stays put will vary. Manufacturers may boast that their system ensures little slippage, but generally there are some disclaimers involved. Lightweight foam is most likely to ride upward, especially during a heated exercise session. When slippery with sweat, silicone or polyurethane-covered forms may slide around more, particularly outward and downward on the chest. Some women find it more comfortable to tuck the form into a bra pocket while exercising, even if they would normally rely on adhesive or another system to hold it in place. One woman offered a different solution. "I drape a gym towel over the shoulder of the side where I wear a breast form. It works best when I'm strength training, but gets hot when I'm doing a cardio workout—then I just stare down anyone who is staring at my chest!"

TAKE A TOUR

If you have access to the Internet—at home, at a friend's house, or even at the local library—you can take a virtual tour through the options for breast forms and clothing. Or call several companies (see Resources) to request their catalogs. That way you can see what is out there without feeling pressured to make any decisions or purchases. When you feel ready to discuss choices or go for a fitting, you'll be familiar with what's available. A sampling includes the following:

- Amoena (amoena.org and thebreastcaresite.com) carries many styles of breast forms and shapers, as well as practical, traditionally tailored postmastectomy bras and swimwear.
- Still You Fashions (stillyoufashions.com) has a small array of beautiful, very feminine camisoles and lingerie. The company has its own style of gel-filled breast form.
- Airway (surgicalappliance.com) has a good range of breast forms and bras (including a bra that is seamless). Some of the breast forms have a comfortable microfiber backing to absorb perspiration or a pocket that holds polyester fluff to allow a more customized shaping. A small collection of swimwear to suit most figures is available through the company's printed catalog.
- Camp Healthcare (camphealthcare.com) has a variety of traditional and lightweight breast forms for women who have had a lumpectomy or mastectomy. The company also sells helpful accessories, such as StayDry Ovals (disposable pads that go on the back of the form), washable breast form covers, and lacy vee-shapes and wedges to add to bras for extra coverage.
- The "tlc" catalog (tlccatalog.org) from the American Cancer Society offers breast forms, lingerie, sleepwear, swimwear, and many other products designed to help women who have had mastectomies or are undergoing treatment for breast cancer. A very soft, loose camisole or bra for use during radiation treatments is available.
- Lands' End (landsend.com) has several attractive mastectomy swimsuits and the option of separate tankini tops and bottoms.

The more active you are, the more you'll want a form that will stay in place. Ask a fitter to describe your options.

Caring for Breast Forms

Any breast form you buy should come with instructions for cleaning and care. The products you use may make a difference in how soon you'll have to buy a new one. Lotions, soaps, and cleansers may have ingredients that gradually erode the outer shell. The cleanser or spray supplied by the manufacturer or a mild soap without perfume or deodorant, such as Ivory, is usually best.

Common sense dictates that safety pins and other sharp objects should be kept well away from gel-filled forms. One manufacturer even suggests removing rings and jewelry before touching a breast form because a gemstone or rough edge might cause damage. Sunlight and heat can speed wear and tear on certain materials, so store forms according to instructions.

A form filled with polyester fluff easily can be refilled as necessary to keep it in shape. Manufacturers of other types of forms may supply a cradle that fits the form when you're not wearing it.

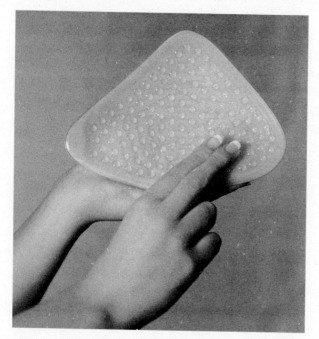

Figure 6.4 Adhesive breast form.

Figure 6.5 Velcro breast form.

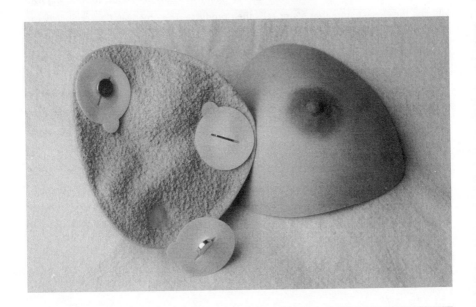

Figure 6.6 Magnetic breast form.

THE RIGHT FIT

Where should you go to be fitted for a breast form? Specialty lingerie shops, department stores, and some medical equipment suppliers or pharmacies may have a basic or broad selection of forms and, possibly, a fitter who can help you. Lady Grace and Nordstrom's are two examples. Better still in many instances are hospitals that have a boutique with specially trained personnel who can help.

A few options include:

- The Friends Boutique at Dana-Farber Cancer Institute in Boston
- The Memorial Boutique at the Breast Center at Memorial-Sloan Kettering Cancer Center in New York City
- Ernie's Appearance Center at Baylor University Medical Center in Dallas
- CareWear at the University of Wisconsin Comprehensive Cancer Center in Madison
- Reflections at UCLA's Jonsson Comprehensive Cancer Center

Hospitals that do not have such services may send someone to talk with you about breast forms during your stay if you have a mastectomy. Reach to Recovery volunteers from the American Cancer Society do this; so do sales representatives from specific manufacturers. Of course, there is always Internet shopping. Although there really is no way for you to ensure proper fit or handle the merchandise, many company websites have a locator that will help you find the closest store that fits or sells their products. The American Cancer Society can help you in this search, too.

Before you make a trip to any store or supplier, call ahead to find out who will be helping you. Whenever possible, choose a certified mastectomy fitter. The American Board for Certification in Orthotics and Prosthetics or the Board for Orthotist/Prosthetist Certification ensures that a person has received training and passed qualifying exams. Manufacturers may provide their own training as well, but that would be limited to their products. Ask about experience and how large a selection of products will be available to you. Inquire whether the fitter knows of new products through continuing education classes or conferences where medical goods are showcased.

If you do a little research ahead of time, you may know generally what types of forms you are interested in learning more about. That knowledge can help you find someone who can serve you well.

Custom Breast Forms

One step closer to the real you are custom-made breast forms. Currently, a plaster-casting technique or three-dimensional body scan is used to create the form, which then hugs the exact contours of your chest wall. Thus, it looks more natural and feels more comfortable than commercial forms.

Custom forms echo the coloring and shape of your breast fairly closely. One company offers twenty-one color choices, for example, and another company sixteen—not perfect, but both a far cry from the typical two to three options of commercial forms. Even your nipple can be re-created in the mirror image of your natural breast and the color matched, if you choose. If you plan to have a bilateral mastectomy, the casting can be performed beforehand, or you can choose the breast shape you prefer while ensuring that the final form will be shaped to fit your chest wall.

Two custom forms available at this writing are ContourMed (contourmed.com or 888-301-0520) and Radiant Impressions by Camp Healthcare (radiantimpressions.net or 800-492-1088). Both must be fitted by a trained consultant.

Who Pays?

Insurance varies widely, so check with your insurer directly about what will and won't be covered.

The Women's Health and Cancer Rights Act of 1998 requires health insurance plans that cover mastectomies to pay the costs of surgical reconstruction and prostheses (breast forms) for women who chose reconstructive surgery, except for appropriate co-pays and deductibles. This applies to every state, but there are certain exemptions for health plans, so it is wise to make sure it applies to you. Check the Centers for Medicare and Medicaid Services for more information (cms.hhs.gov/hipaa/hipaa1 and click on Women's Health and Cancer Rights Act or call 877-267-2323).

If you do not have reconstructive surgery, an insurer might pay for a prosthesis every two years and two bras annually. Find out in advance what will be covered and whether it matters if you choose a breast form in addition to reconstructive surgery. Some companies may not pay for both. Co-pays and deductibles generally apply, and many insurance companies only reimburse you for a set amount for all

BEHIND THE SCENES: FITTING FOR A CUSTOM BREAST FORM

If your destination is reclaiming your body, you can reach it through more than one path. After my mastectomy, I left the hospital with a lightweight puff beneath my shirt. I wore it in public while my drains were in and my chest wall healed. Once I finished chemotherapy, I planned to have breast reconstruction with an implant after an expander had been placed under the chest muscle to gradually stretch the muscle and skin. Because all of this would take a while, I had a custom breast form made two months after my surgery.

The form I chose required plaster casting of my intact breast. If you decide to do this, be sure to wear old clothes and shoes—the plaster drips! The fitting room was kept on the cool side during casting because Julie Durmis, a certified mastectomy fitter at the Friends Boutique at Dana-Farber Cancer Institute, has found that some women feel overheated as the plaster dries.

Before my fitting, I had chosen the shades I wanted for the finished form. There were three separate color sections—skin, areola, and nipple—to select from a palette of twenty-one color choices. There were also two choices of ready-made nipples, or I could decide to have a custom-fitted nipple made or simply leave the form without one. A natural nipple relaxes or projects depending on temperature or arousal. The choices of nipple for the breast form vary in projection, too—though, naturally, whichever one a woman wears won't change when the temperature does. When a nipple mold is made in a cool room, it is bound to show more projection than would be usual throughout the day. Because of this, Julie recommended selecting one of the standard nipples with a lesser amount of projection.

Along with old clothes, I brought a favorite, comfortable bra to the fitting. It would be used during the chest wall markings and sent to the manufacturer with the plaster cast. Using a thick, felt-tipped pen, Julie marked a series of intersecting lines across my chest at the underarm, below the breast and rib cage, and down the center of my chest. Other marks outlined my bra and nipple. They extended beyond the bra to the upper chest, too, where I chose to have the form shaped to mimic the way my breast tissue previously had tapered. These marks were designed to show up on the plaster cast used to create the breast form.

Ask questions and be active to get the fit you really want. Depending on your surgery, you may have hollowed-out areas on your chest that you want the form to cover. Don't be afraid to request that.

Photos of my chest were taken from all sides and a lotion was applied to the skin surrounding the marked areas to make the cast come off more easily. Use lots of lotion. I could have used more.

A plastic bag served as an apron to protect my pants. Then Julie dipped plaster strips into warm water and gently applied them to the chest wall and intact breast so that the cast extended from below the collarbone, over all of my chest and ribs, and toward my waist. This process may be uncomfortable if surgery has left the chest area numb, tingling, burning, or painful to touch, as it did in my case.

Once the cast had dried, which took about seven minutes, Julie peeled it away. That was the least comfortable part. Afterward, I washed the marker and plaster residue off my skin.

It takes four to six weeks for the plaster cast and photos to be turned into a custom breast form. This particular form is lightweight, feels and looks quite natural, and can be worn while swimming.

durable medical goods, the category these products fall into—for example, $1,500 to $5,000 annually.

While some insurers skimp on costs, others are quite generous. My insurance paid for my custom breast form, which cost more than $2,500. Several months after that, I had a tissue expander placed. They agreed to pay for bilateral forms—a booster for one breast and a hybrid breast form for the side undergoing expansion so that I could keep removing the filler as the expansion went along.

Most hospital boutiques—and possibly other shops, though not usually—will submit the bill directly to your insurer. I found this really helpful. I simply was not up to having to go through the insurance reimbursement process myself.

Keep track of all receipts. You'll need them to submit to insurers, of course, but if your medical bills are high enough, costs not covered may be tax deductible. Ask a tax preparer for more information or check with the IRS.

The Body Unadorned

After breast cancer surgery, some women feel strongly that their bodies need little or no enhancement. Surgical scars may be a badge of courage or just a simple fact of life. Deena Metzger, a writer who chronicled her bout with breast cancer in *Tree*, had a beautiful tattoo entwined across her chest after her mastectomy. The artist and one-time model Matushka made a different statement with bold photographs mapping the new terrain of her body after a mastectomy, which appeared in the *New York Times* in the summer of 1993.

Other women choose to go au naturel partly because of comfort. They don't like the feeling of a breast form and decide against reconstruction because of time, expense, reluctance to undergo more surgery, concern that reconstructive surgery will interfere with athletic pursuits, personal preference, or other reasons. Small-breasted women and those who have had bilateral mastectomies or lumpectomies may find this suits them fine. Larger-breasted women may not like the way clothing drapes or may even feel off-balance physically. Some choose to undergo surgical reduction of the remaining breast so that going without a breast form is more comfortable. A smaller number decide to have a prophylactic mastectomy of the other breast when worries about developing cancer there make this an appropriate choice; this also may make a larger-breasted woman feel more comfortable forgoing breast reconstruction or a breast form.

You might also decide to go natural only under certain circumstances and choose to wear a breast form for others. Just as there are women who shed their bras the moment they walk through their front door, some women prefer to wear no breast form once at home or while sleeping but like the look of one under clothes or whenever they are out and about.

Amanda, for example, usually felt fine about the fact that her lumpectomy left one breast a size smaller than the other, even when nursing a newborn considerably enlarged her other breast further. When faced with a black-tie evening out with her husband's firm, though, she panicked. "I had nothing to wear. I was a uni-boob. I asked a friend for her prosthesis. She came over and brought me a boob and a bra to wear and dresses that would fit. I had cleavage! People spent the whole night wondering—because they knew Daniel's wife had had cancer—where did these come from?"

WHAT TO WEAR

Take a moment to slide open your dresser drawers or look in your closet. Odds are good that you already have plenty of clothes. So what else are you going to need?

Right after surgery, rather than the standard flapping hospital gown, you might prefer to wear an attractive, loose nightshirt with big buttons up the front that can be fastened with one hand. When you're ready to trade this for clothes, it helps to

BEHIND THE SCENES: TWO UNADORNED EXPERIENCES

No statistics tell us exactly how many women choose to leave their bodies as is after surgery for breast cancer, but certainly there are those who prefer to do so. The reasons for their choice differ widely.

Sloan, who had a mastectomy at forty-three, remembered wrestling with her doctors over what to do. They found it hard to credit her resolve when she immediately ruled out reconstructive surgery. One reason she shied away from the surgery was the thought of a longer recovery time that would make her less available to her children. Suggestions that she might wish to wear a breast form instead didn't make much sense to her either.

"I would like to see the option of losing a breast and getting on with your life equally presented," she said. "Almost all of the messages you get from the instant you lose a breast is how can you make other people comfortable? I know some women are more comfortable putting themselves back together so that no one knows. And if they truly want to do that, fine. But if they do that because they think they're not acceptable unless they do it, that's screwed up.

"I didn't need to maintain that illusion for myself and I have never cared about maintaining that illusion for other people," she added. "So it was an easy choice for me." While recovering, Sloan embraced the image of the Amazon warrior women who deliberately removed a breast in order to wield bow and arrow more effectively in battles.

Clothes don't always fit Sloan comfortably, though. She has adapted her look by sometimes swinging a colorful scarf over the side of her chest where the mastectomy was done. But she wishes that someone would learn to make bras and clothes that would accommodate women who make the same choice she did.

Amanda, who had her lumpectomy at thirty-one, also saw no reason to change her body further. The surgery scooped out the side of her breast, leaving it about a cup size smaller than her other one. A highly athletic woman—she went in-line skating six to seven miles a day throughout chemotherapy and continues to windsurf, bike, blade, and rock climb with zest—Amanda concluded she didn't want to wear a breast form to compensate.

"I originally thought, I'll get a little prosthesis and put it in there," she said. "Then I thought, I will be spending more of my time chasing that damn thing around because if I'm climbing or doing something else, it's going to pop out. And I could never stand bras that hook in the back because they bite into me when I exercise. So I said, forget it. This is what it is, this is who I am. You know what? Like it or lump it."

On a few occasions, she has borrowed a breast form to look more balanced, but she has otherwise deemed herself satisfied as is. "There's a Hebrew saying: *Ehyeh asher ehyeh*. I am who I am and I will be who I will be. This is me."

choose soft fabrics and a not-too-tight shirt that opens in front rather than pullovers or sweaters, because raising your arm will be uncomfortable for a while.

Underwire bras and tight clothes that put pressure on tender, healing skin will be out initially, but don't toss your favorite outfits just because they cling to curves. If you enjoyed the way you looked in body-hugging shirts and sweaters, keep them. You'll be able to wear them again. If loose, flowing clothes fit your style better, these can be worn right away.

Bras and Camisoles

Not long ago, the only choice after a mastectomy was an unattractive, seemingly ironclad bra that rose high on the chest to conceal what was missing. If you've been picturing yourself in this, you can safely banish the thought. While most post-mastectomy bras do focus on extra coverage and many sport wider straps, there are far more options than there have been in the past.

Shortly after surgery, you'll probably be issued a soft cotton bra with a front closure and a pocket in the cup to stow a breast form. If you don't need or want to use a breast form, you may wish to loosen up your favorite bra by adding a short strap extender that has hooks on both ends. Although either choice will be looser than your usual bra, it will offer needed support for the remaining breast. A surprising number of nerves and muscles may be affected by your surgery, even with a lumpectomy, so reining in jiggling helps.

Some women prefer to wear a loose camisole. A few beautiful camisoles in simple white or bright colors with lace trims now are designed for postsurgery needs with a pocket for breast forms. Specially designed soft T-shirts with these pockets are another choice.

After you have healed, you can probably return to wearing your favorite bras or camisoles with shelf bras. A puff can be anchored with safety pins to the shelf bottom of a camisole. If lingerie you've enjoyed in the past seems too revealing, consider breast forms or enhancers that could help fill in where necessary, or add coverage with a wedge-shaped bra or camisole insert or lacy vee-shapes that can be sewn in.

Several companies make a variety of pretty or practical bras designed to hold breast forms. A soft cup can smooth your outward appearance. If you never owned a bra that fit well, this is the right time to shop for one. Don't be embarrassed to ask for help. A good fit is essential for comfort and may even help ward off lymphedema if you had nodes removed. A bra that is too tight or one that has narrow shoulder straps can obstruct the flow of lymph fluid along the remaining channels, potentially triggering troublesome swelling. More lymphedema precautions can be found in Chapter 3.

If you usually go without a bra, you can still do so. If you wish to wear a breast form, choose one that adheres to the chest. Typically, this option works best for small-breasted women. Alternatively, you can have pockets to hold a form sewn into your favorite clothes. There is no need to wear a breast form if you do not want to, of course.

Clothing

Once your body has healed, you can decide what part of your wardrobe to keep and what to give away. Not surprisingly, you may wonder if you need to toss more if you had a mastectomy than if you had a lumpectomy, which is usually easier to conceal. Outfits that skim your body tightly and necklines that dip low may seem too revealing now—or you might look just fine in them. Partly, that depends on the extent of your surgery and plans for reconstruction or wearing a breast form.

Take your time. If you feel self-conscious at first—whether you wear a breast form, had reconstructive surgery, or left your body as is—consider a pretty, comfortable vest layered over any top you choose. Don't stock your shelves with loose sweaters unless you enjoy wearing them. If you look gorgeous or elegant in a particular outfit, hang on to it. Sticking with your style rather than adopting one that seems drab to you is a good idea. If you feel charged up about changing your look radically, give it a whirl. Just pack your old clothes away for a while before you dispose of them, in case you decide to return to the old you.

Sports and Exercise Attire

What can you wear while exercising? Initially, the most difficult part of your workout may be lifting your arm overhead to get into your top. One simple choice is a form-fitting, sleeveless or cap-sleeve athletic top with a shelf bra. Try one with a scooped neckline and a back that swoops low. This way you can step into it and slide it up your torso so that your arms move downward through the sleeves in comfort. The bottom of a puff can be attached to the inside of the bra shelf with a safety pin to prevent it from riding up. Or a breast form, particularly one that is custom-made or well fitted to the chest, can be tucked inside the shelf bra. Check periodically while you are exercising to make sure the puff or form remains in place or toss a towel over your shoulder if you prefer.

Some sports bras and camisoles that have a pocket for a breast form may even come with a zipper in front, which can help enormously if lifting your arms is difficult. Breast forms sometimes slip around uncomfortably when you begin to sweat. The pocket of your exercise wear or a breast form with a microfiber backing will help absorb sweat. Two other options to help soak up perspiration are a washable breast form cover or disposable pads that are placed between form and flesh.

Bathing Suits

Before sinking into a hot tub or diving into water, find out whether any breast form you might wear can stand up to chlorine, heat, or salt water. An inexpensive foam form that can be attached to the shelf bra or cups of any bathing suit with safety pins works decently. A swim form is an alternative. These may be smooth silicone forms or have tiny holes that both allow water in and allow water to be discreetly squeezed out of the form.

Finding a bathing suit that you enjoy wearing may be easier than you think. Companies such as Amoena and Airway design suits for women of all sizes who have had mastectomies. Lands' End also offers a few options, plus the ease of shopping by phone or online. Some suits are decidedly matronly, so you might prefer to search out your own and add a pocket. If you want smoothness, seek out suits with soft cups. Mesh trim above the breast hides scars, while a shirred bodice masks unevenness. Tankinis—or, indeed, any attractive suit—with soft cups or shelf bras are another option.

Still like the look of a bikini? Look for those with tops cut more like sports bras, if you need concealment. Some swimwear companies let you mix and match tankini and bikini tops and bottoms. Or if you finally find the right top but don't really like the match proposed by the manufacturer, consider buying two suits or a separate bottom and wearing the best of each. Black is easiest to match, but you might enjoy a mix of bright colors and patterns. If you're not planning to swim, you may be comfortable with a bikini bottom and a T-shirt or pretty swim cover-up layered over a bra with a breast form in one pocket.

Sleepwear

Sleepwear ought to be comfortable as well as pleasurable to wear. If you do wear a breast form during the day, you might decide not to use it at night, because rolling over or sleeping on your abdomen may be uncomfortable.

If you wish to wear a breast form at night, the bra you were given after surgery, which is looser than usual lingerie, combined with a puff, may prove to be the most comfortable choice. Still You Fashions makes attractive nightgowns with a pocket to hold a breast form. Also, you can sew a pocket into any nightgown or sleep top you enjoy.

7

RESHAPING THE BREAST

◉

While every woman's experience is different, I really felt my recovery gather speed when I took the first step toward breast reconstruction. Four months after my mastectomy, once my chemotherapy was completed and my blood counts had recovered, I had surgery to place a tissue expander that would gradually stretch the muscle and skin of my chest wall. Later I returned for a second surgery to remove the expander and replace it with a permanent implant.

Perhaps I'm not alone in feeling that this marked a turnaround point in my recovery. Certainly I'm not alone in choosing breast reconstruction after a mastectomy. In 2003 the American Society of Plastic Surgeons estimated that more than 68,500 women had reconstructive breast surgery. Many of my patients choose to have the surgery at the same time as their mastectomy to allow for fewer operations and, possibly, soften the impact of the change in body image as well. One reason I waited was that, for my particular breast cancer, it was important to know whether I would need radiation therapy to the chest wall, as explained a little later.

This chapter will detail choices in reshaping your breast and help you balance your hopes for it with the options available. Naturally, reconstructive surgery is not for every woman. If you choose to forgo it or to wait until later, you may wish to wear a breast form or simply leave your body as it is (see Chapter 6).

OVERVIEW: RECONSTRUCTIVE SURGERY

Detailed descriptions of the different breast reconstruction surgeries appear later in this chapter, but a quick overview first will be helpful. Basically, you may choose an implant, which is essentially a silicone bag filled with saline (salt water) or silicone. Alternatively, you may choose a flap procedure that moves skin and fat and often muscle from one part of your body to the chest wall to reconstruct the breast.

Usually, the skin, fat, and muscle flap is taken from your abdomen (a *TRAM flap*) or back (a *latissimus dorsi flap*, or lat flap).

It is a *pedicle flap* if it is tunneled beneath the skin from the donor site to the chest wall so that the blood supply to the muscle remains intact. Otherwise, tissue and blood vessels may be entirely severed and reattached to blood vessels in the underarm or chest areas using microsurgical techniques to reestablish the blood supply. This is known as a *free flap*. It may be done using tissue and muscle from the abdomen in a variation of the TRAM procedure. If necessary, tissue from more distant sites, such as the buttocks or thigh, can be used instead.

Sometimes, flap procedures are combined with a saline implant to fill out the breast. That is common with a lat flap and less common with a TRAM flap.

Reconstruction may be performed immediately after the mastectomy (simultaneous or immediate reconstruction). In this case, a *skin-sparing mastectomy* is commonly done (see Chapter 3). The surgeon removes the nipple and areola with the breast mound but leaves most of the breast skin intact to help achieve a pleasing cosmetic result.

Delayed reconstruction is performed weeks, months, or years after the mastectomy. During the original mastectomy, the surgeon removed the nipple, areola, and breast mound and left just enough skin to allow the skin to lie flat and smooth on the chest wall when the incision was closed. This is a *non-skin-sparing mastectomy*.

Working with a Plastic Surgeon

If you are considering breast reconstruction, finding a plastic surgeon before you have your mastectomy enables her or him to work with your breast cancer surgeon to develop a plan that best lends itself to reconstruction. But how do you find a good plastic surgeon?

If you wish to have simultaneous reconstruction, the breast surgeon and plastic surgeon will need to practice in the same hospital and be able to coordinate schedules. Many academic medical centers and larger community hospitals have several plastic surgeons on staff. Generally, you'd choose your breast surgeon first. She or he would then recommend one or more plastic surgeons at the hospital with whom to discuss reconstruction. After meeting with both the breast surgeon and plastic surgeon, you should feel confident that they are actively communicating with each other about your situation.

If you prefer to have delayed reconstruction, your plastic surgeon can be located at any hospital. In addition to asking the members of your cancer care team, ask friends if they know women who have had breast reconstruction and were pleased with the results. You can also call the American Society of Plastic Surgeons (see Resources) for the names of board-certified surgeons in your area.

Skill and experience count highly. Ask how much of the surgeon's practice is devoted to breast reconstruction. Find out which procedures she or he is most adept at and experienced in doing, and consider whether that meets your needs. Ask to see photos of the best and worst results of the reconstructive procedures the surgeon has performed. Surgery to reconstruct a breast is truly an art—even the best plastic surgeons will admit that the outcome is unlikely to be perfect. One woman may be wonderfully satisfied with the change; another will feel keen disappointment at the gap that stretches between the breast she remembers well and her newly created breast.

Personality may also matter to you. At a minimum, you should feel comfortable asking questions and confident that the plastic surgeon will respond to questions or concerns that arise after the initial appointment. Of one plastic surgeon she interviewed, Lisa said, "It was a real slick office. I felt like I was just in and out, like I was just a number. He was very rushed." Although the surgeon she eventually picked was in high demand, he went at their pace. "We never felt rushed. He was drawing us pictures, showing us books like he had all the time in the day to spend with us because he knew what we were going through."

Consulting with more than one plastic surgeon offers you more than one opinion on your options and lets you observe differences in skills, communication, and how patient-friendly the practice is. "Go with your gut," advised Lisa. "If the doctor doesn't feel right, don't use that one."

Before speaking with your surgeon about your hopes and expectations, take time to think about your priorities for the surgery. Is a reconstructed breast that looks and feels as natural as the original when nude the highest priority? Or are athletic pursuits and minimizing impact on your ability to perform your favorite activity most important? How much does the length of the recovery matter?

While there are a variety of options for reconstruction, they may not all be appropriate for you. Slender women who have little excess body fat may not be able to take advantage of a TRAM flap procedure. Implants are made to approximate small to medium breasts, not large breasts, which makes symmetry harder to achieve for certain women. Radiation may make a difference in whether an implant will work well. A good plastic surgeon can suggest techniques and modifications that can help you attain your wishes, whether that is "two bumps on my chest to make my clothes fit easier," as one woman joked, or a breast that looks and feels very close to natural. The surgeon will assess your physique and activity level and can rank the reconstruction options as they apply to your situation. Although compromises are usually necessary—a more complex procedure with a longer recovery time, perhaps, or a breast that looks rounder and perkier than its mate—hopefully you will be pleased with the result.

The website breastcancer.org or the book *Show Me: A Photo Collection of Breast Cancer Survivors' Lumpectomies, Mastectomies, Breast Reconstructions, and Thoughts on Body Image* (see Resources) can give you an idea of how some women look after various types of reconstructive surgery. If a friend has gone down this path before you, ask detailed questions about the final results. Possibly, she may feel comfortable showing you, too. Other sources of information are Reach to Recovery, Y-ME, Young Survival Coalition, and similar organizations, which may connect you to women willing to share their experiences.

Reshaping the Breast: Implants

A breast implant is a flexible silicone bag filled with saline or silicone, which is placed under the pectoral muscles of the chest wall (see Figure 7.1). Implants best suit women who desire smaller-sized breasts. A relatively narrow rib cage and minimal rolls of flesh at the side of the chest—every woman has some of this tissue and it is usually more apparent after a mastectomy—allow the new breast to be well positioned on the chest. Otherwise, the base of the implant may not sufficiently cover the front of the chest in a woman with a broad rib cage or blend into tissue rolls in the outer chest wall.

For some women, the controversy that surrounds silicone implants (see the sidebar "Silicone Implants" later in the chapter) is off-putting, and they feel more comfortable using saline implants. Others prefer the more natural look and feel that silicone offers.

How Tissue Expander and Implant Surgery Are Performed

If you have very small breasts, it may be possible to place a small permanent implant beneath the pectoral muscle at your initial surgery. However, if your cup size is a large A, a small B, or larger, a similarly sized implant is likely to tear the overlying muscle. In that case, a temporary *tissue expander* is used to gradually and gently

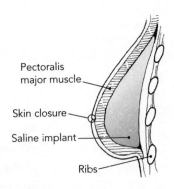

Pectoralis major muscle

Skin closure

Saline implant

Ribs

Figure 7.1 Mastectomy with implant reconstruction. A view from the side. The breast tissue has been removed. The skin lies directly over the pectoral muscles. The implant is placed beneath the muscles and over the ribs.

stretch the chest wall muscles and overlying skin. This creates a pocket that subsequently will accommodate a larger implant.

After the mastectomy is completed, the two closely aligned chest wall muscles, called the *pectoralis major* and the *pectoralis minor*, are exposed. The surgeon separates the muscles along the length of their fibers and gently lifts the pectoral muscles away from the ribs. This forms a pocket into which the expander is placed. Later, the implant will go into this pocket. (See Figure 7.2.)

The expander contains a valve (port), which the surgeon positions directly beneath the skin and muscle. A small quantity of saline may be injected through a needle into the expander. For some women, just placing the expander puts sufficient stress on the muscles, and the surgeon does not inflate it with saline. A drain is placed under the skin to siphon off excess lymphatic fluid. It will be removed in a week or two. The surgeon then stitches the muscle closed and then the skin. Tissue expander or implant surgery takes one to two hours or possibly longer if performed at the time of the mastectomy.

Filling the Expander

After several weeks of healing, the expansion phase is ready to begin. An external magnet is used to locate the dime-sized magnetized port of the expander. Saline is injected through it into the expander. Every few weeks, this will continue until the

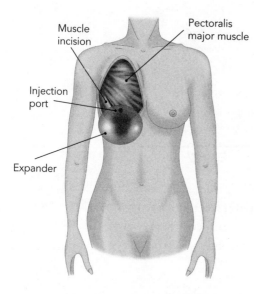

Muscle incision

Pectoralis major muscle

Injection port

Expander

Figure 7.2 Before a permanent implant can be placed, a tissue expander is temporarily inserted under the skin and chest muscles to gently stretch them and create space for the implant.

expander is somewhat larger than the desired size of the implant. Overfilling helps ensure that the skin and muscle over the expander stretch enough to create a more natural droop to the breast, called *ptosis*. When the slightly smaller permanent implant is placed, a natural crease will form below the breast. Once the expansion process is completed, the surgeon removes the expander and places the permanent implant.

If you wish to have a nipple created, a third surgery is performed a few months later, once the postoperative swelling has resolved and the breast has assumed its new shape and position.

My patients often ask me why the tissue expander needs to go under the chest wall muscles. Why not put it directly beneath the skin and on top of the muscle as is done with cosmetic breast augmentation? In cosmetic breast augmentation, skin is nourished by the rich blood supply of the overlying breast tissue. During a mastectomy, however, the breast tissue and its blood supply have been removed. The remaining skin is the thickness of a piece of leather, and its blood supply can be tenuous. Placing a tissue expander directly underneath it would place undue pressure on the already tenuous blood supply and compromise blood flow to the skin. Areas of skin with insufficient blood flow would die off, forming a black scab, a condition called an *ischemic eschar*. Having the healthy pectoral muscle directly beneath the skin augments the blood supply of the skin.

Sometimes, the plastic surgeon chooses to cut the median pectoral nerve, which reaches to the outer portion of both pectoral muscles. The added laxity of the muscle may enhance the appearance of the reconstructed breast in some women. However, the chest muscles affected will be weaker than the muscles on the other side of the body. This is a good point to discuss with your surgeon before surgery.

What to Expect While Recovering from Surgery

Usually it takes several weeks to physically recover from surgery to place an expander and, later, an implant. Talk with your surgeon about the best way to take care of yourself.

Pain

The pectoral muscles are used to lying flat on the chest wall. Pushing them away with the tissue expander can cause a spasm that feels like a charley horse. This muscle spasm pulls the shoulder forward, so posture on that side is somewhat hunched over. I found it took several days for the spasm to stop and the muscles to relax. Narcotic pain medication helped for the first few days; afterward, acetaminophen helped. Although many of my patients found comfort with a support bra, I did not. I didn't wear a bra at all for more than a month. Speak to your nurse or doctor about how pain control might be best managed for you. This is a time to be comfortable, not stoic.

Lifting

The pectoral muscle, which has been stitched closed along the incision line, holds the tissue expander or implant in place. To allow the incision to heal, a plastic surgeon typically will restrict heavy lifting for six weeks. If you overuse your arm and the muscle stitches weaken, the implant may shift and move to your outer or lower chest wall.

Range of Motion

Initially, raising your arm at the shoulder will be nearly impossible. Many plastic surgeons recommend limiting your shoulder range of motion to ninety degrees (parallel to the ground) for the first several weeks to allow muscle stitches to heal. I preferred wearing clothing with large front buttons that allowed me to easily slide my arms into the sleeves and button up. With the passage of time and after performing upper body stretches described in Chapter 11, pain and stiffness lessen, comfortable upright posture returns, and everyday tasks and enjoyable activities become possible again. You can, however, start a gentle walking program as soon as you feel up to trying it, even while the drains are still in. One woman who had tissue expanders placed at the same time as her double mastectomy noted that her breast surgeon estimated she'd be able to play tennis again in eight weeks. "It didn't happen," she said. "It took a little longer than that, but I healed fairly nicely."

What to Expect During Tissue Expander Inflations

Each time the tissue expander is inflated, it's likely you'll feel discomfort or pain in the pectoral muscles, which may go into a spasm for several days. Usually, this can be eased by taking acetaminophen, ibuprofen, or a similar medication. Ask your surgeon which would be best for you. Stress relief techniques that relax you may help a bit, too. As the muscles loosen up again, weakness and discomfort recede, and strength returns.

A dear friend of mine, who is also a patient, asked whether the metal port of her tissue expander would set off the airport security alarm as she traveled to Geneva. I had been in an airport several weeks earlier and no alarms went off. So that she could travel with minimal worries, she asked her plastic surgeon to write a medical note describing her condition.

How Will the Breast Look After Healing?

No matter what shape an implant has in the box, once it goes beneath the pectoral muscle the body attempts to shape it into a circle. "They're just round," said Audrey of her saline implants, "that's not a real breast." They look fine under clothes, she added, which was a big reason why she decided on the reconstructive surgery.

Juliana, who had been well endowed by nature, found her saline implants offered some pleasing advantages. "I could wear a tank top. I didn't have to wear a bra. I was a size D before and I went to a C. I liked being a little bit smaller," she said. "I had the expanders put in right away and I think two weeks later I had my first expansion. I healed fairly quickly."

Saline implants sometimes show ripples when a woman is standing or sitting. Salt water is a liquid. Like any liquid, it responds swiftly to the pull of gravity. As a semisolid, silicone moves more naturally within the implant, and rippling of the top of the breast when you are upright is less likely to happen. Opting for silicone implants after having had a TRAM flap procedure that did not work out well, one woman said she liked the idea that it was much more lifelike than saline implants. "A bag of saline in my breast just didn't appeal to me."

Occasionally, an implant may slip out of place. Juliana had that happen almost immediately after her surgery when her overexuberant toddler kicked her in the breast while tussling with her. The implant flipped upside down—not a complication that could be foreseen, though her plastic surgeon had warned her to be quite careful while the reconstruction healed. Audrey has noticed that one of her saline implants sometimes migrates an inch or so over beneath her arm; a quick shove pushes it back into place. That said, both women count themselves largely satisfied with the way they look.

What Will the Breast Feel Like to Touch? How Will Sensation Be Affected?

A breast reconstructed with an implant never will feel exactly like the breast that was removed. Saline implants feel firmer than natural breast tissue. Silicone, which has more give to it than saline, comes closer to approximating the feel of breast tissue.

Usually, sensation in the reshaped breast is noticeably limited. Many of the sensory nerves to the skin of the breast emerge from between the ribs. During a mastectomy, these microscopic nerves are divided while the breast is being removed from the chest wall. That leaves the chest wall skin insensate, so pleasurable sensations are usually muted or entirely lost. With healing, there may be periods where the surgical site is itchy and scratching brings no relief. Some women experience *dysesthesia*, an odd, bothersome sensation whenever the chest wall is touched. Women who live in colder climates may notice on a cold day that the chest wall where the implant is placed, which now lacks the insulation of fat from the breast, loses heat more rapidly than the rest of the body.

SILICONE IMPLANTS

At one time, silicone implants were a popular way to enhance a breast as well as reconstruct one. In 1992, on the heels of reports suggesting a link between these implants and certain autoimmune disorders such as lupus, scleroderma, and rheumatoid arthritis, neurological symptoms such as multiple sclerosis, and chronic ailments such as fibromyalgia and chronic fatigue syndrome, the FDA limited their availability. Now only women who agreed to join a clinical trial could choose a silicone implant. This disappointed some women, who liked the more natural look and feel silicone supplied, and relieved others, who were concerned about possible health risks.

Since 1992, research has continued and much of it fails to support earlier concerns. A National Cancer Institute study of 13,500 women who had silicone implants placed for cosmetic reasons found that after an average of thirteen years, this group had no greater risk for most causes of death compared to two separate control groups: the general population and four thousand women who had had other plastic surgery. Slightly higher risks of respiratory tract cancers and suicide proved significant among women with implants, though the reasons for this were unclear.

In 2001 an FDA-sponsored study of about 350 women found those with ruptured silicone implants were no more likely than those with intact silicone implants to report persistent symptoms like fatigue, joint pain and stiffness, or connective tissue diseases like scleroderma, lupus, chronic fatigue syndrome, or Sjögren's syndrome. The major difference noted was that women with ruptured implants more often reported having fibromyalgia, a syndrome marked by pain at many sites in the body, sleep troubles, and fatigue. Other studies will be needed to confirm or refute this.

Both silicone and saline implants may rupture as the material ages or is put under stress. Silicone gel can migrate beyond the natural capsule of scar tissue that forms around an implant to the chest wall, armpit, arm, or abdomen. It may cause local scarring, tenderness, or knots (called *granulomas*), prompting a second surgery to remove or replace the implant. Saline, by contrast, is safely absorbed by the body, though a woman typically chooses surgery to replace the implant for cosmetic reasons.

To minimize the possibility of silicone migration, implant manufacturers have created a triple-layered shell as well as a new cohesive, silicone polymer that is almost like a gummy bear—if the implant is cut with a knife, the gel stays in place. When compared with traditional liquid silicone implants, the cohesive polymer is firmer to the touch, though still softer than a saline implant. The cohesive gel implants are available in Europe and through clinical trials in the United States.

In 2004 the FDA requested additional information from manufacturers of silicone implants before they would be allowed back on the market. Among other recommendations, the agency asked for better data on rupture rates and connective tissue ailments. Currently, silicone implants are still available to women with breast cancer who participate in a clinical study.

Mentor and Inamed are the two companies participating in the FDA trial (mentor corp.com and inamed.com). The Mentor and Inamed websites list physicians who use these implants but do not specify those participating in the trial.

The National Academy of Sciences has published a layperson's booklet titled, *Information for Women About the Safety of Silicone Implants*. A single free copy is available through Y-ME. (See Resources.)

How Will the Breast Change over Time?

One aspect of breast implants that sometimes surprises women is that the reshaped breast is likely to look perkier and rounder than breast tissue normally does. This may be fine if you have a bilateral mastectomy and reconstruction. However, if only one breast has been reshaped, it's likely to look increasingly different over time as its mate continues to respond to gravity and changes related to age. If you gain or lose a significant amount of weight, your natural breast will become larger or smaller, while the breast with the implant will be mostly unchanged. Sometimes, this size discrepancy can be addressed through surgery on the natural breast, as described later in this chapter.

How Will Muscles and Activities Be Affected After Implant Reconstruction?

When it comes to implant reconstruction, you may need to make some trade-offs between form and function. Beneath clothes, a breast implant looks quite comparable to a breast reshaped by muscle flap surgery. Yet when a woman is nude, an implant may present the least natural appearance. When it comes to function, however, breast implants are least likely to interfere with the activities you enjoy compared with muscle flap reconstruction. In fact, some women choose implants for exactly this reason.

Given my physique, I was not a candidate for a TRAM flap. I am an avid cyclist and skier as well as a surgeon and so was not willing to sacrifice the use of the latissimus dorsi muscle of my dominant arm for breast reconstruction. I am also relatively small-breasted, so the choice of an implant was the obvious one for me.

Implant reconstruction does create some limitations in arm mobility and strength, as described next. Usually, these are temporary and resolve as healing occurs and muscle strength returns.

Shoulder Range of Motion

Initially, outward motion is limited, and it may not be possible to raise your arm higher than shoulder level. Spasms, pain, or scarring in the muscles in this area— the pectoralis of the chest, the latissimus dorsi of the back, and the coracobrachialis, which runs in the underarm area from the back of the shoulder down the upper arm—all contribute to motion restriction. The stretching exercises described in Chapter 11 will help you regain full shoulder motion. Some women also benefit from physical therapy, which may include heat packs to relax the muscle, massage to break down scar tissue, and passive stretching. A word of caution about heat packs: the surgical site is usually numb, so to avoid risking a burn, the pack should not be too hot. Put a towel between the heat pack and your skin.

Shoulder Strength

Initially, strength in your shoulder and even your arm and hand is affected. I was unable to grip a jar to open the lid and had to change my children's meal plans on more than one occasion. Other simple tasks that were temporarily challenging included opening a large drawer of pots while bending forward from the waist, pulling open a heavy door or pushing a revolving door, and turning the steering wheel away from the side of my body where the surgery had been done (flipping my hand upside down and grasping the top of the steering wheel made this maneuver easier). Part of my recovery was during the winter. Although I did try to ski, planting my poles on the flat catwalks was at best a challenge and at worst ineffective on the side of my surgery.

As pain and muscle spasms subside, strength training to retool the muscles can begin. Like many of my patients, I resumed strength training under the careful eyes of an exercise physiologist to help this along. I started with far lighter weights than I had once lifted and very, very slowly increased to my previous weight amounts.

My ability to bench-press, which primarily uses the pectoral muscles, has not yet fully returned.

What Problems Might Occur with Implant Reconstruction?

Any surgery may have side effects and complications, such as infection, bleeding, problems due to anesthesia, and an unpredictable cosmetic outcome. Fortunately, most women will have an uneventful surgery and recovery.

Among women who participated in a three-year study, the FDA identified a variety of issues specific to implants, including asymmetry, wrinkling, loss of nipple sensation, leaking or deflation of the implant, and the need for additional surgeries or implant removal. Some women experienced more than one of these problems. Implant replacement may be performed to treat implant leakage or rupture, implant migration, scar formation around the implant, or a poor cosmetic result. Implant removal without replacement may be required if antibiotics fail to stop an infection; due to pain in the chest wall or back; or if skin sutures open, exposing the implant, and the surrounding tissue is unhealthy due to a poor blood supply.

How often do problems occur? A 1997 Mayo Clinic study published in the *New England Journal of Medicine* found almost 22 percent of women who had implant reconstruction due to breast cancer had complications requiring further surgery during the first year; by the fifth year, this rose to 34 percent. The likelihood of complications is higher among women who smoke and those with a prior history of radiation to the breast or subsequent radiation to the chest wall.

A few complications and cosmetic problems are described in more detail in the following pages. Clearly, many women will not run into these issues, but it is wise to understand them anyway.

Capsular Contracture

While healing, the body naturally walls off any foreign object—and an implant would qualify—by creating a thin capsule of scar tissue around it. This scarring, called *capsular contracture*, happens with every implant, although usually you can't see or feel it. In some cases, though, the capsule grows thick and harder. Surgeons suggest that women massage the breast with the implant regularly at first to help prevent this. This works sometimes, but not always. If it evolves, capsular contracture can distort the implant into a firm sphere and may even shift its placement on the chest wall. In advanced stages, the site becomes painful, often prompting surgical removal of the implant and scar capsule.

Implant Leak or Rupture

Breast implants are not expected to last a lifetime, as every manufacturer's package insert states, so additional surgery to replace one is likely at some point. According to the Institute of Medicine, one study on saline implants reported a rupture rate of 16 percent over the course of six years. A second study, which looked at silicone gel implants and expanders, found a rupture rate of 18 percent. When a saline implant leaks or ruptures, the reconstructed breast deflates either quickly or over several days, an event readily observed by the woman. As a semisolid, silicone may stay within the scar tissue capsule, in which case a leak or rupture may be less noticeable, or it may migrate beyond it. Usually, a ruptured implant is exchanged for a new implant during an outpatient surgical procedure.

Skin Ischemia

After surgery, the surgical site will be observed for *skin ischemia*, which is dead skin at the edges of the mastectomy. If the blood supply to that region of the skin becomes inadequate, the edges of the skin abutting the incision initially turn deep red and then blacken like a scab. In most cases, the area of ischemic skin is small and will heal spontaneously or can be trimmed off in the surgeon's office. At worst—and this is very uncommon—not enough healthy skin remains to adequately cover the implant. The implant would need to be removed and the ischemic skin edges trimmed away to promote healing and minimize the chance of infection.

Inability to Proceed with Reconstruction

Occasionally, the blood supply to the chest wall skin may not be sufficiently hearty to survive a mastectomy compounded by skin tension caused by an implant. This is particularly true if the skin has undergone radiation, which permanently alters blood vessels in the skin. Sometimes, such tenuous skin is observed or suspected in the operating room during a mastectomy. If so, the surgeon may choose to minimize chest wall skin tension by not placing an expander or implant at that time.

RADIATION AND BREAST IMPLANTS

Radiation affects skin and blood vessels, which can have repercussions for breast reconstruction, especially when a woman chooses implants. Small studies confirm that if radiation is done after reconstructive surgery, it is far more likely for capsular contracture to occur or for an implant to break through the skin (extrude) than if radiation is not required as part of treatment. In 2001 an offshoot of the Michigan Breast Reconstruction Outcome Study reported that women who had radiation after reconstruction with implants experienced complications more than twice as often as those who did not have radiation. The rate of capsular contracture, for example, was 26 percent versus 10 percent, and infection occurred in 37 percent of the women studied versus 19 percent. Such problems may require corrective surgeries.

If you have had radiation to the breast or chest wall or if you may need it, talk with your plastic surgeon and radiation oncologist about the timing and type of reconstructive surgery that would work best for you. Muscle flap surgeries, which bring their own blood supply to the chest, may be a good choice.

When this happens, the woman will awaken from the surgery without a reconstructed breast and with a flat chest wall. In six weeks or so, when the surgical site has healed and a blood supply between the skin and underlying pectoral muscle has been established, she will probably be able to return to the operating room for placement of a tissue expander.

RESHAPING THE BREAST: TRAM FLAP

A second option for reconstructing the breast is a procedure that uses lower abdominal skin, fat, and the *rectus abdominis muscle*—that is, the TRAM flap. The "T" in TRAM refers to the transverse—horizontal—incision in the abdomen. Women who have extra fat in the lower part of the abdomen are ideally suited for this. At least a portion of the blood supply to the muscle must be intact and hearty, rather than having been severed by previous abdominal surgeries or affected by radiation treatments.

How TRAM Flap Surgery Is Performed

These two vertical, elongated rectangular muscles form the center of your abdomen and are responsible for the "six-pack abs" of infomercials (see Figure 7.3). Each extends the full length of the abdominal wall from the front-central fifth, sixth, and seventh ribs to the pubic bone. When one breast is being reconstructed, one muscle is used. When both breasts are being reconstructed, both muscles are used, one for each side. For some women, however, this could weaken the abdomen too much. In that case, the surgeon might recommend bilateral implants.

Covering the muscle is the *fascia*, a sheet of thin tissue. On the underside of the muscle, the fascia acts like a piece of plastic wrap separating the rectus muscle from the abdominal organs.

The blood supply to the muscle runs on its undersurface. In the upper part of the muscle, it is called the *superior epigastric vessel*. In the lower part of the muscle, it is called the *deep inferior epigastric vessel*. One or both of these vessels will supply blood for the TRAM flap reconstruction.

First, the surgeon will make a horizontal (*transverse*) elliptical incision, like an elongated eye, in the lower part of the abdomen (Figure 7.4). The incision extends from hip bone to hip bone and includes the underlying fat. One rectus muscle is exposed, and the fascia on either side is cut open. The surgeon then detaches the muscle from where it is anchored to the pubic bone and cuts the blood supply to

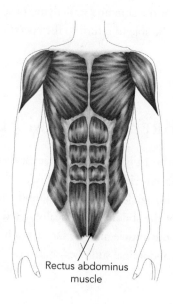

Rectus abdominus
muscle

Figure 7.3 The rectus abdominis muscles consist of two vertical muscles which make up the center of the abdominal wall. They run from below the chest wall to the pubic bone.

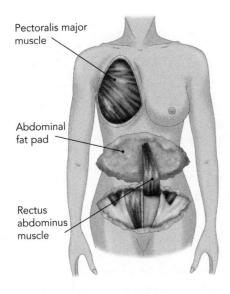

Pectoralis major
muscle

Abdominal
fat pad

Rectus
abdominus
muscle

Figure 7.4 In TRAM
flap surgery, skin, fat,
and muscle from the
lower abdomen are
transferred to the chest
to reconstruct the
breast.

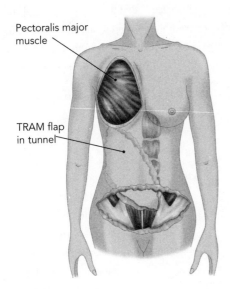

Pectoralis major
muscle

TRAM flap
in tunnel

Figure 7.5 In pedicle
TRAM flap surgery, the
muscle flap is only
partially detached. It is
then tunneled beneath
the skin to the chest,
where the muscle,
abdominal fat, and skin
are used to form the
breast mound.

the lower portion of the muscle, too. The muscle flap with its attached fat and skin is now ready to use to reconstruct the breast.

In a pedicle flap procedure, the blood supply to the upper portion of the muscle is maintained, and the flap is flipped from its position in the abdomen to the chest (Figure 7.5). The surgeon creates a tunnel of skin and fat reaching from the

Free Flap Procedures

Best known of the free flap procedures is a variation of the pedicle TRAM described. Instead of leaving part of the muscle and blood supply anchored at the ribs, the surgeon cuts the muscle and the blood supply to both the upper and lower portions of the rectus muscle. The entire flap is then moved from the abdomen to the chest wall (Figure 7.6). Using highly specialized microsurgical techniques, the surgeon forges entirely new connections for the blood vessels.

Another free flap option bypasses the abdominal muscles and takes only skin and fat tissue from the abdomen. Called a *deep inferior epigastric perforator* (DIEP) tissue flap, this delivers a tummy tuck while entirely sparing the muscles that allow you to do sit-ups and keep your lower back strong. Two other sites that surgeons sometimes plumb for tissue are the buttocks (a *gluteal flap*) or the outer thigh (a *lateral thigh flap*). Usually, these procedures are chosen if you have had previous surgeries that preclude the use of the TRAM or lat flaps.

One advantage to free flap techniques is that no tunnel is needed to bring transplanted tissue to the chest wall. One disadvantage of the free flap is that the new blood supply may fail, so that the transplanted tissue dies off either entirely or in certain areas, a complication called *necrosis*. As a result, certain spots on the reconstruction will feel firmer and, possibly, look puckered or otherwise differ from surrounding skin (this can occur in a pedicle flap, too). At worst, it means the flap must be removed.

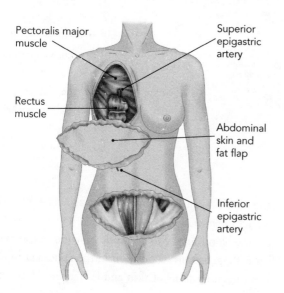

Pectoralis major muscle

Superior epigastric artery

Rectus muscle

Abdominal skin and fat flap

Inferior epigastric artery

Figure 7.6 In free TRAM flap surgery, the muscle, abdominal fat, and skin are completely detached from the abdomen. The blood vessels of the flap are reconnected to blood vessels in the underarm or chest. The flap is then surgically reshaped to form the breast mound.

abdomen to the chest. The muscle flap is rotated at the point where it attaches to the ribs and is passed through the tunnel. The blood supply from the superior epigastric artery has been left untouched and serves as the blood supply to the flap. Because the creation of the tunnel during a pedicle flap disrupts the nerve supply to the skin in that region, the abdominal wall may become permanently numb.

The surgeon next trims, shapes, and sews the flap into place to re-create the breast mound. The skin of the new breast is then sewn closed, after which the surgeon turns to the abdomen and sews together the edges of the fascia. A piece of mesh may be positioned over the fascia and sewn into place to further secure the abdominal wall. Then a new spot for the belly button, or *umbilicus*, is fashioned. The surgeon makes a small incision in the wall of the upper abdomen, brings out the umbilicus at this spot, and sutures it into place. Finally, the incision on the abdomen is sewn closed. The drains inserted under the skin of the reconstructed breast and in the abdomen to siphon off excess lymphatic fluid are usually removed a week or two after surgery.

TRAM flap surgery takes about two to eight hours with an experienced team and may take longer when a mastectomy also is being performed that day. A second surgery may be needed in a few months to contour the new breast and possibly revise scars. A third may be needed to create a nipple.

What to Expect While Recovering from Surgery

Recovery from TRAM flap surgery is lengthy, especially if you are also undergoing chemotherapy. Usually, it takes six weeks to three months before strength and energy improve enough for a woman to return to most activities, though it may take up to a year before you truly feel like yourself. The first three days, said Lisa, she wanted to die. "I'd say you pay a price for about three weeks, then you start to feel better, then it starts to become worthwhile."

Pain

When I see my patients in the hospital after a TRAM flap procedure, they rarely point to the chest area—where the sensory nerves were divided at the time of mastectomy—as the primary site of pain. Rather, it is the lower abdomen that is uncomfortable. If the skin and fat tissue in the lower abdomen had been lax before the surgery, it is easier to close the incision with minimal tension. The flatter the abdomen before surgery, the tighter the final closure, which can increase pain. While you are healing, lying on your belly will not be comfortable.

A variety of medications ranging from narcotics to acetaminophen can help control inevitable pain at the breast and donor site. A bra is usually off limits for two to four weeks during the initial healing phases because any pressure on the flap's blood supply can place the flap at risk. A loose-fitting camisole can be comfortable. Talk to your nurse or doctor if you have any trouble with pain.

Range of Motion

At first, you may find it hard to stand up straight and walk without bending over, and it will be difficult to reach overhead. Tightness in your abdomen and hip flexors (muscles that link legs to trunk) contributes to this. Gentle stretching will help you regain a comfortable, upright posture. (See Chapter 11.)

Raising your arms to slip into clothes or do other activities may be impossible initially. Consider wearing loose shirts that close in front with large buttons initially. Performing the stretching exercises in Chapter 11 will help ease this.

Lifting

The most important task to avoid while recovering is heavy lifting. To help minimize the chance of developing a hernia, or weak spot, in the abdominal wall, certain activities like vigorous sports (though not walking), overhead lifting, and sexual activity will be temporarily off limits, usually for up to six weeks.

How Will the Breast and Belly Look After Healing?

Because the TRAM flap procedure deploys body skin, fat, and, frequently, muscle, the end result often looks quite natural. There will be a scar on the new breast where the skin of the TRAM meets the remaining skin of the chest. On the abdomen at the donor site there will be a hip-to-hip scar. Like all scars, these will fade somewhat with time. Because skin coloration varies across the body, the match between donor site and surrounding skin on the chest may not blend perfectly. Likewise, the breast itself may not share the shape of your natural breast. To a certain extent, this can be remedied by further surgery; alternatively, the other breast can be reshaped.

With a pedicle TRAM flap, the muscle flap remains attached to the lower ribs on the side opposite the mastectomy. The flap is rotated from the abdomen to the chest surgical site. In some women, the rotation process causes a noticeable lump or bulge at the lower, central part of the ribs. As the muscle shrinks, or *atrophies*, this becomes less noticeable.

The tummy tuck supplied by a TRAM as a section of abdominal fat is transferred to the chest is a boon, according to many women.

What Will the Breast Feel Like to Touch? How Will Sensation Be Affected?

Nothing will feel exactly like the breast that was removed, but because flap procedures move skin, fat, and, often, muscle, the padding of the reshaped breast feels softer and much more like a natural breast when compared with an implant. As with any extensive surgery on the breast—including a mastectomy without reconstruction—nerves will have been cut, so sensation is usually muted or entirely lost. When coupled with a skin-sparing mastectomy, sensation may return somewhat after a TRAM. Expect numbness at the abdominal donor site, too, and over the skin of the tunnel if a pedicle flap is done. "You're completely numb on one whole side of your body for years," said Lisa, who is nonetheless quite happy with the way her TRAM has worked out.

How Will the Breast Change over Time?

Because a TRAM flap is your own tissue, gravity and aging will affect the flap reconstruction much as it does natural breast tissue. Over time, the muscle of the TRAM flap atrophies, or shrinks, so that a greater proportion of the transferred tissue will be fat. If you gain or lose a significant amount of weight, the fat in the TRAM flap will follow suit. While both breasts will respond to gravity and aging as time passes, this will be less noticeable in the reconstructed breast.

How Will Muscles and Activities Be Affected?

Flap procedures affect important muscles, so active women may wish to steer clear of these surgeries. A TRAM can affect your posture, flexibility, and strength. There

A Tale of Three TRAMs

A TRAM flap is a complex operation that takes hours to perform and requires weeks or months of recovery. Yet for many women, it represents real hope after the blows of a breast cancer diagnosis and a mastectomy. Their reshaped breast will be warm to the touch. It will feel soft and look remarkably similar to a natural breast if the relocated tissue and muscle take well to their new home and the surgeon is talented. A breast lift or reduction on the other side, or an implant for added volume, can help in achieving symmetry, too. Though scars are inevitable, the tummy tuck can be an added enhancement. "I had the tightest, flattest stomach," remarked Leah. "I wish I still had it."

Annette and her husband feel the surgery was well worth it. Her reshaped breast looks so good, she said, that a photo of her results is among those her surgeon shows to women considering the operation. It's a "best case," not a "worst case." Her recovery was arduous but proceeded well. "As soon as I had the drains out, I was out walking. I healed really fast. But I was in good shape to start," she noted. Two weeks after her operation, when she could not yet stand up straight, she went on a previously planned cruise with her husband and two children. He entertained; she took a deck chair.

Sit-ups are out nowadays, though Annette returned to running as soon as she could. Practical issues bother her slightly. "They don't make bras for this situation. You don't have any feeling, so if a bra rides up, maybe you feel pressure. You only have one nipple, so you have to protect yourself from weather-related coldness. You want a bra that is flexible, very pliable, because one side is very round and your regular breast isn't."

Life after surgery raised other concerns for Leah. Recalling the way she looked before her mastectomy, she said, "I had a pretty awesome body. I wasn't about my body, but I sure liked it."

While the abdomen can supply a lot of tissue, the harvest wasn't quite abundant enough, so her reconstructed breast was smaller than its mate. She also developed a hernia due to the loss of abdominal muscle. When it was repaired, she had her plastic surgeon add a breast implant behind the TRAM so that her breasts would be more symmetrical. Even so, she notices the difference when she's nude. "My breast, the one from birth, has a very different shape." Once she's dressed, it doesn't usually bother her. "But every day when I get up and I put my bra and panties on, I know I've had breast cancer."

Like Leah and Annette, Andrea has reached out to help many women confronted with breast cancer. She knows TRAM surgery can be a great success. Unfortunately, her experience was not, partly because afterward she needed radiation, which harmed the tissues and blood vessels of her newly reconstructed breast. Lumpiness due to fat necrosis required a biopsy to evaluate the lumps for cancer. A recurring infection took hold, requiring still more surgery. The subsequent wound on the previously radiated skin refused to heal for an inordinately long time. Although she continued to be active—participating in the marathon Avon Walk for Breast Cancer and the 5K Komen Race for the Cure—cramps and pulling pain in her sternum frequently nagged.

Despite it all, her breast looked great, which made her next decision harder. Eventually, Andrea decided to have the TRAM removed and also had a mastectomy on her opposite breast due to other concerns. "Literally, two days after surgery I felt so much better," she said. After the skin heals, she hopes to have implants placed. Already this has been done on the other side. "I would not talk anyone out of a TRAM because I think it's a very viable solution for a lot of people," she said. "I just didn't anticipate my complications, I guess."

are always exceptions to the rule—a long-distance biker can still be free-wheeling after her TRAM, for example.

Rehabilitation begins with regaining range of motion at the shoulder through stretching and, sometimes, physical therapy. Closure of the abdominal incision produces tightness. A progressive stretching program can help restore comfortable, upright posture (see Chapter 11). Walking is also beneficial.

The body *core* includes muscles of the abdomen and back running between the ribs and the pelvis. Strong core muscles minimize the chance of lower back strain and disk problems. Removing one or both of the strong central abdominal muscles during a TRAM procedure weakens the abdomen, which helps support the back. Thus the procedure is not recommended for women with lower back problems. Sit-ups, lifting, and other activities that rely heavily upon central abdominal muscles (like rowing, waterskiing, and windsurfing) are no longer possible for some women. However, the oblique muscles on each side of the abdomen and the transversus abdominis muscle that runs horizontally across the deep central abdomen are unaffected. Strengthening abdominal and back muscles that support the trunk will help you avoid postural problems and low back strain. (See Chapter 11.)

How greatly daily activities are affected is debated and may depend on how active you are. A 2004 study in *Plastic and Reconstructive Surgery* surveyed 124 women who had TRAM flaps using one or both muscles. Four percent (one muscle) and 10 percent (both) rated work performance worse, while 19 percent (one muscle) and 23 percent (both) said recreational performance, such as walking, swimming, and golf, was worse. Forty-two percent (one muscle) and 64 percent (both) felt their abdominal strength had weakened; 16 percent (one muscle) and 12 percent (both) reported back pain that hadn't previously existed.

What Problems Might Occur with TRAM Flap Surgery?

A few issues of concern are outlined in the following sections. Talk with your plastic surgeon about potential complications, and ask what his or her experience has been with the TRAM procedure.

Skin Necrosis

For some women who have TRAM flaps, the blood supply to the skin of the chest may be compromised, so the surgical site may heal slowly and possibly quite poorly. For example, the injured skin may contract, resulting in tightness and decreasing the size of the reconstructed breast. If the skin blood supply is completely inadequate, usually at the edges where chest skin meets the skin from the flap, an area of skin may die off. This is *skin necrosis*. Women who had radiation to the chest area are more susceptible to this. If the surgeon can see areas of damaged skin during surgery, he or she will trim away the affected chest skin and use a larger portion of skin from the TRAM abdominal donor site.

Fat Necrosis

Fat necrosis, or dead fat, occurs when areas of fat in the TRAM flap no longer receive an adequate blood supply. The pockets of dead fat cells can be felt as firm lumps under the skin. In pedicle flaps, fat necrosis most commonly appears in the upper portion of the reconstructed breast, which is farthest away from the blood supply. If there is concern that a palpable lump in the reconstructed breast may be a recurrence of the cancer, the area will be evaluated either with imaging studies (mammogram, ultrasound, MRI) or with a needle or surgical biopsy.

Loss of the TRAM Flap

Only rarely does a pedicle flap fail and need to be removed due to problems with the blood supply. This problem is more common with free flap procedures, affecting approximately 2 percent of these surgeries, although an individual surgeon's experience may differ. Ask your surgeon about this. If a flap fails and must be removed, sometimes reconstruction with an implant or, less often, another type of flap procedure can be attempted.

RESHAPING THE BREAST: LATISSIMUS DORSI FLAP

A third option for breast reconstruction uses the latissimus dorsi muscle, or "lat," a large, triangular muscle that fans out across the lower half of the back. A woman may consider this surgery if she has a slender lower abdomen that precludes a TRAM flap and when a breast implant would not be sufficiently large to match a remaining natural breast.

How Lat Flap Surgery Is Performed

The latissimus dorsi muscle originates from the lower six chest (thoracic) vertebrae, the lower back (lumbar) vertebra, and the part of the hip bone (iliac crest) closest to the spine (Figure 7.7). It converges and tapers upward as it approaches the arm, where it attaches to the underside of the humerus, the bone in the upper arm.

This muscle permits your shoulder to rotate and helps the wing bone, or scapula, on your back to lie flat. You use it when reaching overhead and pulling downward, such as when closing the trunk of a car or planting and pushing off from your poles in cross-country skiing.

During this procedure, the entire lat muscle, the fat above the muscle, and a section of skin over the fat are used. The surgeon first makes a horizontal, vertical, or diagonal incision on the back. He or she then releases the muscle with its overlying fat and skin from its attachments to the spine and hip bone. The blood supply to the muscle comes from the *thoracodorsal artery*, which originates from the

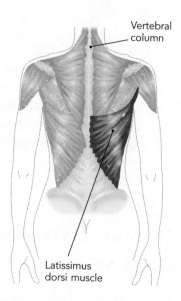

Vertebral column

Latissimus dorsi muscle

Figure 7.7 The lat (latissimus dorsi) muscle stretches from the lower spine and hip bone to behind the armpit.

axillary (underarm) *artery.* These vessels and the portion of the latissimus dorsi muscle that normally attaches to the undersurface of the arm bone—a spot close to the armpit—are left intact. That secures the blood supply to the muscle, so that muscle and tissue remain viable (Figure 7.8).

Next, the surgeon creates a tunnel in the underarm area. The tunnel has skin and fat on the top and the muscles of the side part of the chest underneath. The lat muscle is then rotated from the back, through the tunnel, onto the front of the chest (Figure 7.9). Now it is on the front of the body.

In most women, the lat muscle is thin and wouldn't be large enough when used alone to re-create a breast that matches its twin. Thus, the upper edges of the lat and lower edge of the pectoral muscles are sewn together to create a pocket into which a permanent implant can be placed to provide additional volume.

Drains to suction out the lymphatic fluid that accumulates after surgery are placed under the skin in the chest and back surgical sites. The skin edges from the chest wall are then sewn to the skin edges from the latissimus flap. Finally, the incision on the back is closed.

Latissimus dorsi flap surgery takes two to four hours with an experienced surgical team and possibly longer if performed at the same time as a mastectomy. A second surgery may be needed in a few months to recontour the new breast and possibly revise scars. A third surgery may be needed to create a nipple, if you wish.

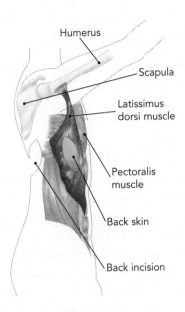

Humerus

Scapula

Latissimus
dorsi muscle

Pectoralis
muscle

Back skin

Back incision

Figure 7.8 The lat muscle is detached from the spine and hip bone. It remains connected near the underarm. The muscle, along with the skin and fat above it, is then tunneled beneath the skin along the side of the body, and repositioned on the chest to form the breast mound.

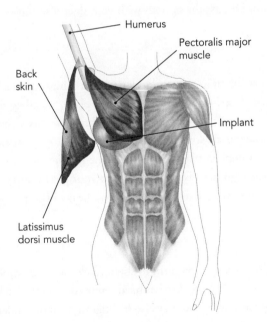

Humerus

Pectoralis major
muscle

Back
skin

Implant

Latissimus
dorsi muscle

Figure 7.9 The lat flap generally provides a small amount of tissue, so an additional implant is often needed. The edges of the lat and pectoralis muscles of the chest are stitched together to create a pocket for the permanent implant.

What to Expect While Recovering from Surgery

Usually, recovery takes three to six weeks, though it may be longer before you truly feel like yourself.

Pain

Muscle, skin, nerves, and blood vessels were disrupted or removed from two opposing sites on your body and the area between, where the tunnel was created. Expect to feel physically bruised after your surgery, though emotionally you may feel encouraged by the thought that you are closer to your goal. While in bed, many of my patients have found having the operative side propped up on pillows and placing their weight on the other side of the body is most comfortable. Your surgeon initially may caution against wearing a bra for at least two weeks until the lat muscle and its blood supply are well established in the chest wall. It is important that pain is well controlled so you can take in deep breaths, thus minimizing the chance of developing *atelectasis*, or small areas of lung collapse. A variety of medication can help you control your pain. Discuss the options with your doctor or nurse.

Lifting

If you had an implant placed at the time of your lat flap, the latissimus dorsi and pectoral muscles were stitched closed to hold the implant in place. To allow the incision to heal, a plastic surgeon typically will restrict heavy lifting for six weeks. If you overuse your arm and the muscle stitches weaken, the implant may shift.

Even if you did not have an implant placed, allowing time for the incision to heal before working the muscles too hard is important. Ask your plastic surgeon how long to wait before you can resume activities that involve heavy lifting.

Range of Motion

Avoid excessive shoulder motion. Raising your arm to slip into clothes or do other activities will be impossible initially. Because skin has been removed from the back, this closure is likely to feel tight and sore. You may also feel tightness in the underarm area and on the chest from the pull of the latissimus dorsi muscle in its new location. Your plastic surgeon may instruct you to not raise your arm at the shoulder more than ninety degrees (parallel with the ground) for several weeks, while the incisions and stitching mend. This also helps the reconstructed breast heal well in its new position on the chest. When the area has healed, your plastic surgeon will instruct you on shoulder range-of-motion exercises. Massage therapy can help release tightness and help restore shoulder mobility.

How Will the Breast and Back Look After Healing?

Because the lat flap procedures deploy skin, fat, and muscle, the end result often looks quite natural. There will be scarring where the chest wall skin meets the skin from the flap, and the skin tone where the two areas meet may not match. Eva found that the relocated muscle atrophied over time, shrinking somewhat so that her breasts were not symmetric. "I think frankly my plastic surgeon didn't want to do it, but he did because it was what I wanted at the time," she said. The difference was compounded when she became pregnant and after she nursed her new baby.

The back will have a sizable scar (though there are ways for a surgeon to minimize this). Like all scars, the chest and back scars will fade somewhat with time. Also expect an indentation where the muscle was removed and a projection of the wing bone (scapula) where the muscle is no longer present to hold it down.

What Will the Breast Feel Like to Touch? How Will Sensation Be Affected?

Because the lat flap procedure moves skin, fat, and muscle, the padding of the reshaped breast feels softer and much more like a natural breast. If an implant is placed beneath the lat flap, the reconstructed breast will feel firmer. As with any extensive surgery on the breast—including a mastectomy without reconstruction—nerves will have been cut, leaving little or no sensation in the reshaped breast. Expect numbness at the back donor site, too, and over the skin of the tunnel on the side of the chest.

How Will the Breast Change over Time?

Most lat flap reconstructions reshape the breast using the muscle flap combined with an underlying implant. The implant may make the breast look perkier and rounder than before. The reshaped breast is likely to look increasingly asymmetric over time as its mate responds more readily to gravity. Also, the natural breast will contain a greater overall percentage of body fat, so if you gain or lose a significant amount of weight, it will change in size to a greater extent than the reconstructed breast.

How Will Muscles and Activities Be Affected?

Active women may want to avoid a lat flap procedure because of its effect on important muscles. There are always exceptions to the rule—an avid squash player who continued her game unhindered, for example.

Posture, shoulder flexibility, and strength can be affected by this surgery. Stretching and, sometimes, physical therapy, including heat, massage, and passive range-of-motion exercises, are necessary to regain full shoulder range of motion and to prevent posture problems that occur as you try to avoid painful actions (see Chapter 11). "It sort of threw off my whole right side and my mobility," said Eva. Occasional shooting pains and itchiness that bothered her have since disappeared. Certain areas on her right side still feel somewhat numb or knotted, but practicing yoga has eased many of the muscle problems she initially experienced.

Normally, the lat muscles help you bring your outstretched arms down to your sides, as when shutting the trunk of your car. They also help if you're trying to pull or propel your body upward, as you might when climbing a ladder or using your arms to assist you in getting out of the tub. Shoulder rotation—for example, flipping your thumb from front to back when your arm is resting at your side—calls upon these back muscles, too. Removing a lat muscle from its normal position can compromise shoulder strength and interfere with some daily activities. You might find it more difficult than usual to use your arm to push yourself up out of a chair, get out of a car, close a car trunk, or remove a box from a high shelf. Decreased strength also may affect racket sports, cross-country skiing, swimming, rowing, or kayaking, rock climbing, and even uphill cycling, though this is not always the case.

Initially, you may use the unaffected arm or change arm and body positioning to help compensate for the loss of strength. Strength-training exercises to build other muscles of the shoulder and back will help remedy the muscle loss and may help you avoid posture problems. (See Chapter 11.) Some can be started fairly quickly, while others must wait until your body has healed. Walking is beneficial right away and can even begin while the drains are still in. Start with a very light program—a lap or two around your home or block—and gradually add to it as your energy and strength return.

What Problems Might Occur with Lat Flap Surgery?

Any surgery carries the risk of side effects and complications. Talk with your plastic surgeon about his or her experiences with lat flap surgery.

One of the most common problems encountered with this surgery is an accumulation of lymphatic fluid called a *seroma* in the back donor site. The latissimus dorsi is a muscle with a large surface area. When the muscle is moved from its normal position raw tissue surfaces created will weep lymphatic fluid for several weeks. Drains siphon the fluid away from the body. After the drains are removed, fluid may continue to accumulate. The seroma may go away as the fluid is reabsorbed or your surgeon can draw it off through a needle.

Some women who have latissimus dorsi flaps may experience capsular contracture of the implant. Very rarely, loss of the flap may occur when blood vessels fail.

ADDITIONAL CONCERNS

Sometimes women decide to take a few more steps to make their re-created breast and new figure look as natural as possible. Surgery to create a nipple or change the shape of the other breast may help.

How Can a Nipple Be Created?

Usually, a nipple and an areola can be constructed about three months after incisions in the breast mound have healed and the new breast literally has had a chance to settle so the nipple will be in the right spot. The projection (how much the nipple protrudes) may be created with breast skin, though cold or arousal will not cause the new nipple to change shape. If the skin is too thin and stretched too tightly from previous surgery, a skin graft can be taken from the thigh or groin. A natural-colored areola can be added by tattooing four to eight weeks after the nipple is created. These tattoos tend to lighten over time.

Some women choose to have the whole nipple and areola tattooed on rather than constructing a nipple. Others don't bother. "I want a tattoo, but I don't know what I want and where I want it," said Audrey, who seemed certain that the last place she'd choose would be on her breast. Either way, the lack of projection can leave you feeling like you have one headlight on and one headlight off, as one of my patients wryly observed. Of course, you can change your mind and do nipple reconstruction at a later date.

Latex nipples are another option. They are sold by some companies that make breast forms and even some lingerie shops. (See Chapter 6.) A roll-on adhesive allows you to attach the nipple to skin.

How Can Differences Between the Breasts Be Handled?

No woman has breasts that are exactly alike. Women who simultaneously have bilateral mastectomies and reconstruction have a good chance of achieving symmetry. Some women having a unilateral mastectomy are concerned about asymmetry between their breasts. They may decide to have their plastic surgeon lift the unaffected breast (*mastopexy*) or make it smaller (*reduction mammoplasty*), as did Betty more than a decade after her mastectomy. The prosthesis she had worn so that her breasts would appear symmetric was very heavy, so the reduction made a real difference. "I felt better because it wasn't that heavy." Others, like Leah, who had a TRAM flap procedure, chose to leave the remaining breast untouched and instead wear a booster or balancer (see Chapter 6) beneath the breast that is somewhat smaller than the other.

Who Pays?

Under the Women's Health and Cancer Rights Act of 1998, health insurance companies that pay for mastectomies must cover the cost of breast reconstruction afterward. Surgery to achieve symmetry through a breast lift or reduction of the opposite breast is typically included if performed at the same time as the recon-struction. However, once the reconstruction is completed, you may be required to pay for any additional surgeries or scar revisions that you might desire for improvements.

The usual co-pays and deductibles apply to reconstructive surgery, and there may be other exceptions as well. Call your insurance company to learn more. Be sure to ask exactly what will be covered: will they, for example, pay for a later sur-gery to replace an implant, if necessary, or a lift on the unaffected breast to enhance symmetry? Find out exactly what fees you will have to pay. Be aware, too, that some private plastic surgeons charge additional money to supplement the fee paid by insurance.

8

YOUR SKIN

◉

Draped neatly over muscle, bone, and underlying tissue are millions of skin cells laid down in an orderly strata of interlocking tiles. When intact, your skin repels bacterial boarders and other agents that could cause infection. It traps much-needed moisture, helps regulate body temperature, and raises a shield against damaging ultraviolet rays.

Speaking as both doctor and patient, I know that the very treatments that successfully keep breast cancer at bay may affect skin in a variety of ways. Surgery requires your body to jump-start the healing process. Some effects of chemotherapy and radiation resemble changes due to aging and sun damage. Others may prompt dry skin, sun sensitivity, or an allergic response.

Any list of possible skin troubles is bound to set your mind racing. Will you experience every one? That didn't happen to me, and it's unlikely to happen to you. When problems do crop up, the solutions noted in this chapter and others supplied by your cancer care team or a dermatologist may help make you feel better. Equally important, this may keep your treatment proceeding as planned. While certain products are suggested here, your cancer care team or a dermatologist may have other recommendations based on their experiences and your specific needs.

SKIN AND SURGERY

One truly remarkable feature of skin is its ability to heal. Even before I left the operating room on the day of my mastectomy, a collection of growth factors, blood components, and skin cells had begun to mobilize to protect my body and seal off the incision made by my surgeon. After your surgery, your body responded—or will respond—that way, too.

WORKING WITH A DERMATOLOGIST

Not every woman undergoing breast cancer treatment needs to see a dermatologist. Your cancer care team is experienced in dealing with treatment-related skin problems. The following are a few good reasons to see a dermatologist:

• Hard-to-handle skin reactions or infections
• Acne that isn't easily treated with over-the-counter preparations
• Cosmetic concerns, such as enhancing skin or handling skin discolorations, blotches, spider veins, and scars

Your nurse or doctor may be able to recommend a dermatologist who has expertise with cancer treatments. You might also contact a cancer center near you or the American Academy of Dermatology (aad.org or 888-462-DERM) to find dermatologists in your area.

Although close to miraculous, the healing process explained next always leaves a scar in its wake. However, you can take steps to enhance the way your body heals after surgery and minimize or possibly revise scars.

Phases of Healing: Inflammation, Regeneration, Remodeling

The phases of healing—inflammation, regeneration, and remodeling—overlap at times.

Beneath the top layer of skin, or *epidermis*, blood cell fragments called *platelets* oozing from broken blood vessels in the *dermis* attach to divided collagen fibers to plug the wound. Along with a protein called *fibrin*, the platelets form a soft clot that helps staunch blood flow and pull together wound edges. Later, it will harden to a scab.

The surrounding tissues swell with fluid that dilutes harmful substances and nurtures specialized cells, such as *neutrophils*, which destroy microorganisms that can cause infection, and *macrophages*, which clear cellular debris. Although *inflammation* may be pronounced at this point, it should ebb fairly quickly. When a wound is clean and all goes well, the cells associated with inflammation usually disappear within five to seven days.

Below the scab, *regeneration* is under way. New blood vessels bud and then fuse across the wound to shuttle nutrients and oxygen to the site. New epidermal cells migrate across the wound bed to knit together the gap above the dermis. Deep in the dermis, cells called *fibroblasts* synthesize supportive collagen fibers that replace fibrin to help strengthen the new tissue. Over the course of two weeks, the scab sloughs off to expose an unbroken sheet of new skin cells.

Remodeling—a process that goes on for years—begins in earnest about three weeks after surgery. During remodeling, collagen fibers are continuously manufactured, broken down, and rearranged in the dermis. The fibers are bundled in cross-linked patterns that resist stress.

Raised (*hypertrophic*) scars occur when too much collagen is produced and too little is broken down. During the third to ninth month of healing, scars can become surprisingly thick, red, and bumpy. Such scars usually relax and grow paler over the course of three to six more months.

Keloid scars are also raised and are somewhat itchy but spill irregularly beyond wound boundaries. They stem from unchecked collagen production. While this eventually stops, the overgrowth of tissue will not improve on its own as hypertrophic scars sometimes do. Keloids are more likely to affect people of African or Asian descent.

Strength Returns Gradually

Over the course of six to twelve months, scar tissue gradually grows stronger. Initially, the tissue is quite weak, but its strength begins to pick up by week three as increasingly strong cross-links of collagen are built. By the end of six weeks, 80 percent of tensile strength will return (thus the well-known advice from doctors to avoid heavy lifting until that time). It will creep upward to 90 percent by the end of a year. The new skin, though, will never be as strong as it was before surgery.

Enhancing Healing and Minimizing Scars

Physics plays a surprisingly big role in scarring, notes Charles A. Hergrueter, M.D., a plastic surgeon at Brigham and Women's Hospital in Boston with extensive experience in breast reconstructive surgery. When skin is under tension—as it frequently is when a surgeon closes an incision after removing tissue during a mastectomy or adding tissue or volume during reconstruction—scars are more obvious than if the skin is more relaxed. Similarly, scars that cross large muscles or areas of the body engaged in lots of movement, such as the back and shoulders, often widen over time. Scars that lie along skin creases or parallel to lines of tension in the skin tend to heal in the least eye-catching way. Whenever possible, surgeons plan incisions with these issues in mind.

Keeping infection at bay encourages the skin to heal cleanly. Katherine, whose lumpectomy became infected—partly, she believes, because the cancerous cells were buried quite deeply in an abundant breast—found her final scar larger than it would have been had it healed without this trauma. Her chemotherapy, which started on schedule, slowed healing further.

What you and your surgeon have the least control over are quirks of biology. Some people simply scar more than others.

Talk with your surgeon about ways to help enhance healing and minimize scars, such as those outlined in the following:

• After your surgeon removes the bandage, if new skin has not yet fully covered the wound, keep the skin moist by applying bacitracin ointment (or another product recommended by your surgeon). Opinions differ on bandaging, but Dr. Hergrueter usually recommends continuing to bandage the wound until the new skin is formed and then leaving it open to air.

• Once new skin covers the wound, some experts suggest gentle daily massage for the first six months or so, which appears to help heal the site and settle down scars. Your surgeon may have a preference regarding what to apply. Vitamin E is a useful moisturizer and lubricant for this massage, though research is mixed on whether it helps healing in other ways. Put a small amount of vitamin E on a fingertip and massage the scar gently with it. Another choice is the over-the-counter ointment Mederma, though again, there is little firm data to show whether it helps healing other than as a moisturizer.

• Silicone sheeting or silicone gel, which can be bought over the counter in pharmacies, encourages new scar tissue to grow in smoother, flatter, and more evenly colored. A few examples of these products are ReJuveness and ScarEase and the reusable silicone sheeting sold at some pharmacies. Silicone sheets have been shown in studies to reduce keloids over time. Typically, these must be worn over the scar

WHAT AFFECTS HEALING?

Healing is a complex process that can be helped or hurt by many factors. Some—such as your age—are out of your hands, but you can have an impact on others:

- **Smoking:** By cutting the amount of oxygen that reaches the tissues, smoking impairs healing. Quitting smoking aids healing and your health.
- **Nutrition:** Vitamin C, vitamin A, zinc, and protein, carbohydrates, fats, and fatty acids are all essential to healing. A healthy diet (see Chapter 12) plus a multivitamin should supply sufficient nutrients. If you are having trouble eating, consult a nutritionist. Remember, too much of a good thing—zinc, for example, which is called a *trace mineral* because the body only needs a very small amount of it—can actually be harmful in larger quantities. Typically, it is hard to get too much of vitamins or minerals through diet, but easy enough to do so through supplements.
- **Diabetes:** A higher risk of infection and impaired blood supply can slow healing in diabetics. Tight control of blood sugar helps.

many hours a day for months. Some products have their own adhesive system, while others must be held in place with hypoallergenic tape. Be aware that these products may cause redness, rashes, or itching in some women.

- Keep scars covered with clothes or liberally applied sunscreen (at least SPF 45) during the first year. Sun can darken a scar, making it more apparent.

SKIN AND ANTICANCER DRUGS

Skin cells are continually replaced by the body, though this turnover slows somewhat as you age. Like other rapidly dividing cells, skin cells can be harmed by certain anticancer drugs. This may contribute to patchy skin thickening or thinning, discoloration, and dryness. Certain drug regimens that push women temporarily or permanently into menopause deprive the skin of estrogen, which may affect the elasticity and dryness of skin.

Several anticancer drugs may prompt hypersensitive skin reactions, so that rashes, itching, and redness may occur. Docetaxel (Taxotere), doxorubicin (Adriamycin), 5-fluorouracil (Adrucil; abbreviated as 5-FU), methotrexate (Mexate), and paclitaxel (Taxol) are among the drugs that sometimes do this. Skin discoloration over the veins being used to administer the drug may happen with 5-FU or Adriamycin, while cyclophosphamide (Cytoxan) sometimes darkens nails or creases in the palm or soles of the feet.

Blotchy spots and tiny, tangled capillaries called *telangiectasias* or pinhead-sized spots called *cherry angiomas* may crop up more frequently, too. These particular skin changes also owe a debt to time, genes, and sun damage, though some are probably accelerated by treatment.

Sometimes, the culprit behind skin reactions may be a drug given to calm certain side effects of treatment. Prednisone, a steroid given to minimize nausea and vomiting, may trigger acne, for example.

Although most of these problems will disappear once you finish treatment, you may find them distressing. The following are tips on handling some of the most common problems that beset skin and nails as well as options for pampering your skin during or after treatment.

Dryness

Like an ill-fitting wool suit, dry skin feels uncomfortably tight and itchy. Very dry skin is more likely to crack, which hurts and invites infection, especially while your immune system is weakened. Whether anticancer drug regimens or the natural state of your skin is to blame for dryness, these steps may help:

- Make it a daily habit to get enough water and other fluids. Chemotherapy regimens are often dehydrating—doubly so if nausea makes drinking difficult or vomiting is a problem—and can require extra fluids to help push drugs through your body. If necessary, experiment to see what liquids (soda, perhaps, or soup or herbal tea) sit best on a queasy stomach. Eating watermelon, cucumbers, lettuce, and other fruits or vegetables with a high water content may help.

- When showering or bathing, water should be warm, not steaming hot. Long soaks or showers are relaxing, but ten- to fifteen-minute stints are better for skin.

- Wash with mild soaps or cleansers, such as Dove, Basis, or Neutrogena. Because soap clears away natural skin oils along with dirt and odors, though, try to lather up only where necessary and give the rest of your skin a reprieve.

- Pat skin dry with a towel rather than rubbing, which can cause further irritation.

- Water softens skin, so use moisturizer while it is still damp. Choose fragrance-free emollient products, such as Cetaphil, Lubriderm, or Eucerin, and facial moisturizers that do not clog pores (noncomedogenic). Moisturize your hands several times a day and before bedtime. If your skin is especially sensitive, avoid products with alcohol, which is drying, and lanolin, which may cause allergic reactions. One exception is no-soap hand cleansers. These products do have alcohol, but work so well to help quell germs that they are worth using when there is no place to wash your hands.

- Winter winds and indoor heat can be drying, too. Bundle up properly to protect tender skin before venturing outdoors. Try a humidifier in the bedroom and other places where you spend a lot of time.

Itching and Rashes

Certain chemotherapy drugs may trigger itchiness and sometimes rashes. While scratching an itch is surely an elemental pleasure, the blissful pain only temporarily flips the "off" switch on nerves that conduct itch impulses. When the pain recedes, the itch rebounds, starting the cycle again. Too much scratching can easily breach the skin, setting the stage for an infection, especially if your immune system is below par due to treatment. Try these tips instead to root out the underlying cause or help quash it:

• Rashes and itching can be a sign of a drug allergy or merely an unpleasant side effect of certain treatments, so tell your care team if you experience either. "I broke out in hives," recalled Greta, during treatment with Adriamycin and Cytoxan. "Red, blotchy things. I looked like I had poison ivy." Antihistamines often subdue itchiness. If they fail to do so, antidepressants, sedatives, or tranquilizers might offer relief, according to the National Cancer Institute. Corticosteroid creams are sometimes prescribed to help clear up a local rash. Because cancer treatments often suppress immune function, it may take longer than usual for your skin to heal properly.

• Try a cool, damp washcloth on itchy areas. A colloidal oatmeal bath can ease overall itchiness.

• During treatment, skin may become ultrasensitive to irritants in soaps, moisturizers, clothing, and wigs, among other items. An irritant in my wig, for example, sparked a rash and open sores that took weeks to heal. Shield your skin physically from irritants when necessary, as I did by wearing a cotton wig liner after the sores healed. Weed out potential irritants by using mild, fragrance-free soaps and shampoos. Forgo dyes and fragrances in laundry detergents, too. When washing clothes, use less detergent than usual and rinse twice. If the water is still sudsy, run an extra rinse cycle and make a note to cut down detergent further. Skip fabric softeners, which can contain irritants.

• A dusting of cornstarch helps soak up perspiration and cuts down irritating friction that can lead to heat rash. Sometimes, though, cornstarch feeds yeast infections, especially when applied to skin folds, so go lightly.

• Breathable fabrics like cotton are best for clothes and sheets because they lessen the buildup of perspiration and heat, which can trigger itching.

• Just as scratching interrupts nerve impulses that broadcast itchiness, distractions of other sorts may work. Meditation, deep breathing, or visualization can help redirect your focus; so, too, might an engrossing book or TV show, a conversation, or a change in activities.

• Vaginal itching and discharge or discomfort is often a sign of overgrowth of certain natural vaginal flora, such as yeast. Tell your care team about this.

Infusion Site Reaction

A few chemotherapy drugs, notably Adriamycin and Taxol, can seriously irritate or harm skin if they escape from the vein. An infusion site reaction (*extravasation*) occurs only if the drug leaks from a vein. It happens rarely—reports on all types of cancer suggest it occurs in 0.6 to 6 percent of cases—but is one reason why doctors sometimes suggest that a port be placed beneath the skin so that the drugs reliably can be injected directly into the bloodstream. Nurses who administer chemotherapy take great care with these drugs, of course.

With a minimal reaction, irritation marked by redness, aching, pain, or tightness at the injection site or along the vein may occur. Usually, this will heal on its own as long as the area is small. About one-third of the time, though, an ulcer may form or some skin tissue dies. At its worst, this may require removal of affected tissue and a skin graft.

Tell your nurse immediately about any skin discomfort, burning, tingling, itching, or pain during chemotherapy, as well as signs that crop up days or weeks later, such as injection site swelling, redness, pain, dark discoloration, peeling, or blistering. When caught quickly while the IV is still going, damage is more likely to be limited and the skin may be quickly treated with appropriate measures, such as stopping the infusion and removing the IV, elevating the affected area, and applying cold packs or heat. Sometimes, an antidote is used on the skin as well.

Numbness and Tingling

Numbness, tingling, or pain in the hands and feet or occasionally other outlying areas of the body is a sign that nerves are inflamed or harmed. Sometimes, the sensation is likened to pins and needles or the muffled feeling of wearing a sock or glove, though it also can appear as sharp, brief pains or extreme sensitivity. Called *peripheral neuropathy*, these sensory problems are most often tied to a few chemotherapy drugs. It affects up to 49 percent of women taking Taxotere and 60 percent of those on Taxol. Weakness and loss of balance and coordination can occur if motor nerves, which affect movement, are involved.

Fortunately, peripheral neuropathy sometimes stops on its own after treatment is under way and may be reversed once treatment ends, though this can take months. At this time, the best way to handle the problem is to report any of the symptoms just described to your cancer care team. Be sure to mention any trouble you have performing normal activities, such as using utensils, buttoning a shirt, typing, or walking. If the symptoms are mild, you may be able to continue with treatment; if not, it may be safest to stop treatment and consider other options.

Hand-Foot Syndrome

Redness and peeling on hands or feet are a possible side effect of certain chemotherapy drugs, such as Adriamycin or 5-FU. Tingling of the palms or soles turns into a burning sensation and swelling a few days later. Blisters and peeling may occur.

Hand-foot syndrome is very uncomfortable and may require stopping chemotherapy until the skin heals. A variety of treatments, such as corticosteroids and vitamin B$_6$ have met with mixed success. Usually, simple measures offer some relief. Cleanse affected skin to avoid infection as directed by your care team. To lessen swelling, raise the affected area and apply cold compresses. Take pain medications approved by your nurse or doctor.

Acne

"During chemo my skin cleared right up," laughed Amanda. "I never had a blemish at all." Not bad for a woman who admits her skin care regimen is slapdash at best.

Yet not everyone who goes through cancer treatment finds that to be true. Acne begins when overactive sebaceous (oil) glands and dead skin cells combine to clog pores. Hormonal changes brought on by certain treatments for breast cancer may help set the stage for outbreaks. Open comedones (blackheads) and closed comedones (whiteheads) pop up even on skin that has been clear for years. Sometimes, whiteheads, which house inflammatory and bacterial substances, evolve into larger eruptions called pustules or papules.

I noticed acne flare-ups on previously smooth skin during my treatment. One eruption was so severe it could have temporarily derailed my chemotherapy had my skin not been treated promptly by a dermatologist.

These steps may help keep skin smooth and handle mild outbreaks:

• Wash your face gently with a mild soap twice a day. (If that makes skin too dry, try washing just once a day.) Use your fingertips rather than rubbing with a wash-cloth, which may irritate skin. Pat skin dry.

• Choose noncomedogenic moisturizer and makeup to avoid clogging pores. Crème-based makeup has oils that can add to the problem. Anytime you wear makeup, be sure to remove it at night.

• Picking or squeezing harms skin, sometimes spreading inflammation and infection and scarring it. Don't do it or allow it during a facial.

• Ask your cancer care team or a dermatologist to recommend over-the-counter acne preparations, particularly if your skin has been very dry or you have had rashes. Many over-the-counter products contain benzyl peroxide, which helps keep pores open and inhibits bacterial growth. Other common ingredients are salicylic acid, sulfur, or resorcinol, which makes existing eruptions dry and peel. Sometimes, these ingredients can further irritate sensitive skin.

Professional care or a prescription preparation, such as antibiotics or a topical retinoid, may be necessary. I needed to have a pustule on my cheek lanced by my dermatologist during my treatment. That prevented an infection from progressing and helped me avoid scarring while allowing proper healing. This should be done by a dermatologist or your nurse or doctor—squeezing pimples yourself will only make matters worse. If necessary, a dermatologist may suggest injecting cortisone into an eruption to help clear it up.

Skin Discoloration: Streaks, Blotches, and More

A few chemotherapy drugs may trace dark marks along vein pathways, especially in darker-skinned women. Discoloration may also show up on the creases of the palms of your hand or soles of your feet or on your face or elbows. Sun sensitivity triggered by a medication may be at fault. Usually, such discoloration clears within a few weeks or months of the final treatment; sometimes, as with Cytoxan, it may take six to twelve months to fade. The brown, pinprick-sized discoloration at each IV infusion site on my arms began clearing about six months after my chemotherapy ended.

Blotchy so-called age spots may seem to pile up at a more rapid clip. Whether that reflects treatment-related hormonal changes, previous sun damage, newly acquired sun sensitivity, or another process is unclear.

Of equal concern for many women is a temporary overall change in skin tone. "That's the chemo glow," said one of my patients. "It's like a shadowy, skeletal look almost, like your skin is really transparent." To ease these problems, try the following:

• Minimize exposure to sun, especially if you are taking medication that makes you more sensitive to its rays (see the sidebar "Sun Sensitivity" later in this chapter). Avoid tanning salons entirely.

• Camouflage discolorations (see the sidebar "Cover-Ups" later in this chapter) and hide the chemo glow with artful makeup. Consider attending a free Look Good . . . Feel Better workshop, where trained volunteer cosmetologists offer makeup tips and give out kits packed with cosmetics to complement various complexions. Call 800-395-LOOK or check online at lookgoodfeelbetter.org for makeup tips and local programs. Another good resource replete with how-to photographs is *Facing the Mirror with Cancer: A Guide to Using Makeup to Make a Difference* by makeup artist Lori Ovitz with Joanne Kabak. (See Resources.)

• Wear colors that perk up your complexion rather than highlight green or pallid undertones. "You know that color palette business?" asked Katherine. She found wearing colors that were best for her—especially around her face—really made a big difference.

• Ask your care team or dermatologist whether creams and lotions that contain the bleaching agent hydroquinolone or glycolic acid would be appropriate to lighten patches of discolored skin. This works poorly, however, on darker-skinned women, who may be left with blotchy areas of coloration. Because these products can be irritating, they are best prescribed and overseen by a nurse or doctor on your cancer care team or a dermatologist.

• Consider having a chemical peel. Often touted as a way to freshen skin and erase fine lines, chemical peels may also partially wipe away age spots and some other discolorations. The solutions that are swabbed on prompt layers of skin cells to separate and slough off. The depth of a peel depends on application and the chemical solution chosen. A light peel leaves a red glow that fades by the following day. This is the *only* type of peel recommended during chemotherapy. It should be performed when blood counts are in the normal range and are expected to stay there for several days. A superficial peel is usually followed by several days of scaling; a medium or deep peel, which can be painful, trips off swelling, blisters, and peeling that take one to two weeks to subside. New skin beneath a peel is tender and must be protected from sun. Although chemical peels are often offered by aestheticians at spas and salons, going to an experienced dermatologist is safest.

Spider Veins and Red Dots

After her chemotherapy treatments, Andrea started to notice tiny, wiggly clusters of spider veins (telangiectasias) and pinhead-sized red dots (cherry angiomas) on her skin. These slightly aberrant blood vessels appear on skin for many reasons, including the effects of certain chemotherapy drugs and radiation, genes, hormonal changes, and aging. Cherry angiomas and the smallest spider veins can be treated with *laser*, an intense beam of light that seals shut the blood vessels. *Sclerotherapy*, which works well on larger spider veins, requires injections of saline (salt water) or other chemicals through a very fine needle. Over time, the collapsed vessels are absorbed by the body. While erasing spider veins, either technique can cause some discoloration that takes up to a year to disappear and more than one treatment may be necessary. Discuss the best approach and the likely outcome with your dermatologist.

Nails

One of the lesser casualties of chemotherapy drugs may be your nails. Darkened nail beds, dingy or yellowish discoloration, streaking, flecks, brittleness, and dryness are problems you may notice as treatment goes on. Bands or ridges in nails can also develop as normal growth cycles are interrupted. Time should erase these lin-

SUN SENSITIVITY

Several anticancer drugs, including methotrexate, Adriamycin, and Taxotere, increase sun sensitivity during treatment. This leaves your skin more vulnerable to sunburn and accelerates discoloration and other signs of sun damage, like wrinkles, freckles, and age spots. Long after radiation therapy, skin can also be especially vulnerable to sun, so cover up well or put sunscreen (at least SPF 30) on it.

Newly bare skin—such as a bare scalp—can provide quite a target, as one woman found after basking in the sun without a wig for a short time. The next day, when she wore her wig at a professional conference, she repeatedly shoved it askew while scratching her suddenly itchy scalp skin. Luckily, a good friend and colleague helped her out by tugging it back in place for her.

The following tips can help protect your skin:

- Talk with your care team about whether any of your treatments will boost sun sensitivity.
- Sun is strongest between 10 A.M. and 4 P.M., so limit exposure during these times as much as possible.
- Wear a wide-brimmed hat that casts shadow on your face, ears, and neck. Choose very tightly woven clothes or clothes designed with sun protection in mind, such as products by Solumbra (sunprecautions.com or 800-882-7860) and Coolibar (coolibar.com or 800-926-6509). Long-sleeve shirts and pants are best.
- Half an hour before sun exposure, apply a broad-spectrum sunscreen that blocks UVA and UVB rays on lips, hands, and any other skin that will see the sun. Don't assume that an SPF 15 sunscreen is enough for anything other than a brief walk, warns one dermatologist. If you are going to be outside longer, wear at least SPF 30 sunscreen. Remember to reapply sun protection every two to three hours.
- Skin irritation can be a problem with some sunscreens that contain PABA (para-aminobenzoic acid), Parsol 1789, or heavy fragrances. So-called nonchemical products designed for sensitive skin, which rely on zinc oxide or titanium dioxide to physically block sun rays, may be a better choice if you have sensitive skin. Again, apply thirty minutes before sun exposure. Rub in well to avoid white streaks. Apply foundation over it if your skin still looks too light for your liking.

gering reminders of treatment, but you can also try the following tips while you wait:

- Wear gloves during activities like gardening or dish washing that could dry out nails or breach cuticles and affect surrounding skin.

- Even if you love swooping fingernails, consider cutting back. Nails kept reasonably short and neatly filed are less likely to break. Artificial nails sandwiched atop natural nails may offer an inviting place for bacteria or fungus to set up shop and multiply.

- Cover discolored nails in any shade of polish you enjoy. Just choose polishes that don't contain formaldehyde, which can dry and stain nails. Likewise, pick polish removers without acetone, an ingredient that also leaches moisture.

- When treating yourself to a professional manicure, choose a shop that looks sparkling clean rather than one that is simply inexpensive. Some salons may be less scrupulous than necessary about cleaning clippers and other tools. By bringing your own manicure set, polish, and polish remover, you can be doubly sure of cleanliness and ingredients.

- Whether your manicure is done at home or at a nail salon or spa, cuticles should be pressed back gently rather than clipped. Clipping may nick the live cuticle and provide a foothold for infection.

- Be cautious about nail-strengthening products, which can contain irritating chemicals. Try a product out by using it on a single nail for a week or two to see if irritation occurs.

- Tell your cancer care team if nail beds or cuticles redden, hurt, or change in any way.

Skin and Radiation Therapy

Unlike chemotherapy, which wends its way through the body, radiation is typically aimed at the breast or chest wall and, possibly, lymph nodes beneath the arm or around the collarbone. Despite this focus, radiation does damage some healthy cells caught in its path. This affects healing and can prompt such problems as sunburn-

COVER-UPS

Makeup can hide a multitude of minor imperfections. Use it on a lumpectomy scar, a radiation tattoo, or annoying skin discolorations that peek from a favorite outfit. Dermablend, a specialized cosmetic much like a heavy, slightly greasy foundation, is one option. Stick concealers or thinner, lighter body foundations, which are less likely to come off on clothes, can also do the trick. Try these tips for concealment:

1. Select the concealer shade closest to the skin near the spot you wish to blot out.
2. Start with a moisturizer so that the concealing product spreads more easily. If the skin you're covering is red, follow this by patting on a little green-tinted foundation to help correct the color.
3. Now put a dab of concealing product in the soft hammock of skin between your thumb and the first knuckle of your forefinger. Use a finger on the opposite hand to rub it lightly. That warms the product so it will be easier to spread. Dot a little bit of the concealing product on the scar, tattoo, or discoloration. Smooth it evenly across the skin. Add more only if necessary.
4. Feather the edges with the side of a finger or a tiny makeup brush so that it blends into the surrounding skin.
5. As an optional step, set the concealer with a translucent blotting powder.

If the cover-up is on your face, follow these steps with a facial foundation and your usual makeup, if you like.

like skin irritation and redness, peeling, skin thickening, swelling or shrinkage, and discoloration. Some of these changes are temporary, while others may be long lasting.

I tell my patients that radiation is a bit of a wild card. Currently, it isn't possible to predict who will breeze through practically unscathed and who will experience skin problems. It may ease your concerns somewhat to know that one 2003 study of 265 women that evaluated the cosmetic outcomes of lumpectomy plus radiation noted that 48 percent of the women participating experienced excellent results with no skin changes and very minor, or no, differences in size between their breasts at the six-month mark.

If you do run into problems, talk with your radiation oncology nurse, who can make specific recommendations. The tips laced through the sections that follow can help, too. Caring for your skin properly will make you more comfortable and may also help to prevent interruptions in treatment that could influence its effectiveness.

Healing After Radiation Therapy

Just as when healing takes place after surgery, cells called *fibroblasts* that manufacture supportive collagen must migrate to radiation-treated tissue to help it heal. Some of these fibroblasts show radiation-induced abnormalities and produce more collagen than usual. This causes skin thickening called *fibrosis*. Inflammatory substances and cells also show up in greater amounts than normal, and some blood vessels become blocked. Because blood brings oxygen and nutrients to the tissues, this compromises healing. Fewer blood vessels and thickened skin make it harder for platelets and inflammatory cells, such as neutrophils and macrophages, to reach the tissues, which can slow healing. Sometimes, tiny superficial spider veins appear.

Once radiation has been used on the breast or chest wall, the muscles may stiffen and skin in that region may not heal quite as easily as it once did. Incisions or wounds may take longer to close. Sometimes infections get such a good grip that it is hard to subdue them. That said, most women who have previously undergone radiation heal uneventfully after surgery.

General Skin-Care Tips

• Before using any soaps or products on skin that will be in the radiation field, ask your radiation team for specific recommendations. Salves and moisturizers, for example, should not be applied right before treatments because this can contribute to skin irritation.

• Put away antiperspirants containing metallic ingredients, such as aluminum chlorohydrate, and talcum powder, because these products may affect radiation beams. Try a light dusting of cornstarch, which cuts down on friction as well as odors, or crystal deodorants, which are sold in some natural foods stores. Because cornstarch may encourage yeast growth, ask your radiation team if this makes sense for you.

• Keep skin clean and dry. Report any discomfort, peeling, or blistering to your radiation team.

• Cover up well and avoid spending time in the sun. Wear a broad-spectrum sunscreen when outside (see the sidebar "Sun Sensitivity" earlier in this chapter).

Dryness and Itching

During radiation therapy, the epidermis thins out. Oil glands and sweat glands also can be harmed, which makes skin drier. Minimize dryness and attendant itchiness with a simple skin care regimen. Take short, warm, rather than long, hot, baths or showers. Wash the irradiated area with a mild soap, or temporarily avoid lathering it at all. Pat or air-dry skin slightly, then apply a gentle moisturizer, such as Lubriderm, while skin is still moist. Choose skin products that are fragrance-free, hypoallergenic, and preferably without drying ingredients like alcohol. Sometimes, cortisone cream is used to help control itching. Ask your radiation team about this, if necessary.

"Sunburns" and Dry or Wet Peeling

During the first few weeks of radiation, breast skin may look and feel like you've sustained a minor sunburn. That's as bad as it gets for some women. Sometimes, though, the burn worsens as radiation treatments continue, especially in skin folds and on

RADIATION RECALL

Just as you might recall particularly dramatic events, your skin appears to store cellular memories, too. Skin exposed to radiation during breast cancer treatments may redden, itch, burn, or possibly even blister and peel on the sites of earlier bad sunburns or when chemotherapy is given. Known as *radiation recall*, this may last just hours or for several days. Tell your doctor or nurse about this. A cool, wet compress may help ease the burn, and donning soft, loose clothes will make you more comfortable.

the undersurface of heavier breasts. About two to three weeks after radiation begins, skin may redden dramatically and peel or flake off a bit as it does after a sunburn.

Sometimes, this worsens to blisters with raw, moist areas beneath (*wet desquamation*), though typically not until four to six weeks of treatment have passed. "The last four days, I couldn't wear bras. I couldn't have any material touch me," said Amanda.

Report any burns or peeling—minor or not—to your radiation team. While no product has been proven superior, your radiation nurse may recommend daily use of salves like aloe vera, Aquaphor, Lubriderm, or Biafine. Gel pads may also be recommended to help cool the burn.

Any blisters or sores that develop should be carefully treated. Usually, gentle cleansing is recommended. A thin layer of a burn ointment may be suggested as well. Nonstick coverings that block bacteria and water but allow air to permeate will help skin heal properly. If the covering cannot be held in place by a bra or camisole, be sure any tape used to hold it is applied to skin beyond the radiation field. Occasionally, treatment must be stopped until skin heals sufficiently.

If wearing a bra becomes uncomfortable or impossible, go without one if you can or try wearing a soft, loose camisole designed for women undergoing radiation therapy (tlccatalog.com is one source) or a soft, loose cotton T-shirt.

Discoloration

Skin color changes such as redness or tanning may remain for six months or more. Darker-skinned women may find it lasts longer. Sometimes, women notice other pigment changes, such as darkening or lightening of the nipple and areola after radiation treatments.

Red or darkened, itchy skin may respond to cortisone cream, which you should use if your care team recommends it. Occasionally, discoloration is a sign of infection, which may require antibiotics.

Other Changes

Breast or chest wall tissue may swell or shrink somewhat due to radiation. Swelling may recede as the skin heals, though it is sometimes permanent. When swelling occurs in a woman who had a lumpectomy, it may even be welcome if it helps even

Tattoos and You

The pinhead-sized tattoos placed on your chest to mark the radiation field may be nearly unnoticeable to others, especially if your skin is freckled. Yet to some women, these blue dots may loom large as a constant reminder of breast cancer.

Generally, radiation oncologists prefer that the tattoos remain in place just in case radiation is ever needed to treat the other breast. Because radiation should not be repeated in the same tissues, good guideposts delineating the area to avoid are important.

If the tattoos are very distressing to you, as is true for some of my patients, talk with your radiation oncologist about whether to have any of them removed. A dermatologist can do that with a ruby laser. Usually, the dot that is most visible—and therefore most upsetting— is the one at the sternal notch where your collarbones meet. One of the radiology oncologists I work with suggests that a woman bent on removing this tattoo should have a series of photos of the radiation field taken that includes it. This record might help later on if radiation to the other breast is ever necessary.

One simple, though temporary, way to conceal the tattoo is by using a cover-up product (see the sidebar "Cover-Ups" earlier in this chapter).

out a breast that lost a considerable amount of tissue during surgery. "Right now, my breast is so much bigger than it was after surgery," Amanda observed. "They said the swelling would go away after two years, but it didn't." Sometimes, swelling represents a collection of lymphatic fluid (a *seroma*) that has been walled off by a radiation-induced scar capsule. Again, when swelling plumps up breast contours in a way that is pleasing, you may be happy to leave it as is, which is what some of my patients do. If not, the fluid can be drained with a needle.

Who Pays?

Skin reactions or infections should be covered by health insurance. Co-pays and deductibles will apply. Most likely, any procedures considered cosmetic will not be covered. I did find out, though, that my insurance company would pay for treatment-related skin problems. So, for example, a chemical peel for chemotherapy-induced brown spots (the medical term is *melasma*) or laser therapy for broken capillaries might be covered. Call your insurance plan for specific information.

9

YOUR HAIR

◉

Family photos taken before autumn 2003 show me with straight, golden brown hair cascading down the length of my back. In newer photos, the hair framing my face is curly and just a few inches long. Despite the kindness of people who tell me I look quite chic, short hair is tied in my mind to chemotherapy. Like so many changes that stem from a breast cancer diagnosis, it simply wasn't my choice.

As you may also find, some breast cancer treatments can be undeniably hard on hair and scalp. Best known are the effects of certain chemotherapy drugs. By targeting any quickly dividing cells, these drugs are successful in killing rapidly dividing breast cancer cells. Yet at any given time, 90 percent of hair follicles on the scalp are also in the process of dividing while in a growth phase that can last for years. Only 10 percent of hair follicles are in a resting phase. Thus, while quelling cancer cells, chemotherapy may also harm active hair follicles, resulting in hair loss or thinning.

Unlike the physical changes of surgery and radiation, which can be readily camouflaged, hair loss on the scalp, eyebrows, and eyelashes cannot. This red flag for illness summons very emotional reactions. Some women say they cried less over cancer surgery than they did over losing their hair. Others, such as Juliana, considered it a temporary setback. "Losing my hair did not bother me. I'd just had a baby. I gained weight and I lost it. My philosophy was this: I'm giving birth again, I'm nauseous, I can't eat, but instead of getting fat I'm losing my hair. It's temporary, it will grow back." She bought a wig but also a cap that proclaimed "No Hair Day," which served as a remarkably good conversation starter. "If I went to a party, I'd wear my wig." Otherwise, she found she preferred the cap.

BREAST CANCER TREATMENTS AND HAIR LOSS

Hair loss (*alopecia*) is not a sign of whether or not a treatment is working. Some treatments are simply more likely than others to have this effect, as explained in the following. Ask your doctor how likely you are to lose your hair during treatment so you can make your plans accordingly.

Chemotherapy

When you're already awash in concerns, worrying about whether you'll lose your hair can be the icing on the cake. Some anticancer drugs have no effect on hair, others thin hair, and still others virtually guarantee significant hair loss. One in two people taking the combination of oral cyclophosphamide, methotrexate, and

---

COMMON CHEMOTHERAPY CULPRITS

Some chemotherapy drugs most likely to cause hair thinning or loss are the following:

- Cytoxan: depends on dose and duration when used alone for advanced breast cancer
- Docetaxel (Taxotere): 78.5 percent
- Doxorubicin (Adriamycin): virtually 100 percent
- Gemcitabine (Gemzar): 15 percent
- Paclitaxel (Taxol): 87 percent (when Taxol is used alone, hair typically thins over the first eight weeks and regrowth begins after six months even while the drug is still being given)

These combination therapies cause hair loss and thinning as well:

- AC (Adriamycin and Cytoxan): 100 percent
- ACT (Adriamycin and Cytoxan followed by Taxol): 100 percent (hair will not grow back until after the full course of treatment ends)
- CEF (Cytoxan, epirubicin, 5-FU): 95.5 percent
- CMF (Cytoxan, methotrexate, 5-FU): 50 percent

5-fluorouracil (Cytoxan, Mexate, Adrucil, abbreviated CMF), for example, do not experience hair loss. For those with lush hair, thinning associated with CMF may be less noticeable. The drug trastuzumab (Herceptin) won't affect hair at all because it doesn't affect rapidly dividing cells. Yet the commonly used regimen called AC, which is Cytoxan and doxorubicin (Adriamycin), causes significant or complete hair loss by the beginning of the second cycle in nearly all women.

Hair loss usually begins about two or three weeks after a chemotherapy treatment and accelerates in four to eight weeks. Toward the end of each cycle, fuzzy stubble may start to grow in only to fall out again several weeks after the next cycle.

Ultimately, whether you'll notice any effect on your hair depends on the drugs used, the dosages, the time between chemotherapy cycles, the number of cycles, and how the drug is given (orally versus intravenously).

Premature Menopause

If you have not yet reached menopause, chemotherapy treatment may result in early ovarian failure commonly called *premature menopause*. Dipping estrogen levels affect the scalp, and hair may not be as thick or luxurious as it was.

Hormonal Therapies

Only occasionally do hormonal therapies cause hair thinning. Anastrozole (Arimidex) does not prompt hair loss or thinning. Tamoxifen (Nolvadex), on the other hand, triggers hair thinning in 2 to 4 percent of women. Letrozole (Femara) causes thinning in about 5 percent of women.

Radiation

As long as radiation treatment is confined to the breast or lymph nodes beneath the arm, it won't affect the hair on your head. Any small hairs growing around the areola may fall out, though, and if the radiation field includes a part of the underarm where hair grew, you may lose it in that area as well.

Hair Care During Chemotherapy

Whether or not they cause hair loss, all chemotherapy drugs tend to be drying and most treatments for breast cancer can make you feel bedraggled. Your body is working overtime to help repair damaged cells, an endeavor that may be absorbing much of its energy and available nutrients. Judicious pampering may counter some of these effects. It can also raise your spirits and return a measure of control over your body at a time when so much is out of your hands.

Good Hair Care Techniques

Good hair care helps keep thinning hair healthy and assists in sidestepping brittleness and breakage. Although details differ somewhat depending on whether you're caring for hair or scalp alone, the following tips can help you to look and feel better:

• **Shampooing:** Wash your hair with a gentle pH-balanced shampoo. Avoiding daily shampoos is probably kindest because the suds strip off natural oils. You can use a shampoo intended for chemotherapy- or radiation-related hair loss, such as Brian Joseph's Formula 1 (brianjosephs.com or 800-889-8960), although this isn't necessary. Do avoid products with heavy perfumes, which might irritate newly sensitive skin, and alcohol, which might dry the scalp.

• **Conditioning:** Condition hair to cut down on tangles. Again, avoid products with heavy perfumes or alcohol.

• **Brushing:** Brush your hair daily. Not brushing won't keep it from falling out—it just leads to nests of loose hair and tangles. A brush with soft bristles is easier on a tender scalp. Work through snarled hair carefully with a wide-tooth comb. A no-tangle spray can help. Hold your hair gently above the snarl while sliding the comb through bite-size pieces of it.

• **Chemical processing and heat exposure:** Temporarily ban bleaching and other harsh chemicals, blow dryers set on high, curling irons, and curlers, all of which can damage hair. If you usually color your hair and don't expect to lose much or all of it, ask your hairstylist whether touch-ups will be a problem.

BEHIND THE SCENES: "HAIR ISN'T YOU"

"Hair isn't you. You're you. Hair is just an accessory," says Nick. Nick should know. He's cut and styled hair for many years.

Six years ago, when his wife, Annette, temporarily lost her hair during breast cancer treatments, Nick shaved his head, too, which buoyed her spirits enormously. It also led to some interesting mix-ups. "Which one of you is having therapy today?" asked a nurse when the duo arrived for one of Annette's chemo sessions. "*Please.* Do I look like the kind of person who would shave my head, eyebrows, and eyelashes just to come to see you guys?" asked Annette. "No."

Annette bought a top-of-the-line wig, which Nick cut and styled. "I wore it one day and couldn't stand it," she recalled. "I couldn't feel anything. The wind caught it. I looked into a window on the street and my hair was standing straight up. I took it off and put on a baseball cap."

Some days she wore the wig. Usually, though, the baseball cap, a scarf, or bare scalp suited her better. A wig worked best for suburban jaunts where people were apt to stare or look away hurriedly, while baldness was acceptable—chic, even—in the city.

Once chemotherapy ended, Annette's hair began growing back almost immediately. Soft fuzz appeared first. As the hair lengthened, she noticed its texture had changed to soft, flat loops dubbed "chemo curls," which she likened to the pelt of a lamb. Her new hair grew in gray and wouldn't hold coloring for many months. It hardly resisted the scissors when cut, and the ends seemed to wear down to hollow, quill-like points, remembered her husband, who kept it neatly trimmed. Over time, though, the curls relaxed and the normal texture and strength of healthy hair reasserted itself.

• **Styling:** Avoid hair sprays and gels that are drying. Putting stress on hair by braiding it or working cornrows in—or even through tight clips or ponytails—is not a good idea right now.

• **A new do:** Consider embracing a new look. A chic, short hairstyle will have fewer tangles and be easier to keep up than long, flowing locks.

COMPLETE HAIR LOSS

If you are undergoing certain types of chemotherapy, simply running your fingers through your hair may have unhappy consequences. Presiding over strands of falling hair and constantly picking it off pillows, clothes, and other landing sites is utterly disheartening. "When it flies out of the sunroof in your car—oh, my god," said Annette, who had that experience one windy day en route to an outing that was supposed to be fun. "I remember just crying with my friend."

Ultimately, hair loss is for a very good cause, though it may be hard to keep this in mind. Once treatment ends, be assured that your hair will grow in again. Meantime, get the skinny on what to expect and learn about wigs, wraps, turbans, and hats.

Scalp Discomfort: The Beginning

With chemotherapy regimens that are known for causing complete hair loss, scalp discomfort, burning, stinging, or itching may begin within one to three weeks of the first treatment. Termed *dysesthesia*, this precedes the actual hair loss. Touching, shampooing, combing, or even a gentle breeze may produce scalp tenderness and pain. The hair follicle is a very active portion of the scalp, continuously growing and shedding hairs. Chemotherapy directly injures actively dividing cells and thus affects the hair follicle, too. Discomfort frequently continues until the hair loss is complete. Hair often begins to grow back between chemotherapy cycles, and, unfortunately, discomfort may recur as these new hairs are shed during the next round of treatment.

Hair Loss: The Middle

Normally, a woman might shed fifty to one hundred hair shafts daily. This represents hair that is at the end of its growth cycle, so the shaft end that is in the scalp is dry. Hair loss with chemotherapy also affects hair shafts that are in their active growth phases. When these hair shafts fall out, the tip of the hair that was in the scalp follicle is still moist. The hair may appear somewhat sticky. When lost while showering, it may cling to skin or the side of the tub. Each time she showered, said one woman with a swayed back, she noticed that her short hair strands all collected in the small of her back.

Rather than coming out whole, brittle hair may splinter close to the scalp. When that happens, the slightest touch to the remaining root may cause discomfort. One woman discovered that stripping off these stragglers with lint tape made her whole scalp feel more comfortable.

Many women find the skin of their scalp is exquisitely sensitive to hot or cool water in the shower and to any sort of breeze. Bare skin sunburns easily and winter winds can be brutal without sufficient coverings. Hair offers more protection than most of us imagine from heat, cold, sunrays, and errant blasts of air-conditioning. Knowing about these ultimately temporary physical changes and making necessary adjustments will help you weather them.

Some women prefer to get a jump on hair loss by shaving their heads to the nub in a buzz cut. You can do this right away when hair starts falling out or wait until the day comes when you can't take it any longer. Any hairstylist or a pal with a good pair of scissors and an electric razor can do the trimming. Be very careful about nicks if shaving cream and a regular razor are used.

Bare Scalp: Just Temporary

Bare scalp responds well to tender care and needs it just as much as, if not more than, a full head of hair. Here are some guidelines to follow:

- **Shampooing:** Shampoo clears away dirt, oily buildup, and dead skin cells, keeping the field free for hair follicles to rebound once treatment ends. Again, it's helpful to choose a gentle pH-balanced shampoo without heavy perfumes or drying alcohol. Spend a minute or two massaging your scalp while in the shower. Inactive hair roots will loosen from the scalp when massage is performed with firm pressure using the flat of your fingers and palm against the grain of hair growth. Massaging also stimulates blood flow to the scalp, which encourages hair growth after treatment.

- **Moisturizing:** A dry scalp is itchy and uncomfortable. Plus breaks in the skin encourage infection to take hold. Moisturizing your scalp helps to maintain the integrity of the skin so it doesn't become uncomfortably dry and so that it can better tolerate the synthetic materials that are used in the cap portions of wigs. Any moisturizer is fine. If your skin is sensitive to perfumes, lanolin, or alcohol, try to avoid products that contain any of these.

- **Sun protection:** Wear a hat or sunscreen to ward off damaging rays if your hair is thinning or your scalp is bare. Where sunscreen is concerned, SPF 15 is sufficient only for brief exposure. Otherwise, it's safest to cover up or use SPF 30 or higher.

- **Insulation:** Wear a cap to help retain body heat during cool weather or air-conditioned seasons and while sleeping. Breezes blowing on an unprotected scalp can be uncomfortable. Set fans and air conditioners in the right directions.

Tools of the Trade for Thinning Hair

Not everyone needs these tools, but if your hair is likely to thin or fall out, a small investment is worthwhile:

- Lint brushes help with cleanup as the hair sheds onto pillows, furniture, and clothing.

- Lint tape pressed onto a closely cropped scalp will help remove inactive hair shafts.

IRRITATED SCALP: ALLERGIC REACTIONS TO WIGS

Wigs may trigger a rash on sensitive scalp skin. Usually, this is *contact dermatitis*—that is, a skin reaction to an irritating substance or allergen. If you notice redness, itching, irritation, a rash, or skin breaks, stop wearing the wig temporarily and call your cancer care team for advice. The culprit may be the backing material, the glue, or other substances used in the wig. Depending on the cause and extent of the rash, treatment may include temporarily not wearing the wig, a topical steroid cream, or a moisturizer to help the skin heal.

When you are ready to resume wearing your wig, a skullcap between your scalp and the wig can minimize exposure to the allergen. Skullcaps, or wig liners, are made of flesh-colored soft cotton, possibly with some spandex to help keep their shape, or the nylon material of pantyhose. As one woman found, they may peek out from under the wig, particularly toward the nape of the neck. "Sometimes friends or others pointed this out. After a while, I couldn't have cared less."

- A drain catcher for your shower or tub is an inexpensive alternative to phoning the plumber and paying the price to unclog drains. A screw in the center of many tub drains can be unscrewed to release the metal drain plate so that a drain catcher fits in the opening. Other drains may have a central metal bar that will prevent a good fit. If so, flip the drain catcher over so that it looks like a little garden hat sitting on top of the drain. Any hardware store can supply one of these.

- A satin pillowcase will not tug or snarl thinning hair the way a cotton pillowcase might do.

- A hair net, turban, or mesh cap worn to bed at night will keep loose hairs corralled.

- A soft cotton sleeping cap covering your bare scalp will help keep you warm.

WIGS

Until you become accustomed to it, your newly bald pate will seem strange. Although a naked scalp can initially look quite startling, with time, some women are pleasantly surprised to find it dramatically spotlights eyes, cheekbones, and other features. You may feel comfortable leaving your head uncovered or decide to wear a wig some of the time or coverings most or nearly all of the time. This choice, at least, is yours.

If your doctor believes hair loss is likely, try to schedule a wig consultation before treatments start. That way, your hair color, texture, and cut can be assessed and captured more easily if you do decide to wear a wig. Plus, you can have one ready when you need it. Otherwise, hold on to a lock of hair just in case you decide to match it later, and find photos that show the hairstyle you like best. These needn't be photos of you. Some women take this opportunity to live life as a blond, zap in highlights or jazz up color with impunity, adopt a cut with more pizzazz than their usual one, or even choose more than one wig. "I bought a redhead, a blond, and a brunette," Amanda ticked off, "because if I'm going to be bald, I'm going to have fun with it."

Of course, losing your hair temporarily doesn't automatically mean you need to buy a wig. Personal preference and life circumstances differ. Some women cover their heads only as comfort dictates with a stylish or funky cap, hat, scarf, wrap, or turban. A smaller number wrest a confident fashion statement out of being bald. Others feel naked and miserable without hair. Some work in jobs where being impeccably coiffed and dressed matters deeply, or they worry that signs of sickness or vulnerability will make others shun them at work or on the street.

Choosing a Wig

If you do consider a wig, there is plenty to learn. Wigs can be entirely synthetic and machine-made or artful hand-sewn constructions employing human hair. Depending on materials and construction, they may be easy to style or have genuinely bad hair days of their own. Because most wigs are designed to wear over hair, a scratchy backing can be a true liability on a bare scalp.

A variety of techniques can be used to make wigs. The labor that goes into a wig and the quality and length of the hair or fibers used affects the overall price. The cost might seem quite reasonable or leave you gasping. When selecting a wig, consider the options described next. A personal appointment will enable you to see the differences firsthand and ask questions since terms may vary.

Hair Content: Synthetic, Human, Blended

Wigs may be 100 percent synthetic fibers, 100 percent human hair, or a blend of both.

Human hair is thinner and cooler than synthetic fibers. Two basic grades of human hair wigs exist. Grade B wigs often use hair from Asian countries, which is typically dark in its natural state and may not hold color well if you prefer lighter hair. Grade B hair is often attached to the wig base by machine. Grade A is various natural shades, often from Russia or Europe. It is tied by hand to the wig base. Humidity, wind, or rain can cause bad hair days for either grade of human hair, however. Washing and styling by a wig care professional is usually required every seven to ten wearings to keep human hair wigs looking their best. This can be done at the store where you purchased the wig, or you can ask your hairstylist for a recommendation. Frequent at-home touch-ups, possibly with a blow dryer or rollers, help, too.

Although synthetic fibers are thicker and do not appear as natural as human hair, wigs made from them may offer you a wider range of colors and highlights and tend to hold their shape despite wear and weather. Blended wigs with fairly high human hair content—say 50 percent—draw on the best of both worlds: a more natural look plus the advantages of synthetic fibers. Usually, synthetic and blended wigs can be washed every seven to ten wearings, given a gentle squeeze or blotted dry with a towel to rid them of excess water, and shaken out to revive styling. Wigs with any amount of synthetic fibers should not be combed or brushed when wet. This disrupts the inherent style.

Wefting, Monofilaments, and the Quest for a Natural Scalp

Wefts are thin strips of backing material to which hair or fibers are attached. A wefted, or open-weave, 100 percent machine-made backing is least expensive but will not look natural where the hair is parted.

A monofilament cap costs more but may be worth the investment. This tight-woven mesh looks more like natural scalp when hair is parted because strands of hair are attached to it separately by machine or hand-tied to more closely mimic hair patterns on the scalp. A monofilament cap may have wefting toward the bottom, where hair thickness matters less to the look.

Machine-Tying Versus Hand-Tying

Machine-tied wig hairs or fibers tend to be more evenly distributed and fuller at the top than would normally be true, which contributes to a somewhat artificial look. A stylist can thin and shape these wigs, though, to look more natural. Artful hand-tying, which may be done for just part of the wig (such as the top of the head, where it matters most) or all of it in a custom wig, makes a wig look more like a naturally full head of hair. Hand-tying boosts the price, however.

Prestyled or Custom-Made

Prestyled wigs are available in a wide variety of looks. They may have human hair, synthetic fiber, or a blend. They are far less costly than custom-made wigs. Custom-made wigs can be produced in any style you specify but typically take six to eight weeks or longer to make.

Prices

Many professionals agree the natural look of the monofilament top makes more of a difference to your appearance than the type of hair or fibers you choose, so ask whether wig prices include it. If not, you might pay an additional $100 to $150. Wigs made of 100 percent synthetic fiber can cost as little as $40 from a catalog or between $200 and $500, depending on quality and length. A good-quality, machine-made, synthetic wig in a short style might cost $200 to $250, for example, while its shoulder-length cousin would be closer to $300 to $400. A good-quality blended wig might cost $400 to $500 in a short style or closer to $800 to $900 for a shoulder-length style. Human hair wigs can be purchased online for as little as $99, though bargains like this tend to be poor quality. A better quality of hair with a monofilament cap might more typically cost $600 to $3,000. Again, hair length will make a difference and very high-quality hair will cost more. Custom-made wigs may cost thousands of dollars—as much as $3,000 to $8,000 or more.

Wig prices will vary depending on where you live and what services are being offered. A personal fitting, selection, styling, alterations for a comfortable fit, and good advice all cost money, but bargain wigs are sometimes quite disappointing. Shop around to get what you need at a price you can afford.

Wig Dos

When shopping for a wig, look for the following:

- **A good selection:** Whenever possible, choose a local shop that offers plenty of options in line with hairstyles that you like, rather than just a range of cuts that seem too dowdy or trendy. Look at shorter styles if you think you might adopt a shorter haircut before starting treatment rather than having your hair length change drastically more than once. Take a look online or in catalogs (see the sidebar "Where to Shop" a little later in this chapter) to get acquainted with styles and prices. Buying through a catalog or the Internet may seem simpler but makes it impossible to touch and try on wigs.

- **An expert fitting:** Your head should be carefully measured front to back, ear to ear, and circling the circumference of your usual hairline. That way, the right size (petite or large, for example) can be selected. Wigs have adjustable tabs or bands for a tighter fit once the basic size is chosen. Some wig shops can alter the backing to make it fit more snugly or construct a custom cap for you.

- **The right wig backing:** A backing that looks reasonably natural and feels fairly comfortable is the Holy Grail for women buying a wig. When the hair is parted, does it look like scalp lies beneath? Can you part the hair at any spot? How scratchy does the backing feel? Will a few washes soften it? If it fails to soften up enough, you can wear a wig cap liner. Unfortunately, cap liners may bunch slightly, peek through at the nape of the neck, or just feel too hot. If so, try a light dusting of cornstarch on the backing. It acts as a buffer between a tender scalp and wig and helps soak up any perspiration.

- **Flattering color:** Choose a color that is at least a shade lighter than your own hair. Chemotherapy may make you look wan or give skin a grayish or greenish cast. Darker hair colors sometimes look overly harsh in comparison.

- **Extra style:** If you can't afford a custom-made wig, don't worry. Select a basic color, cut, and texture that you enjoy. Then let a hairstylist help you customize the wig by trimming and thinning it to achieve a more natural look. Often, this can be done at the shop where you bought the wig, or you can ask your own stylist to do it. Depending on the wig, you may also be able to have it cut again several months later when you want a new look.

- **Soft hairline:** A soft look along the hairline or bangs makes a wig appear more natural. Slightly longer bangs can cover thinning eyebrows, too. If you dislike bangs, even a few stylish wisps on temples and brow will help hide the backing. Another option is a fall that comes attached to a headband an inch or two wide, which fits snugly across the forehead and around the face. The hair is affixed to the inside of the headband and the attached wig-cap underneath. These pieces are quick to put into place and require very little fuss.

- **Ease in styling:** Be sure there is someone you can call for further tips or styling, if necessary. This is where shopping locally really pays dividends. And have a backup plan—a hat or scarf you like wearing or an alternate wig—just in case your wig needs expert attention.

TOOLS OF THE TRADE FOR WIGS

Choose shampoos, conditioners, wire brushes, and wide-tooth combs or picks made especially for the type of wig you buy. Styling gels, mousses, and hair sprays should be compatible, too, or the wig could be damaged. Ask about these products when you buy your wig because they differ depending on wig construction and the type of hair used. An inexpensive wire stand that won't stretch out a damp wig while it is drying is helpful, too, though some wigs can simply be tossed over a doorknob to dry. Ask before doing that!

A few drugstores stock these items, and you can find them online, through catalogs, or at wig shops, hospital boutiques, and hairstyling salons that sell wigs. Following are a few good sources:

- Boutiques at hospitals, such as the Friends Boutique at Dana-Farber Cancer Institute (dana-farber.org/bou or 617-632-2211) or Images at Massachusetts General Hospital (massgeneral.org/visitor/salon.htm or 617-726-3211)
- The "tlc" catalog of the American Cancer Society (tlccatalog.org or 800-850-9445)
- Paula Young Catalog (paulayoung.com or 800-343-9695) or its affiliate, Especially Yours (especiallyyours.com or 800-748-6910), which offers more extensive options for African American women

Wig Don'ts

Try to avoid these pitfalls:

- **Insufficient care instructions:** Don't just get a quick rundown on care instructions. Ask for written instructions or try to take good notes. How you wash and dry a wig and whether it needs frequent styling or just a quick squeeze to get the water out and a shake to let hair fall back into place depends on the materials employed.

- **Unexpected heat exposure:** If your new wig has any synthetic fibers, avoid unexpected and obvious heat sources. Opening a steamy dishwasher or hot oven or using curling irons or blow dryers are verboten if you are wearing a wig that has even a touch of synthetic hair. Doing so will frizz and melt the fibers. Naturally, open flames are to be avoided, too. Blow dryers and curling irons are generally fine for human hair wigs, but other heat sources are best avoided. When in doubt about whether a wig might have any synthetic fibers, don't take a chance. Some wigs touted as 100 percent human hair may not live up to their name.

• **Overstyling:** Don't try too hard to sweep or lacquer every hair into place. That looks more artificial.

"Hat Hair," Hairpieces, and Hair Extensions

A lesser-known alternative to wigs are hairpieces designed to be worn under a hat. These may be bangs attached by Velcro to a head covering or a full fall of hair held on by crisscrossing elastic strips that leave the scalp bare, which can be worn with any hat. A shorter version of the three-quarter wraparound fall can be held in place with Velcro attachments to the hat. One woman so appreciated the cooler temperatures offered by her "hat hair" compared to the heat generated by a wig that she bought it in different styles and colors.

Other hairpieces make thinning hair look thicker or fill in bald spots. These typically have clips or combs that you can attach beneath the top layer of your hair. Brushing strands of your own hair over this gives the hairpiece a natural look.

Where to Shop

You can buy a wig, a hairpiece, and assorted head coverings in many places. Cancer centers and hospitals often have a boutique or appearance center with trained sales staff attuned to the concerns of people undergoing cancer treatment. Breast cancer organizations may be able to give you names of wig fitters in your area. Word-of-mouth recommendations may lead you to shops or stylists who offer both good selections and an emotionally sensitive environment. A quick look under "Wigs" in your local yellow pages or even in the aisles of a nearby department store will turn up other choices. The "tlc" catalog of the American Cancer Society and several companies that specialize in products for women with breast cancer sell wigs, hairpieces, and a wide variety of hats, turbans, wraps, and other head coverings.

You can buy these items at many of the same shops that sell wigs or through catalogs.

A wish for long hair without the wait can be granted through hair extensions, which are essentially woven into or glued onto short hair that has grown in after chemotherapy is completed. Weaving and a protein-bond gluing process are more expensive than other options, such as hot gluing, but some stylists say less likely to damage long-awaited hair growth. Before a weave can be done, it's best to wait for about four inches of hair to grow out. That way, the extension blends in far more naturally. Hair extensions can be quite costly. Prices will reflect the amount and quality of hair used and how it is attached, as well as how long it is expected to last. The stylist's experience and how chic the salon is matter, too.

A "volumizing" or partial extension designed to make thinner hair look lush and thick might cost $600 to $900, while full extensions that add length all around might be $600 to $2,000 or higher. Ask the stylist to show you before and after pictures and check with several salons. With careful brushing, shampooing, and, yes, conditioning, extensions typically last two months or, less likely, up to four to six months.

Who Pays?

While Medicare does not pay for wigs, some private health insurance companies do pay for one deemed medically necessary, and a few states have laws that insist on this. Ask your doctor to write you a prescription for a *"cranial prosthesis,"* and check with your insurer for details. Be persistent and use the medical term. Stories abound of women turned down for "wigs" by customer care representatives who failed to mention that a cranial prosthesis might be covered as part of cancer treatments. Boutiques in hospitals may submit the bill directly to the insurance company, whereas most freestanding stores require payment at the time of purchase and will give you a receipt to submit for medical insurance reimbursement.

The American Cancer Society and Y-ME both offer wigs free to women who can't otherwise afford them, though what is available varies. They accept donations of gently used wigs, too.

The cost of a wig may be tax-deductible if you itemize deductions on your tax returns. Keep your receipts and check with the IRS or a tax adviser.

Hats, Turbans, Scarves, Caps, and Wraps

If you find wearing a wig too hot or uncomfortable, don't like the look, or prefer to have days with little fuss, the choices are practically endless. I enjoyed wearing a baseball cap or the bandana with Sponge Bob cavorting across it that my daughter gave me. If that doesn't suit you, consider other options. Pick up a bright kente cloth or fleece pillbox. Cover up with a cloche or bucket hat. Tie on a Gucci scarf or a well-worn bandana. Try a turban Greta Garbo might have lounged in. Wear a warm, furry winter hat, a chic beret, or a crocheted skullcap on jaunts outside. Learn how to twist and tie into place a colorful wrap that hugs the scalp and complements your eye color. Scarves and kerchiefs may come with bangs or even ponytails attached, if you like that look, or may be padded to provide the illusion of hair tucked underneath.

Hats have been known to blow off in a high wind, which can be quite embarrassing. Buying one with an adjustable inner strap or padding the headband to make it fit more snugly will help. Likewise, a stretchy cotton headband with a mix of spandex can help anchor hats and slippery scarves while providing a soft buffer. An added benefit is that a headband covers a bare scalp that peeks through at the temples, brow, and nape of the neck. Some hats incorporate a headband with just this idea in mind.

These items can easily pile up, as friends are apt to start searching them out in lieu of flowers and other warm gestures. You can find plenty on your own or visit the same places that sell wigs and hairpieces, as well as practically any clothing store.

Body Hair: Brows, Lashes, and More

Eyebrows, eyelashes, hair on legs and arms, underarm and pubic hair, and even nose hair may succumb to chemotherapy, too. Again, this depends partly on the drugs, dose, and number of cycles given. Just as with the hair on your head, you may or may not lose body hair even if you know of someone who did on the exact same regimen.

Tying a Wrap

You can buy wraps with long, loose tails (Figure 9.1) that fit the head fairly snugly or use a large square scarf. Slippery materials like silk tend to slide, so consider cotton or very light, soft wool. Another option is to put the scarf on over a cotton headband to help hold it in place.

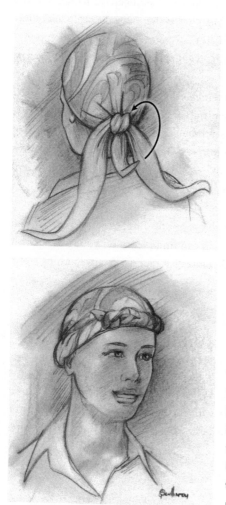

Figure 9.1 First, make a triangle. Drape it on your head so that the material dips down an inch or two onto your forehead and tie the ends at the base of your neck. Neatly tuck the bottom of the triangle over that knot. Twist the loose ends of the scarf and bring them up to your forehead. Knot them there once or cross them and bring the ends back to the nape of your neck. Tie the ends there or tuck them under the circle of material formed by the twist.

WANT MORE ON MAKEUP?

Want to brighten up a look washed out by treatments? Steer away from browns, neutrals, and nudes in eye shadows and lipsticks. Try a more brightly colored lipstick than usual or a mauve or plum shadow instead of earthier tones. The American Cancer Society partners with cosmetic industry giants to sponsor Look Good . . . Feel Better workshops. During these, trained volunteer cosmetologists offer valuable tips on makeup, wigs, wraps, and other accessories. The participants may have many helpful tips of their own to share, too. The workshops are free and so are kits packed with cosmetics to complement various complexions that are given out. Call 800-395-LOOK or check online at lookgoodfeelbetter.org.

You may be pleased enough to take a break from shaving or waxing your legs, if indeed you do so, but other losses can be more unsettling. Typically, body hair, particularly eyebrows and eyelashes, grows less quickly than the hair on your head. That's actually good news because it means the hair follicles divide less rapidly and are thus less likely to get caught in the net thrown out by chemotherapy. Thinning, rather than complete hair loss, may occur. Ultimately, any hair lost is likely to grow back—where you want it as well as where you might prefer to go bare.

Legs and Underarms

Because so many women put in time and effort trying to make their legs and underarms look baby smooth, hair loss here may be less bothersome than in other spots. "You don't have to shave!" said Annette wryly. "Look on the good side."

If hair is growing back between chemotherapy cycles and you'd like to see less of it, waxing or shaving is usually safe. Try a small patch test to be sure it doesn't cause undue skin irritation. One note of caution: shaving underarms with a razor blade should be avoided if you have had lymph nodes removed, particularly if you have lost sensation here due to surgery or radiation. An altered underarm lymphatic network combined with nicks and cuts may make lymphedema more likely. Consider waxing or laser hair removal instead, or at least use an electric razor to avoid nicks. Looking into the mirror while shaving this spot will help, too, if loss of sensation is an issue, because the visual input will help compensate for the loss of tactile input.

Eyebrows

Eyebrow hair is slower growing than that of the scalp. For a given chemotherapy cycle, many of the hairs may not be in an active growth phase, and thus the brows may experience thinning, sometimes in patches, or complete loss only after multiple cycles.

Brows created from human hair can be bought at some cosmetic shops or online. These come in a few shades and can be shaped to your preference. A special adhesive is used on the brow before the eyebrows are set in place. Oil-based makeup remover works well to take these off, according to the manufacturer.

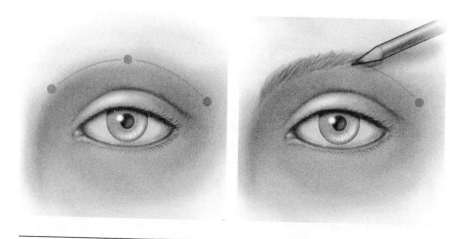

Figure 9.2 If you've lost your eyebrows entirely, you can follow these steps to pencil them in. Run your fingers along your brow bone above your eye to feel the way it curves. Make three dots to help you form a natural looking arch. Hold your finger or a brow pencil against your nose and place the first dot on the brow bone. The second dot goes on the brow at the midpoint of your pupil when you are looking straight ahead. Angle your finger from the bottom of your nose to the outer edge of your eye to place the third dot on your brow. Next, create the desired curve and width of the brow using an eyeliner brush dusted with taupe or light brown eye shadow. Then use lightly sweeping strokes with a brow pencil to create the illusion of hairs. Light cross-hatching in the opposite direction adds texture. Not dark enough? Try adding a little darker eye shadow over it. It probably will take some practice before you can do brows easily this way.

REPLACE MAKEUP REGULARLY

Makeup, especially products used near the eyes, should be replaced regularly to avoid bacterial buildup. Some dermatologists recommend tossing mascara and eyeliner every six months and replacing other products every year. When you are undergoing chemotherapy, your immune system may be weaker, so it is especially important to be vigilant about replacing products frequently. Never share products with a friend or use opened samples or testers at cosmetic counters.

Makeup offers other options. A tiny brush coupled with taupe or light brown eye shadow can create a natural look that builds on thinning brows (Figure 9.2). Stencils of varying thickness can be bought in many pharmacies and department stores to help with that or to use when penciling in eyebrows. Stencils can be somewhat tricky to place correctly, but with practice they can be very helpful, especially if your hands are unsteady.

Eyelashes

Lashes put up a great defense against airborne dust and grit, especially on windy days. If lashes have thinned or disappeared, wearing sunglasses or regular glasses outside will help. False eyelashes are tempting, but the adhesive used to anchor them can irritate the sensitive skin of your eyelids. Infection, though unlikely, also is possible, so it's probably best to forgo false lashes.

Also, during chemotherapy, the tear duct is more susceptible to blockage. Irritants in the glue of false eyelashes may exacerbate this condition. If a blocked tear duct occurs, laying warm compresses on the inner eye usually resolves the problem; if a day or two of this does not do the trick, talk with your doctor about an ophthalmologic evaluation.

Artful makeup can help promote the illusion of lashes. Choose eyeliner pencils that are soft or soften them slightly with a few seconds of hot air from a blow dryer to avoid scratching or pulling at delicate skin. Gray or plum eyeliner, both a softer shade than black, sets off many eyes nicely.

Remaining lashes will seem thicker with mascara. Try a thickening, lengthening mascara for best results. When using mascara, take the wand out of the bottle and let it dry slightly for a minute before applying it. Replace mascara tubes frequently. After multiple uses, the tube can harbor bacteria, which may set the stage for an eye infection during a time when chemotherapy has weakened your immune system.

Pubic Hair

Certain chemotherapy drugs, such as Taxol and Adriamycin, may cause pubic hair to thin or fall out, a subject some women feel very uncomfortable discussing. "When I was diagnosed, one of the women who called me was a friend of a friend," recounted Amanda. "I asked her if I was going to lose all my hair. She said, 'Oh, you lose the hair on your head, the hair on your arms.' I asked, 'Do you lose your pubic hair, too?' That made her so uncomfortable. These were clearly things she didn't talk about." Some people find this bare skin appealing, while others feel more exposed and upset than ever. Usually, the hair grows back. When it does, you may be uncomfortable for several days. "It was so unbelievably itchy," said Amanda. Try as she might, she failed to find a nonchalant way to relieve the itch, though it fortunately subsided in a week or so.

Nose

The small hairs that line the inside of your nose may disappear, too. That may not strike you as particularly significant but can leave you sniffing more than expected, especially when you have a cold, during winter weather, or during a heated exercise session. It can be bothersome at other times, too. Keep tissues handy, advises Annette. "Every time you put your head down your nose runs. You write a check and all of a sudden, it happens. You don't even feel it coming."

WHEN WILL HAIR GROW BACK?

It varies. Soft fuzz may appear within a few weeks to a month after treatment ends. The more hearty true hair roots from which stronger, longer hair will grow will take a bit more time. Usually, hair grows at the rate of about half an inch a month. Your hair may grow back exactly as you remember it, or its color and texture may change somewhat. If you are near menopause or pushed into it by your treatments, your hair may feel a bit coarser than it once did. So-called chemo curls—that is, decidedly curly hair growing in where straighter hair once lay—are not uncommon. Often, this curlier hair relaxes over time, though that may take a year or two. The initial fuzz that comes in may be light in color, and the true hair that follows may be darker than your original color, which had sun exposure to lighten it over the years. Some women experience increased or complete graying.

Coloring, Straightening, or Perming Hair

One woman who disliked her new short gray hair swore by Grecian Formula in the early months. "That way, when it was tiny, tiny, tiny, it just looked dark," she explained. Later, she had her hair colored professionally. You, too, may be eager to make some changes once your hair begins to grow in again, especially if its color or texture is noticeably different from the look you once enjoyed. Before coloring, straightening, or perming your hair, though, it is wisest to first check with your doctor. That's especially important if your scalp received any radiation or if you are still receiving treatment.

Usually, coloring can be done safely once the early fuzz disappears and the first half inch to two inches of new hair appears. Sometimes, as Annette found, the new hair will not hold color properly and must grow out further before it will. Ask a hair colorist for advice if this is true for you. Trimming the first fuzzy growth once or twice before attempting to add color can help. Plus, a darker shade or a coloring process that uses two pigments rather than a single color may work.

Chemicals used in straightening or perming may be too harsh for new hair and tender scalp. Straightening hair too quickly may also backfire because it will have to be done again fairly soon to keep new growth smooth. Again, ask a dependable stylist and try to be patient while hair grows in. Before attempting to perm hair— which will make it shorter, remember—it's probably safest to wait for four to six inches of healthy hair growth rather than risk frizzing and further damage. Just as bad, as one stylist noted, unless the hair on top of the scalp has grown down to the ears, you are likely to look like a "pouf-head."

10

YOUR SMILE

◉

When you are hip deep in the concerns and appointments that occupy the early weeks after a diagnosis of breast cancer, seeing your dentist may be low on your priority list. Yet it is surprisingly important to help ensure that your teeth and gums are in good shape.

I scheduled a checkup with my dentist for a cleaning several weeks after my biopsy confirmed that I had breast cancer and before I started chemotherapy. Why? Overall, roughly 40 percent of people undergoing therapy for a variety of cancers, including breast cancer, experience dental problems during treatment. Difficulties may include mouth sores, which are a common problem among women who have certain types of chemotherapy; periodontal disease, which affects gums and underlying structures that support teeth; accelerated tooth decay; dry mouth; and changes in taste.

Any dental woes can be trying, of course, but the mouth is also a prime source of infections that can spread through the bloodstream. Sometimes, treatment must be changed or halted in order to quash a dental complication before it gets out of hand. Before you start to worry too much, though, realize that many, if not all, dental troubles explained here may pass you by—particularly if you actively seek good dental care before treatment starts and quickly attend to problems that come up.

BEFORE YOU START TREATMENT

Any treatment for breast cancer—whether surgery, anticancer drugs, or radiation—stresses the immune system. Chemotherapy drugs often temporarily suppress infection-fighting white blood cells as well as platelets and other agents that aid in blood clotting. A hobbled immune system slows healing and may allow a simmering or dormant infection, such as early gum disease or herpes simplex type I (a virus that causes cold sores), to surface.

Thus, it's a good idea to call your dentist for a thorough checkup and cleaning once you learn you will be treated for breast cancer. Explain the situation so that it is easier to get a prompt appointment and the attention you need. If possible, bring information on your treatment plan and your current blood test results. Your dentist also may wish to speak with your cancer care team before or after your checkup.

During a thorough checkup, your dentist should do the following:

- Take medical and dental histories, including information on whether you have had herpes simplex type I cold sores in the past

- Obtain x-rays to evaluate potential problems, such as cavities and gum or bone conditions, and to provide a baseline to help assess any changes due to treatment

- Look for periodontal disease and cavities as well as for signs of asymptomatic infections and treat these problems, if necessary

- Correct irritations, such as bridgework, dentures, or other restorations that rub against gums or soft tissue

- Assess whether you suffer from dry mouth

- Decide whether you might benefit from fluoride therapies

- Clean your teeth and advise you on the best way to care for them during your treatment

If you do need any extensive dental work, such as gum surgery or tooth extraction, ask your cancer care team when to schedule it. Depending on your situation, you might be urged to proceed quickly or to wait until after your treatment finishes. Whenever possible, experts recommend scheduling dental work at least seven to ten days before chemotherapy. Because radiation to the breast or chest wall can affect your immune system, it's wise to speak with your dentist about the proper time for dental work if this will be part of your treatment.

Good dental hygiene can help you stay on track for treatment, so close attention to routine care of your teeth at home is wise. Review your dental care regimen with your dentist to see whether he or she suggests any modifications.

Dental Hygiene 101

Here is a quick review of basic dental care. Pay particular attention to the following during treatment:

- **Choose a good brush and use it.** Choose a toothbrush with soft or extra soft, rounded bristles. Soften its bristles further each time you brush by wetting them with warm water. If even this is too harsh for overly tender gums, cotton swabs or a clean, thin washcloth wrapped around a finger can help you clean tooth surfaces gently. Electric toothbrushes, such as the Oral-B Professional Care 7000 Series, which features a three-dimensional rotation pattern, or Sonicare, which relies on high-speed vibration of individual bristles, resemble professional cleaning tools used by your dentist. These devices do a good job of cleaning teeth when used properly. As long as the bristles of their brushes are soft or extra soft, it's fine to use them during treatment—in fact, some women swear by them. I started using a Sonicare toothbrush with a two-minute timer during chemotherapy, and at my first dental visit after treatment, I had very little plaque buildup. If you have trouble reaching the corners of your mouth, you'll reap the greatest benefits from an electric toothbrush. No matter which brush you choose, though, it is consistent application—brushing after each meal, if possible, and brushing for at least two minutes—that counts.

- **Choose the right toothpaste.** Always choose toothpaste with *fluoride*, which helps prevent cavities. Toothpastes labeled "tartar control" rebuff *plaque* (a sticky film on teeth that speeds decay). These toothpastes tend to be more abrasive, however, and may trigger sensitivity in teeth and gums. If you have a brand of fluoridated toothpaste you like—with or without tartar control—it's probably best to stick to it during chemotherapy, rather than risk irritation with a new product. If your teeth are sensitive to cold, heat, acidic or sugary foods, or touch, consider using toothpaste designed for sensitive teeth.

- **Floss, too.** Floss gently once a day to remove plaque from between teeth. Certain brands of floss, such as Glide, which is made from a high-tech synthetic fiber, are designed to slip easily between tight teeth. Dental tape, which is broader and flatter than traditional floss, does a better job of scraping off plaque on widely spaced teeth than floss does. When your blood counts are low, your gums are likely to bleed easily, making infection more likely. If bleeding occurs, you can skip flossing temporarily, though you should start up again as your counts rise. If gums continue to bleed easily or bleeding is hard to stop, tell your nurse or doctor.

(continued)

- **Irrigate your mouth.** Saliva bathes teeth and moves debris along. Even mild dehydration is likely to put a crimp in saliva production, a problem worsened by certain chemotherapy drugs and also by antidepressants. Try to drink water and other sugar-free fluids frequently to stay well hydrated. Swishing warm salty water around your mouth after meals and before bed or possibly every few hours helps, too, especially if saliva is in short supply. Adding a bit of baking soda, which helps neutralize acids in the mouth, is sometimes suggested. One such recipe combines one-quarter teaspoon baking soda and one-eighth teaspoon salt with a cup of water. After swishing with this, rinse with plain water. If you prefer a commercial mouthwash, sidestep brands with alcohol, which can be irritating; a mild mouthwash, possibly with baking soda, will treat tissues more kindly. (Also see "Dry Mouth" for tips on dealing with one.) Should you use an irrigating device, such as a Waterpik? These appliances can flush out debris from deep gum pockets and around bridges or other restorations, but they do not remove plaque. You may want to avoid using them during cancer treatment, because they can injure tender gums and may force bacteria into underlying tissue, where it can gain entry to the bloodstream. Talk to your dentist before using these devices during treatment.

EMBARKING ON TREATMENT

During the course of your treatment, you may experience some of the problems described in the following sections. Try the tips suggested and ask your cancer care team for their recommendations.

Dry Mouth

For many of my patients undergoing chemotherapy, dry mouth (*xerostomia*) is a real trial. A mouth almost as dry as dust with thick, tacky saliva is more than just an annoyance. Not only can a dry mouth cause difficulty eating and swallowing, changes in taste, bad breath, and irritation and infection of mouth tissues, it also raises the risk for tooth decay and gum disease. When the saliva shortage is prolonged, it severely inhibits the remineralization process that replenishes tooth enamel dissolved by acids in the mouth. With the protective enamel stripped away in spots, the number of cavities begins to rise within as little as three months after dry mouth begins.

If you have dry mouth, you can help fend off these problems by paying special attention to preventing tooth decay and taking steps to boost the flow of saliva:

- Use fluoridated toothpaste regularly.

- Talk with your dentist about fluoride rinses and treatments. You may need a fitted mouthpiece that can be filled daily with fluoride gel or drops. Sometimes, a fluoride rinse or a gel swabbed onto teeth, or possibly a combination of approaches, is recommended.

- Suck sugar-free lemon drops or chew sugarless gum. Other flavors are fine, though mints may irritate and sting if your mouth tissues are tender. Ice chips work well, too.

- Drink plenty of sugar-free liquids, including water and diet drinks (although sorbitol, an artificial sweetener, causes diarrhea in some people). Carry a water bottle with you wherever you go.

- Rinse your mouth with salt water or swishes that combine baking soda, salt, and water every few hours to help clear your mouth of debris.

- Try over-the-counter artificial saliva products, such as Salivart Synthetic Saliva, Saliva Substitute, or Biotene oral*balance* Mouth Moisturizing Gel. Typically, these products are used once in the morning or before each meal and again before bedtime. Occasionally, prescription drugs that encourage saliva to flow more freely, such as pilocarpine (Salagen), are recommended.

If a dry mouth makes it hard to eat, you may find that soft or pureed foods, smoothies, soups, and stews go down more easily. Adding gravy or broth or dunking foods in any mild broth or drink can help, too.

Usually, dry mouth gradually improves after treatment. If chemotherapy has been intensive or radiation to the head was necessary, as it is for a very small percentage of women with late-stage metastatic breast cancer, dry mouth may take years to improve or may be permanent.

Mouth Irritations and Sores

Any inflammation or infection of the tissues in the mouth is known as *stomatitis*. One such problem is mouth sores, or *mucositis*, an unpleasant, fairly common side effect that afflicts two out of five people during chemotherapy. Normally, the cells forming the top layer of the soft tissues in the mouth divide rapidly. Old cells are discarded and replaced with new ones every nine to sixteen days. In addition to cancer cells, chemotherapy also singles out these rapidly dividing cells lining the mouth. The usual suspects—among them, 5-fluorouracil (Adrucil; abbreviated as 5-FU), doxorubicin (Adriamycin), methotrexate (Mexate), and paclitaxel (Taxol)—are implicated. Research suggests other factors play a role, too. Dry mouth and other irritants, such as ill-fitting bridgework or restorations, can raise the risk of mouth sores. Poor oral hygiene may give bacteria that accelerate mouth sores a chance to flourish, a problem that worsens when blood counts are low.

Usually, mouth sores triggered by chemotherapy start with redness and a burning sensation. Ulcerations occur five to eight days after drugs are administered. The sores may appear pretty much anywhere on the soft tissues of the cheeks, tongue, base of the mouth, soft palate, or back of the throat. They last from seven to fourteen days, generally healing by themselves.

While they last, mouth sores are painful and unpleasant. They interfere with chatting, eating, and drinking—or even the desire to do so—and can slow treatment until they clear up. Occasionally, mouth sores lead to more widespread infection by bacteria that must be treated by antibiotics or other medications and can result in hospitalization.

Prevention

Sucking on ice chips or medicated ice pops for thirty minutes starting five minutes before your chemotherapy session begins may help prevent these sores by constricting blood vessels in the mouth so that less of the drug reaches them. This technique made it to the small screen in an episode of "Sex and the City." "When Samantha went for her treatment, they were all eating Popsicles," Juliana said. "A bunch of people called and asked, 'Are you getting Popsicles?'" Experts disagree over how well this approach works. Ask your doctor or nurse about this.

Thus far, studies disagree over whether glutamine supplementation has any protective value. Vitamin E, beta-carotene, and other antioxidants have been researched, too, also with mixed results.

Remedies

Remedies for mouth sores abound, although most are aimed at stopping the pain they cause rather than treating them.

- So-called magic mouthwash—a combination of topical painkillers and buffering agents—coats irritated tissues and provides pain relief. A prescription product called Gelclair, which forms a film over irritated tissues, has been successful in relieving pain for some people suffering from mouth sores. Warm salt-water swishes, sometimes mixed with baking soda, are also recommended and may be better at easing discomfort than hydrogen peroxide, which is sometimes suggested. Glycerin can dry out the mouth, so it's best avoided. Pain relievers, such as acetaminophen, may help a bit, but check to see if you can take these.

- Cold or room-temperature foods may be less irritating than hot or warm foods. Likewise, soft, soothing foods, like cooked cereals, soft or cooked fruits, mashed potatoes, ice cream, smoothies, cottage cheese, yogurt, pudding or custards, and scrambled eggs, may be gentle to tender tissues. Acidic foods, such as tomatoes and citrus, and spicy foods or foods with rougher edges may cause more pain. Experiment to see what works well for you.

- Avoid toothpaste with mint or other flavors that could irritate tissues and mouthwash or rinses that contain alcohol.

- Moisturize your lips with petroleum jelly or a lip balm that you like. Naturally, steer clear of flavored or medicated lip balms that sting.

Candidiasis

Chemotherapy is not the only cause of mouth sores. *Candidiasis*, which looks like small, white, curdlike clumps or flat red lesions, is a fungal infection caused by yeast. Yeast exist peaceably in the mouth and other sites on the body but may multiply as illness, medication, or immune suppression affects other flora that keep it in check. Candidiasis can be treated by antifungal drugs in pill, lozenge, or liquid form. While nystatin in a liquid suspension has been used frequently, some experts question its effectiveness; it coats affected tissues but is not absorbed well once swallowed. Chlorhexidine rinses are also recommended at times, though research on effectiveness is mixed and some data suggest it lessens the effects of nystatin. Sucking on clotrimazole lozenges may be more helpful, especially if you are suffering from nausea. Three other promising antifungal medications are amphotericin (liquid or pill), ketoconazole (pill), and fluconazole (pill).

Herpes Simplex Virus

Another organism that causes mouth sores is the virus herpes simplex type I. The virus may be spread by someone who has it, or it can remain dormant in the body once a woman has gotten it and surface when her immune system is suppressed. Unlike mucositis, which begins fairly soon after chemotherapy, mouth sores caused by a dormant herpes virus generally start about eighteen days after drugs are administered. Typically, a burning, tingling sensation quickly gives way to tiny red lesions and then fluid-filled blisters, which break open.

If you have ever had mouth sores caused by the herpes simplex virus, tell your cancer care team and your dentist. Acyclovir can help prevent painful herpes outbreaks as well as treat them.

Periodontal Disease

Periodontal disease is a catchall term for a variety of dental troubles ranging from gum disease to problems with the underlying structures that hold teeth firmly in place. *Gingivitis*, the earliest form of gum disease, is marked by reddened, swollen, bleeding, and sometimes tender gums. Advanced *periodontitis*, a far more serious problem, undermines the bony support structures of teeth.

According to the American Academy of Periodontology, 30 percent of the population may be genetically predisposed to gum disease, which increases their risk of developing periodontitis sixfold. Perhaps not surprisingly, women who have chronic gum inflammation or periodontal disease before cancer treatment starts are likely to have worse bouts during periods when the immune system is depressed. Luckily, identifying and treating these problems early can stop their progression.

Periodontal disease gets a foothold when plaque is not regularly removed from the *sulcus*, a shallow trough where the gum meets the tooth. Without proper cleaning, plaque bacteria can build up there like leaves in a gutter. Successive layers of bacteria keep oxygen from reaching the innermost recesses of the sulcus. These bacteria thrive in an oxygen-free (*anaerobic*) environment. Toxins released by the bacteria inflame surrounding gum tissue. The surface of the plaque hardens into *calculus*, which further irritates the gums. A healthy immune system sends a legion of antibodies to combat the bacteria, but immune suppression cuts down this response and may allow other bacterial flora in the mouth to grow unchecked.

As periodontal disease worsens, enzymes released as a by-product of the immune response start attacking the gum tissue itself. Connective tissue attaching the tooth to the gum is destroyed first. That creates a larger pocket between tooth and gum, which leaves the exposed portion of the tooth root vulnerable to cavity-causing bacteria. Ligament and bone come under attack, and finally, the tooth loosens in its socket, sometimes to the point where it will fall out.

Prevention

Good oral hygiene habits help but may not be enough for people predisposed to gum disease. A dental checkup before treatment starts will help identify problems, the simplest of which—gingivitis—can almost certainly be corrected before chemotherapy begins.

Treatment

Treatment varies depending on the stage of periodontal disease. If extensive work is necessary, your dentist and cancer care team should discuss the best way to proceed.

BONE MARROW TRANSPLANTS

While bone marrow transplants (BMT) were a common treatment for breast cancer in the past, they are performed infrequently nowadays. High-dose chemotherapy used during BMT considerably raises the risk of treatment-related dental woes, such as dry mouth, infections, mouth sores, and bleeding. Sometimes, a complication called *graft-versus-host disease* triggers bouts of inflammation, ulceration of soft tissues, and dry mouth that can last weeks to even a bit longer than a year after treatment.

During treatment, frequent dental assessments and care are advised. Antibiotics may be recommended before any dental work, including cleaning, is done. Daily use of fluoride gel is often suggested.

After a transplant, blood counts may be low for up to a year. Postpone elective dental work, but see your dentist regularly to head off problems and call for advice about any changes or discomfort. Tell your cancer care team immediately, too.

- **Scaling and root planing (debridement):** Scaling removes accumulated plaque and calculus above and below the gum line. Your dentist may scoop damaged tissue from the bottom of the gum pockets to spur the healing process; this is called *curettage*. The final step—root planing—smooths the root surface so that gum tissue can reattach to it more easily. These procedures are usually performed with local anesthesia.

- **Drug therapy:** Short courses of oral antibiotics as well as antibiotic and antiseptic medications applied directly to gums can cut down on bacteria and inflammation. Sometimes, this regimen, along with regular debridement, can avert the need for surgery.

- **Surgery:** Occasionally, surgery is necessary with moderate to advanced disease. A specialist known as a *periodontist* surgically removes degenerated gum tissue and reduces the depth of the pocket before the tooth root can be properly cleaned. This is recommended only when it will prevent loss of a tooth and when more conservative measures have failed.

- **Maintenance plans:** After initial treatment, the focus is on keeping plaque in check. Usually, a good plan includes visiting the dentist or hygienist every three months, brushing and flossing regularly, and using an antimicrobial mouth rinse, but your dentist and cancer care team may wish to tailor the plan differently during breast cancer treatment.

Changes in Taste

A dear hometown and college friend of mine, who also became a patient, likened the metallic flavor that stays tenaciously in the mouth for days or weeks after treatment with certain chemotherapy drugs to a taste you might expect after licking metal deck furniture. Repeatedly. Eating, drinking, and brushing her teeth did nothing to banish the awful flavor. "I couldn't get rid of the taste," she said. To help dispel it, she stocked her cabinets with peppermints—a smell she eventually found loathsome—and chewed Arm & Hammer baking soda gum.

Some of my patients swear by butterscotch or lemon drops. My children bought me lots of hard candy, and I went through pack after pack of cinnamon gum. Whatever you prefer, you may need to use it constantly, which means you'll go through quite a bit. Stick to sugarless candies and gums rather than products with sugar. The bacterial by-products of sugar breakdown release acids that harm the teeth. Calories add up, too.

In my case, the metallic taste seemed to fade more slowly with each chemotherapy session. With the first cycle, it began a week after the chemotherapy infusions and lasted about a week. It took longer to disappear with each successive cycle. After the final cycle, it was a good two to three months before the taste was completely erased and food started tasting like it should. As time went on, there were periods in the day when I would notice a metallic taste and times when I didn't have it at all. Eventually, I'm glad to report, it petered out entirely.

Even when anticancer drugs are not the culprit, bacteria or dry mouth often leaves a nasty taste. Good oral hygiene, lots of liquids, and taking steps to ease dry mouth may help you make some headway here.

Taste Bud Trouble

Chemotherapy may temporarily harm taste buds while pursuing cancer cells. Some women complain of losing a good deal of their sense of taste, a side effect called *dysgeusia*. One evening during her first round of chemotherapy, Amanda decided to make a Thai lime soup for her husband. Futilely, she kept squeezing lime into

Stressful Grinding

Bruxism—tooth grinding due to stress, misaligned teeth, or, possibly, certain antidepressants—can wear down and chip away enamel. Teeth become more vulnerable to decay and jaw muscles may ache. A mouth guard fitted by your dentist helps protect teeth at night. Stress relief techniques or changing medications may be necessary, too.

it, wondering why the soup didn't taste like much despite repeated jolts of juice. After one sip, her husband puckered up alarmingly. Fishing out a few loose hairs that also had not added much to the flavor of the soup, he joked, "*Thanks*, honey! You're done with cooking."

Sometimes, lost or muted sensations of taste do not occur until after chemotherapy is finished. Usually, you'll regain your sense of taste within a few months after treatment ends, as Amanda did.

Brightening Your Teeth

A number of my patients say that their teeth looked dingier after chemotherapy. Only a few of the drugs used during breast cancer treatment are known to discolor teeth. One is chlorhexidine, an antimicrobial medication sometimes used for treating mouth sores or periodontal disease. Luckily, chlorhexidine actually discolors plaque that sits on your teeth—not the teeth themselves—so a good cleaning can take away much of the stain. When the stain sits atop teeth this way, it is called *extrinsic discoloration*. Smoking and coffee, red wine, tea, cola, and berries can cause it, too.

Intrinsic discoloration often affects the dentin, the soft layer below the enamel. Dentin normally yellows slightly as you age, a tint that becomes even more apparent as the enamel thins out as you grow older. Stains can also accumulate on dentin if enamel isn't there to protect it. Exposure to tetracycline antibiotics in the womb or during childhood and too much fluoride in the early years of life are two other examples of agents that cause intrinsic discoloration. Sometimes, it occurs when a nerve or blood vessel in the pulp is harmed, a problem that is not easy to correct.

Brightening your smile can give you a real lift. I found it a nice way to mark the end of my treatments. Rather than risk irritation to tender gums and the tooth sensitivity peroxide bleaching agents can cause, though, hold off on over-the-counter whitening products and professional whitening until a few weeks after you finish with your treatments. Once you start feeling better and your immune system has rebounded, whitening should be safe, but check with your dentist first, especially if you have had periodontal disease or very sensitive teeth. The following recommendations can help you sidestep stains or erase them.

Good Habits

Brush (or at least rinse) after meals and after potentially discoloring drinks or food, such as coffee, tea, or berries. If you smoke, quitting will certainly make a difference. A Sonicare toothbrush with a soft-bristled brush can help scrub away chlorhexidine and other extrinsic stains; a professional cleaning is likely to be even more helpful, although your cancer care team may prefer that you wait to do this until after your treatment is finished and your blood counts have risen.

Over-the-Counter Whitening

Over-the-counter whitening products may employ a buffing agent, a bleaching agent, or a white pigment that temporarily colors the tooth. Some contain a combination of these whiteners.

Helps a Bit

Whitening toothpastes (Crest Vivid White, Rembrandt Plus, Arm & Hammer Advance White, Colgate Sensitive Maximum Strength Plus Whitening, and others) help a bit with extrinsic stains over time. These products use a buffing agent like silica that physically removes surface discoloration, a low concentration of bleaching agents like hydrogen or carbamide peroxide, or a white pigment like titanium dioxide. Check with your dentist before using these regularly because some are quite abrasive and may potentially damage enamel. If enamel wears down enough, the dentin is exposed and can stain, too.

More Helpful

Over-the-counter bleaching strips or gels, such as Crest Whitestrips and Colgate Simply White Night, do a reasonably good job of removing extrinsic stains. Usually, these products employ a 10 to 22 percent peroxide bleaching agent. The higher concentration may be more likely to cause gum irritation or tooth sensitivity.

Professional Whitening

Whitening is usually faster and brighter when done with prescription products for home use and procedures by your dentist.

- Prescription bleaching strips or gels that you squeeze into a mouthpiece fitted to your teeth are available through your dentist. These products typically have a higher concentration of bleaching agent than over-the-counter products and thus do a better job on extrinsic stains and certain intrinsic stains.

- Chair-side bleaching by a dentist may involve an ultraviolet light or laser ("power bleaching") to remove extrinsic and certain intrinsic stains. Some experts question whether light or laser adds much, however.

- A dentist can remove an intrinsic stain if a tooth nerve is dead by putting a whitening agent inside the tooth. The tooth is capped with a temporary filling, so this stays in place for a few days.

Professional Cover-Ups

Bonding, crowns, or veneers are other ways dentists can cover hard-to-remove intrinsic stains or chipped discolored teeth.

Costs

Costs vary from less than $10 for toothpaste to hundreds or even thousands of dollars for some professional services. Bonding, crowns, or veneers are costly; chair-side bleaching is less so. Talk to your dentist about this.

Easing Aftereffects

Usually, after treatment stops, you can return to seeing your dentist twice a year. If you haven't had a dental checkup in a while, it's a good idea to schedule one now even if the thought of more needles and sharp instruments holds you back. Plucking up the courage to go is especially important if you have been suffering from dry mouth, which makes cavities and periodontal disease more likely.

Behind the Scenes: Delaying the Dentist

Twice a year a pleasant postcard with smiling teeth may nudge you to see the dentist. No matter how polite that reminder is, though, it cuts little ice with Andrea. "I have an aversion to the dentist," she admitted.

"First of all, they tell you not to go to the dentist while you're on chemotherapy," she said. "That's fine. I don't really want to go anyway." After she had finished her treatments, she still couldn't bring herself to make an appointment, even though she knew it was important to do so. "I actually had a physical anxiety attack. I couldn't do it. I couldn't make an appointment."

While many dentists do all that they can to ease anxiety—even offering distractions like videos or prescribing nitrous oxide (laughing gas) for those who cringe at the slightest twinge—they may be facing additional hurdles with certain women who have been treated for breast cancer. After months of enforced appointments and repeated rendezvous with sharp needles, it makes sense that some women might be reluctant to sign on for any more procedures—even one as outwardly harmless as a professional tooth cleaning.

If you have always worried about visiting the dentist or you develop concerns about it, you aren't alone. This is one hurdle you would do well to jump, though, because dental woes tend to worsen with time and lack of attention. These tips may help:

- **Find a gentle dentist.** Ask your friends and doctors for recommendations. "I shopped around," said Andrea. One of her friends, a hygienist, recommended a dentist who worked in a pediatrics practice. "She actually made the phone call for me."

• **Communicate your fears.** "I walked in and said to this woman, 'If you hurt me, I will kill you,'" Andrea joked. "I said, 'I'm not happy about being here, but I really have to be here.'" You may phrase that sentiment differently, but being direct will help your dentist and hygienist devise ways to make appointments easier.

• **Agree on hand signals.** Before any procedure starts, arrange hand signals with your dentist, so that he or she knows when you need to take a break, suggests the American Dental Association. Having control in this way can help ease your anxiety.

• **Try stress relief.** Deep breathing isn't easy with a mouthful of dental appliances, but it can help calm you if you do it before opening your mouth. While you are reclining in the dental chair, inhale deeply through your nose to a slow count of three. Exhale through your mouth just as slowly to the same count of three. As you exhale, relax your shoulders and allow your body to sink deeper into the chair. Repeat several times.

• **Try distraction.** Watching a movie on a small screen supplied by your dentist or listening to soothing music through headphones can help drown out noises you dislike.

• **Ask about sedatives.** Antianxiety medication, such as diazepam (Valium), or a sedative can be prescribed to help you get through the procedures. Ask your dentist about this and be sure to tell her or him if you have taken medications.

"She's been very good," said Andrea of the dentist she selected. "I still go to her."

For additional information on finding a dentist in your area, check the American Dental Association website (ada.org) or call 312-440-2500.

Part III

REGAINING YOUR BALANCE: EXERCISE, NUTRITION, SEXUALITY, AND MORE

II

GET MOVING: ANY ACTIVITY IS BETTER THAN NONE

◉

At their one-year checkup, the most common question my patients ask is, "What can I do for *myself* now?" All have had surgery. Some have had radiation or chemotherapy or both. Usually, their passage from the hands of one caring health professional to the next is finished, leaving an appeal in its wake. "Everyone has done something to me and for me. Now I want to do something for myself."

At one time, I had few well-substantiated suggestions to offer. Now I have an excellent one. A growing number of research trials show that, if you have been diagnosed with breast cancer, exercise is one factor within your control that can make a very real difference to your life. What can it do? Exercise has been shown to help improve long-term survival, decrease the chance of breast cancer relapse, and minimize treatment-induced fatigue, bone loss, and muscle wasting. What's more, it can help you regain flexibility, strength, and endurance; ease certain side effects of treatment; and boost your quality of life.

I recommend embarking on an exercise program as close to the moment of your diagnosis as possible or continuing with your current program to reap all these benefits. I know it may be the last thing you feel like doing, but I believe it can honestly save your life. It also can make you feel better about yourself. As you go through treatment and afterward, you can modify activities as needed.

Some of the material in this chapter also appears in the *Brigham and Women's Hospital Breast Surgery Guide*, developed by staff of the Comprehensive Breast Health Center at Brigham and Women's.

The Bottom Line: Improving Long-Term Survival

Every woman who has breast cancer wonders about her long-term survival. Each treatment she receives aims to improve her prospects. Now mounting scientific data suggest that exercise is also a factor in helping women outlive their diagnosis.

My colleagues at the Harvard School of Public Health presented one such study in 2004 at the annual meeting of the American Association for Cancer Research. Their data were drawn from the Nurses' Health Study, which began enrolling more than 120,000 female registered nurses ages thirty to fifty-five in 1976 and has surveyed them for lifestyle factors and chronic disease every two years since then. Between 1984 and 1996, more than two thousand study participants were diagnosed with breast cancer; follow-up through 2002 showed that slightly more than two hundred died from it. The researchers found that even modest amounts of activity—such as an hour spent walking at a rate of three miles per hour, three to four times a week—lessened the likelihood of breast cancer recurrence and improved survival when compared with being sedentary. Further analysis suggested heavier women might reap even more benefits. Although most of the active nurses walked for an average of more than four hours a week, activities varied. Cycling, aerobics, and yoga or stretching activities were also popular.

Easing Side Effects of Treatment

Side effects of breast cancer treatment can make it difficult or impossible to be physically active on any given day. The day after my mastectomy and, later, my tissue expander placement, a very short walk was all I felt up to doing. Several days during my chemotherapy, I simply did not feel well enough to leave the house. On days when fatigue got the better of me, I spent my scant waking hours on the couch watching videos. Yet I knew that my breast cancer treatment was accelerating the loss of my bone and muscle, so I went to the gym any day I felt well enough to get there. I made physical activity my priority even if it was the only thing I could check off my to-do list. Truly, anything is better than nothing.

Chemotherapy

During chemotherapy, a woman may experience weight gain, a decrease in lean muscle mass, and accelerated bone loss. Fatigue, a common side effect, can make it hard to start or maintain an exercise program. But exercise can actually help ease some common side effects of chemo.

Gaining Weight

Studies show that 50 percent or more of women receiving chemotherapy gain weight. Usually, women add five to fifteen pounds, but higher gains are not uncommon. Factors that make weight gain more likely include longer chemotherapy regimens; the steroid prednisone; receiving chemotherapy through pills, not IV infusion; and being premenopausal or experiencing premature menopause.

Muscle burns calories twice as efficiently as fat. During chemotherapy, muscle mass typically shrinks while fat tissue increases. Called *sarcopenia*, this means that your body burns fewer calories than it otherwise might. A forty-year-old woman undergoing chemotherapy usually experiences a 2.5 percent increase in body fat—that's the equivalent of what might happen in ten years to a healthy forty-year-old.

Gaining too much weight during chemotherapy may have a negative impact on longevity. A 1990 Mayo Clinic study of 330 premenopausal women receiving chemotherapy noted their average weight gain was approximately thirteen pounds. The researchers found the risk of death was 1.6 times higher for women who gained more than thirteen pounds compared to those who gained less. Although there was a trend toward a higher rate of recurrence over the course of five years among women who gained more than thirteen pounds, this was not statistically significant.

Added fat tissue appears to boost estrogens circulating in the bloodstream, which might play an important role in recurrence of the breast cancer as well as the development of a new breast cancer. Here's where the science gets tricky. Body fat contains two important enzymes called aromatase and 17β-hydroxysteroid dehydrogenase. These convert the male hormone androstenedione (which women have in small amounts) into active estrogen.

When women are of normal weight, most estrogen in the bloodstream is tied to a protein, such as sex hormone binding globulin (SHBG). When tethered this way, estrogen is not bioavailable, meaning that it cannot reach vulnerable cells that could be fueled by it. More SHBG means less bioavailable estrogen.

Overweight women have higher amounts of insulin and insulin-like growth factors, which decrease SHBG levels. What's more, obese people have more of a molecule named leptin. Leptin increases the activity of aromatase, one of the enzymes in fat cells that facilitates estrogen production. The combination of greater estrogen production from fat cells and fewer available binding proteins is a double whammy for overweight women. Both boost free estrogen circulating in the bloodstream. Furthermore, greater amounts of fat tissue appear to suppress the immune system, which may also have a hand in allowing cancers to develop or metastasize.

One 2004 study randomly assigned previously sedentary, overweight women aged fifty to seventy-five to a group that exercised moderately for forty-five minutes a day, five days a week or to a group that did stretching activities. After three months, researchers noted significant declines in three types of estrogens circulating in the bloodstreams of women who exercised. Declines continued—though not significantly—among the exercisers during the course of a year. Meanwhile, estrogen levels rose somewhat in those who simply stretched.

Added pounds, especially added fat tissue, may raise the risk of a breast cancer relapse through other means. Insulin levels tend to be higher in women with more fat tissue. A Canadian study, presented in 2000, followed 535 women for ten years after they had been treated for breast cancer. Those with the highest fasting insulin levels at diagnosis were four times more likely to develop a recurrence and eight times more likely to die than women with the lowest insulin levels.

What to Do. Fend off unwanted pounds and pare down fat with exercise. Strength train to maintain and build muscle mass, and do aerobic activities (walking, swimming, cycling) to burn more calories.

Osteoporosis

Not only are breast cancer survivors living longer now, but they are healthy enough to be concerned about other age-related medical conditions, such as osteoporosis.

My colleagues at Dana-Farber Cancer Institute and Brigham and Women's Hospital measured changes in bone density over the course of a year in forty-nine premenopausal women undergoing chemotherapy. Thirty-five of these women entered chemotherapy-induced menopause. Bone loss of the spine and hip was measured over time. By one year, the decrease in bone density was 7 percent at the spine and 4 percent at the hip. By contrast, the average rate of bone loss for women after natural menopause is 1 to 2 percent a year and 15 percent over the first ten years. Thus, a woman who undergoes permanent chemotherapy-induced menopause can lose five years' worth of bone mass in a single year. To a lesser extent, the women who did not experience premature menopause also had accelerated bone loss, though this was not considered statistically significant.

Breast cancer cells may speed the loss of calcium from bone as well as hinder its integration into bone. It's possible that bone is affected in similar ways during chemotherapy.

These data have serious implications for breast cancer survivors. British researchers evaluated the rate of vertebral fractures in 352 women with breast cancer that had not metastasized and 776 women of the same age who did not have breast cancer. When the study began, the rates of vertebral fracture were the same in the two groups. After three years, women who had been treated for breast cancer had a fracture rate almost five times greater than those without breast cancer. As vertebrae fracture, spinal column segments collapse, causing stooped posture, loss of height, and back pain.

What to Do. Exercise and diet (see Chapter 12) help you maintain bone density at the three most common fracture sites: the spine, hips, and wrists. Daily calcium and vitamin D supplements and possibly medications will help. Weight-bearing activities (strength training, walking) that stress the bone and balance exercises that help reduce falls that can lead to fractures are equally essential.

Fatigue

One of the most common complaints of women undergoing chemotherapy and radiation is fatigue. According to the National Cancer Institute, some small, preliminary studies suggest light to moderate walking or other activities may boost energy, mood, and a faltering appetite, among other benefits.

What to Do. Many factors can contribute to fatigue—anemia, depression, poor appetite, thyroid deficiency (hypothyroidism), dehydration—so do speak with your doctor or nurse about possible solutions. That said, getting even a little exercise is always better than doing nothing. Accumulating activity gradually over the day and paying attention to time spent is more important than focusing on intensity. Try to take a walk or do other activities whenever you feel up to it. Sometimes, a specific time of day—the morning, perhaps, or shortly after lunch—is better than others.

Surgery

Pain from the incision site and spasms of the pectoral muscles on the chest wall may make moving your shoulder uncomfortable. This causes *protective posturing*: your head tilts forward, your shoulder rises and tilts forward, too, and your elbow is flexed so that your hand rests across your abdomen. A mastectomy can cause tightness along the front of your chest where the skin has been sewn together snugly and scar tissue is forming as chest wall skin finds a new home against pectoral muscles. Extending your arm to reach for something will hurt enough to make you use your shoulder less. This disuse shortens chest muscles, which further restricts shoulder mobility.

Particularly with lymph node surgery under the arm, a mastectomy, or reconstructive surgery, scarring can cause *cording*. Underarm muscle tendons or larger lymphatic channels become stuck to the undersurface of the skin as scar tissue forms at the surgical site. When a woman lifts her arm, the skin pulls the muscle outward and a vertical cord is apparent in the center of the underarm. In one series of more than two hundred patients who had underarm lymph nodes removed, arm problems eighteen months after surgery included pain (51 percent), numbness (49 percent), stiffness (37 percent), swelling (27 percent), weakness (18 percent), and limited shoulder range of motion (16 percent).

What to Do

Stretching augmented by physical therapy massage of the surgical site to break down scar tissue will help restore full range of motion (see stretching exercises later in this chapter). Once you have done so, you can safely start a program of strength-training exercises for the arm that will help you recoup strength lost after a period of disuse (see strength-training discussion later in this chapter). Discuss with your surgeon the safest time to start these exercises.

Tissue Expander and Implant Reconstruction

Because this type of reconstruction moves the pectoral muscles away from the chest, it can affect your posture, produce chest wall tightness, and limit arm strength. Before your surgery, good posture depended on a counterbalance. Your pectoral muscles pulled your shoulder forward and the muscles of your back tugged your shoulder backward.

Pectoral muscle spasms may occur following tissue expander placement and after each injection of saline. This feels much like a charley horse. The muscle contracts and shortens so that it pulls the shoulder forward. Along with resulting tightness around the shoulder, you may also feel tightness where skin has been sewn together. Pain, muscle spasm, and skin tightness can cause the protective posturing described earlier. These changes combined with surgical discomfort will make it difficult to lift your arm to reach for something.

When placing the tissue expander, some surgeons deliberately divide the median pectoral nerve, which reaches to the outer portion of both pectoral muscles. By adding to muscle laxity, this may enhance the appearance of the reconstructed breast. If your surgeon cut this nerve, you may notice weakness on the side where you had the surgery.

For me, pulling open a drawer or opening jars was noticeably harder at times. Any activity involving these muscles may hurt, whether you are closing a sliding glass door or pushing up out of a chair.

What to Do. Shoulder motion is restricted for three to six weeks to help keep the tissue expander or implant from shifting to the outer or lower chest wall. Afterward, with your surgeon's formal approval, rehabilitation should include stretching to ease skin tightness and regain shoulder range of motion and comfortable, upright posture. Then you can add strength training to reestablish the balance between your right and left sides.

Reconstruction with a Latissimus Dorsi Flap

After this surgery, many women feel tightness in two areas: under the arm from the pull of the lat muscle in its new location and around the back skin incision from the loss of the skin at the donor site. Tightness in the back can make it difficult to extend your arm at the elbow and bring it forward across your body.

What to Do. After three to six weeks, with your surgeon's approval, stretching the arm and shoulder will help ease skin and muscle tightness, increase your shoulder range of motion, and enable you to regain comfortable upright posture. Massage therapy can remodel scar tissue to decrease tightness and improve shoulder mobility.

Strength training can help you balance the strength between the front and back of your body by building up chest muscles (pectoralis, anterior deltoid) and back muscles (trapezius, rhomboid, posterior deltoid, and teres major and minor). Again, wait until you have your surgeon's approval to start this.

Changing body and arm positions will enable you to engage other muscles to perform certain hard-to-manage motions. For example, shifting stance will help you close the trunk of your car more easily. Instead of facing your car with your arm stretching out forward, turn sideways so that your hip faces the car and extend your arm out to the side before pushing down.

Reconstruction with a TRAM Flap

During a TRAM reconstruction, abdominal skin and underlying fat and muscle are removed. The closure of this hip-to-hip incision may feel tight, forcing you to bend forward at the waist to minimize tension and pain. Standing erect is really hard at first. Prolonged bending can shorten the hip flexors (muscles that link hips to legs), making it hard to straighten your leg. It can also cause lower back pain.

Core muscles—the muscles in your trunk that make up the *central zone*, or *power zone*—stabilize your body as you move. The two rectus abdominis muscles in the central abdomen are part of these core muscles. Normally, they help you bend forward at the waist, bringing your ribs toward your hips, such as in a sit-up. One or both of the rectus abdominis are relocated to the chest wall during a TRAM reconstruction, weakening the abdomen. Chronic weakness of the abdominal muscles can cause poor posture, back strain, and, if uncorrected, a herniated spinal disc and other serious spinal problems.

What to Do. After a TRAM flap, it is essential to heal for a full six weeks to minimize the chance of developing an abdominal wall hernia. Lift nothing heavier than five pounds. Do not attempt sit-ups until your surgeon tells you it is fine to do so. Once you get the OK, gentle stretching of the abdominal wall and hip flexors will relieve tightness and make it possible for you to stand upright and regain a full range of motion.

The loss of strength experienced after surgery occurs mainly because a major abdominal muscle is missing. Strengthening the core muscles—the remaining intact abdominal and back muscles—will help correct this.

Sit-ups that rely on the rectus abdominis can be nearly impossible for some patients. Sit-ups with your knees bent and legs rotated off to the side will recruit the *oblique* muscles (muscles at the sides of your abdomen). Sitting up straight and pulling your belly button in toward your spine works the *transversus abdominis mus-*

KEEP MOVING

Some women remain amazingly active throughout much of their treatment—hiking, running, playing tennis, cycling, inline skating, rock climbing, or windsurfing—while others find they can barely leave the couch. No matter where you fall along this spectrum, get moving whenever possible during treatment. Afterward, adding enjoyable activities to your repertoire can rev you up again.

Katherine, who likes to bike, walk, and garden, felt her energy ebb considerably as treatment dragged on. Months after she was through, taking up the entirely new activity of fly-fishing through Casting for Recovery (see Resources) revived her. "I got into those waders and I got into that stream and I thought: 'I haven't been this comfortable in a year,'" she said. "It felt so good, so relaxing. The water was so cool, but I was dry. I wasn't perspiring. You don't have hot flashes when you're standing in the cool stream. It was like—'*Ah*, I remember when life was like this. This is great!'"

Once a hard-driving, avid exerciser, Greta had sought out triathlons and tough gym workouts. During chemotherapy, she admitted, "I was wiped." She swam when she could, finding this eased stiffness after surgery and extended her range of motion better than stretching exercises had. "I did the breaststroke, I did the sidestroke, and it's much more relaxed. I swear that swimming is what brought my arm back." She also decided to stop treating exercise like a job, opting for kinder, gentler activities. "I signed up for yoga. My husband and I walk twice a weekend. Sometimes we take the kids, sometimes we take the dog."

After she finished her treatments, Sloan wanted to feel better than ever before, yet for a long time she simply didn't. "I didn't totally mistrust my body, but I did lose enjoyment of it." Eventually, she signed up for a program called WeCanRow, which is offered by Row as One Institute. Designed to enhance wellness and rehabilitation for breast cancer survivors, WeCanRow emphasizes physical therapy, stretching, and precautions to avoid lymphedema while offering professional-level coaching in rowing low-slung eight-woman shells that streak along the Charles River in Boston, Massachusetts, and the Grand River in Lansing, Michigan. Sloan credits her active, new pastime of rowing with buffing her muscles and helping her feel truly reconnected with her body.

cle, which forms two panels on either side of the central abdomen and wraps around toward the spine. Obtain your surgeon's OK before beginning these exercises.

Radiation

Sometimes, radiation causes *costochondritis*, an inflammation of the ribs that may trigger pain during exercise involving the chest muscles. Radiation may also stiffen and shorten the pectoral muscles, a condition called *fibrosis*. Radiation to the underarm and collarbone raises a woman's risk of developing lymphedema.

What to Do

Stretching and massage therapy can help loosen up muscles tightened by fibrosis. Report any chest pain to your doctors. Costochondritis is a likely culprit. Your doctors may suggest taking nonsteroidal anti-inflammatory drugs, such as ibuprofen, for a few weeks to relieve pain and quell inflammation.

If you received radiation to the underarm, to minimize the chance of lymphedema, be especially cautious when doing strength training, as explained later in this chapter.

GET STARTED AND KEEP MOVING

Being physically active allows you to take control of your rehabilitation and helps ease side effects, leading to a more complete, timely recovery. A comprehensive fitness program comprises aerobic conditioning, balance exercises, stretching, and strength training.

In the following exercises, a *repetition* means doing an exercise once (such as lifting a weight up and bringing it back down); a *set* is a group of repetitions, or "reps."

Aerobic Conditioning

While one of my patients had enough grit and energy to inline skate six to seven miles a day despite the draining fog of chemotherapy, less rigorous aerobic exercise is just fine. The simplest choice is walking, the number one activity recommended for all cancer survivors. This weight-bearing aerobic activity helps guard against osteoporosis in hips and legs while tuning up heart and lungs. Regular walks also build muscle mass and help control weight.

What to Do

The day after surgery—or at any other time—you may begin a walking program. The American College of Sports Medicine (ACSM) Cardiovascular Guidelines for Cancer Survivors recommends a total of twenty to thirty minutes of walking three to five times a week at a moderate or slightly hard pace. You can also meet this goal with shorter five- to ten-minute walks, resting after each, if necessary.

If you can't manage that, do what you can, preferably walking each day rather than just a few days a week. As you feel better, gradually expand your program. The ACSM program progresses slowly, initially by adding to the number of walks per week and the length of each walking session and, finally, boosting the intensity. How intensely should you work out? If you can carry on a conversation, you are probably at a safe level. If you are huffing and puffing, slow down. If you can sing, you may need to pick up your pace. Progressing slowly helps your body adjust over time and reduces your risk of injury.

A pedometer—you can purchase one at any sporting goods store or at walk4life.com—can help you track daily activity. Let it count your steps from the time you get up until you go to bed. Aim for three thousand steps a day, as your first goal. That translates into thirty minutes of movement. One mile equals roughly two thousand steps and the ACSM recommends slowly building up to ten thousand steps a day.

When I gained steam in my walking program, I bought a heart rate monitor, which helps keep me working in my target aerobic zone. With it, I can make sure my heart rate stays in the zone, rather than going too high or too low. When walking downhill, I pick up the pace to stay in my zone. On uphill routes, I slow down.

Sports activities like an aerobics class, cycling, or running are one way to get exercise, but daily activities—at work, perhaps, or around the house—add up, too. On days when I cannot set aside exercise time, I wear my pedometer on my belt and check it periodically. On some treatment days I couldn't even clock five hundred steps. Other days I felt well enough to walk from my home to the hospital for an appointment, ticking off thirty-five hundred steps in the same half hour it would have taken me to drive or take the subway.

Balance Training

Good balance pays dividends at any age, especially if you are at risk for osteoporosis. Poor balance means you're more likely to take a tumble. A fall combined with a loss of bone density increases the risk of fractures in the wrist, hip, or spine. According to the National Osteoporosis Foundation, one in two women over age fifty will have an osteoporosis-related fracture in her lifetime. Half of all older adults hospitalized for hip fractures cannot return home or live independently. Worse still, nearly a quarter of those aged fifty or older will die within a year of a hip fracture due to complications.

Surgery and breast reconstruction can cause skin tightness, muscle imbalances, and body strength asymmetry, which may alter your posture and balance. A woman who has had TRAM flap reconstruction, for example, might experience tightness around her abdomen and hips, causing her to hunch forward and prompting back pain. Movements as simple as walking, reaching, opening doors, and getting in and out of a bathtub may temporarily be challenging or even hazardous.

Chemotherapy and other medications may contribute to balance problems, too. Fatigue, diminished alertness, and poor concentration can impair judgment and increase the likelihood of falls. Some women taking certain anticancer drugs, such as taxanes, experience peripheral neuropathy, which may affect sensation in the feet.

The balance and stretching exercises in the following pages have been developed by Reebok Master Trainers Josie Gardiner and Joy Prouty, specifically to help you recover from surgery and return to your normal activities as quickly and easily as possible.

What to Do

Balancing while standing still or moving depends on strong legs and flexible feet. Start by doing the two simple balance exercises described once a day and work up to two or three times a day. Hold on to a chair or counter at first for support. Start slowly and work gradually, focusing on movement quality, not quantity. Initially, these moves may be hard to do. Practice should make them easier.

Single Leg Stance

Benefits: Helps you improve balance and control by strengthening the supporting leg and hip on which you are standing.

Starting position: Stand evenly on both feet.

Instructions: Shift your weight over to the supporting leg. Lift one foot off the floor. Try to maintain balance. Repeat on the other leg.

Count, sets, and reps: Hold for five to thirty seconds. Do three to five times with each leg.

Technique and Tips

- Concentrate on balancing on one foot.

- Find a spot straight ahead and stare at it.

- Think of your balance and stability as coming from your core abdominal and back muscles and hips.

- Pull your abdominal muscles in and up.

- Try not to sink into the supporting hip. Pull the hip up and in toward the center of your body.

- Breathe naturally.

Variations

- To make this easier, hold on to a stable surface for support.

- To increase difficulty, perform this exercise with your eyes closed.

Heel Raises

Benefits: Strengthens the gastrocnemius (muscle that runs down the back of the lower leg from the knee to the heel). This improves your stability.

Starting position: Stand evenly on both feet.

Instructions: Lift your heels up so you are standing on your toes and bring your heels back down to the floor.

Count, sets, and reps: Count to three going up and going down. Do three sets of ten repetitions.

Technique and Tips

- Think of your foot as a room. Stand evenly on all four corners. When lifting up onto the balls of your feet, try to stay balanced evenly on the front two corners of the room.

- Breathe naturally.

Variation

To increase difficulty, stand on one foot and wrap your free foot around your ankle. Lift your heel up and bring it back down.

Stretching

After breast surgery, my patients often experience body stiffness, postural changes stemming from skin tightness and muscle imbalances, and decreased range of motion at their joints. In addition, inactivity and holding the body in awkward positions to avoid pain can shorten and tighten muscles and tendons. Stretching is the key to regaining flexibility and the first step in alleviating these side effects.

What to Do

Speak to your surgeon about when you can safely begin a stretching program. If you have had reconstructive surgery, you will be instructed to wait three to six weeks. Otherwise, it is usually safe to begin after your postoperative check, once all drains have been removed, and with approval from your surgeon.

The ACSM suggests that everyone stretch at least three days a week. After surgery, I recommend stretching daily to help you recover more quickly and fully. Perform each exercise three to five times, holding each stretch for about five to thirty seconds. Over time, work up to twenty to thirty seconds to optimize the stretch.

Your flexibility and coordination will improve with repetition and daily practice. The more time you spend doing these exercises, the more you'll benefit and the faster your recovery.

Done correctly, stretching should never be painful. If you feel pain, stop: you went too far or your position is incorrect. Pushing a stretch too far or bouncing activates the *stretch reflex*, a mechanism your muscles use to protect themselves. Your muscles are like rubber bands. When you stretch a rubber band, you feel a force pulling it back to its original shape. If you stretch a rubber band too far, it can snap and break. When muscle fibers are overstretched, a nerve reflex tells your muscles to contract to prevent them from being injured. This can cause pain and damage the fibers, which increases soreness and scar tissue formation.

Stretch when your muscles are warm. Think of a piece of bubble gum. When you first put the gum in your mouth, it's cold and hard. After you chew on it for a few minutes, it becomes soft and pliable. The same is true for your muscles. When you begin to exercise, your muscles are cold and tight. After you warm up, your muscles become more pliable and stretching exercises are more effective. Plan to spend about five to ten minutes warming up with an aerobic activity such as jogging in place before stretching or stretch at the end of other activities. You can skip this warm-up if you've been moving around for a few hours during the day, or you can try a warm shower first if your energy is low.

Control your stretches rather than bouncing or jerking. Slowly stretch the muscle just to the point of tightness, and hold it calmly for five to thirty seconds while breathing smoothly and naturally. When you feel comfortable, try to go a little further, although not to the point of pain. Don't strain to hold any pose. Advance at your own pace. Learn to listen to your body and follow its directions.

Single Arm Overhead Stretch

Benefits: Stretches the latissimus dorsi muscle (side of back from underarm to waist).

Starting position: Lie on your back with knees bent and feet on floor. Hold the affected arm at the wrist with your other hand. Point the thumb of the affected arm at the ceiling.

Instructions: Relax the affected arm and let the other arm do the work. Exhale and lift the affected arm slowly up and overhead as far as possible. Stop at the point of tightness; hold the stretch, then return to the starting position. (See Figure 11.1.)

Count, sets, and reps: Hold each stretch five to thirty seconds (after twenty seconds, you may feel a release in the muscle being stretched). Repeat three to five times, one to two times a day.

Technique and Tips

- Start slowly and only lift the arm to the point of tightness. If you are having trouble, try this: place a pillow on the floor above your shoulder. As you raise the affected arm overhead, press into the pillow. This more limited range of motion may be easier when starting to stretch after surgery.

- Perform the stretch while holding a dowel or a towel shoulder width apart with your palms facing forward.

Figure 11.1 Single arm overhead stretch.

Butterfly Stretch

Benefits: Stretches the major and minor pectoralis (chest muscles). Performed lying down, this stretch helps externally rotate your shoulders back and down and stretches your chest and underarm areas.

Starting position: Lie on your back with your knees bent and feet on the floor. Place your hands behind your head, elbows pointing toward the ceiling.

Instructions: Lower your elbows to the sides toward the floor. Hold the stretch for five to thirty seconds, then return slowly to the starting position. (See Figure 11.2.)

Count, sets, and reps: Hold each stretch five to thirty seconds (after twenty seconds, you may feel a release in the muscle being stretched). Repeat three to five times, one to two times a day.

Technique and Tips

- Slowly lower your elbows to the floor with control.

- Stop at the point of tightness.

- Do not bounce.

- Inhale and exhale, then try to go an inch further.

- Maintain slow, rhythmic breathing—in through the nose, out through the mouth.

Figure 11.2 Butterfly stretch.

- If you are having trouble, try this: place pillows underneath each elbow. As you lower your elbows, try to press them into the pillows. If your operated side or underarm area feels very tight, this is a good way to start this stretch because it safely limits your range of motion.

Supine Stretch

Benefits: Stretches muscles of the back from the shoulder to the waist (latissimus dorsi), the underarm region, the abdomen, and the front of the hip (flexors). Eases tightness from bending forward at the front of the hip, particularly after TRAM reconstruction, and helps you regain comfortable upright posture.

Starting position: Lie on back with knees bent, feet on floor, and arms at your sides.

Instructions
- **One leg:** Try this stretch by itself first. Extend one leg out straight so that your knee touches the floor. Hold for five seconds, then return slowly to starting position. (See Figure 11.3.) Repeat with the opposite leg.
- **Both legs:** When you can comfortably extend each leg, repeat using both legs.
- **Advanced combination:** When you can comfortably extend both legs, and you have also mastered the Single Arm Overhead Stretch, combine the two stretches.

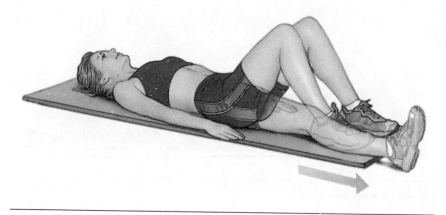

Figure 11.3 Supine stretch.

Count, sets, and reps: Count to five slowly while extending, hold, then count to five slowly while returning to starting position. Breathe normally or count out loud while doing this. Repeat three to five times, one to two times a day. Work up to twenty to thirty seconds for each stretch.

Technique and Tips

- Move slowly and with control.

- Stretch only to the point of tightness.

- If you are having trouble, try this: put a pillow under your head for additional support and comfort.

Wall Climb Front and Side

Benefits: Improves shoulder range of motion to the front and side by stretching the pectoralis (chest), anterior deltoid (front of shoulder), and underarm region including latissimus dorsi (side of back from underarm to waist).

Starting position
- **Front climb:** Stand facing the wall. Place one hand on the wall about shoulder height. Extend your elbow straight, if possible.

- **Side climb:** Stand with the wall at your side. Place the palm of your hand on the wall about shoulder height. Extend your elbow straight, if possible.

Instructions

- **Front climb:** Walk the other hand up the wall as high as you can to the point of tightness. (See Figure 11.4.) If possible, step in toward the wall to increase the stretch, hold for five seconds, and then return to starting position.
- **Side climb:** Walk your hand up the wall as high as you can to the point of tightness. (See Figure 11.5.) If possible, step in closer to the wall, hold the stretch for five seconds, and then return to the starting position.

Count, sets, and reps: Walk up the wall three counts slowly. Hold five counts. Walk down three counts slowly. Repeat both exercises three to five times, one to two times a day. Work up to twenty to thirty seconds for each stretch.

Figure 11.4 Front wall climb.

Figure 11.5 Side wall climb.

Technique and Tips

- Walk the unaffected arm up the wall to get a sense of what your range of motion is and then repeat with the affected arm.

- If the unaffected arm achieves full range of motion easily, then just do this exercise on the affected side.

- You should feel no pain at any time!

- Stop at the point of tightness and try to go a little further each time.

- As the stretch becomes easier, work toward fully straightening your elbow.

Variation

- Once you can fully straighten your elbow, at the top of your range of motion, step in closer to the wall to increase the stretch.

Strength Training

When unused, muscles quickly lose strength and dwindle. In fact, people who do not exercise can expect to lose 30 to 40 percent of their strength by age sixty-five. Surgery leaves many women with muscle imbalances and weaknesses that may hinder their ability to perform daily activities. Chemotherapy combined with post-surgery inactivity speeds muscle and bone loss and prompts fat gain and a lower metabolic rate. A strength-training program can help erase many of these problems, while allowing you to regain strength and abilities.

What to Do

First, get your surgeon's approval before starting any strength-training program. Usually, you will have healed enough to start about four to eight weeks after surgery, but recovery varies. Second, wait until all drains have been removed and you have regained full, upright posture and a complete and comfortable range of motion in your joints. Prematurely starting strength training can cause injury.

The ACSM recommends performing eight to ten strength-training exercises covering all the major muscle groups two to three times a week, with a full day of rest between workouts. (If you had multiple lymph nodes removed, do strength-training exercises for the arms twice a week, rather than three times. Also, please review other precautions explained in "Lymphedema and Strength Training" a little later in this chapter.)

Sets and Reps

Each time you strength train, perform at least one full set of eight to ten repetitions. Start your new regimen very slowly. During your first workout, don't use weights. Instead focus on proper body alignment and practice the motions required to do each exercise correctly. Then select weights light enough to allow you to perform each exercise safely with proper form and a full, controlled range of motion. Once you are comfortable and familiar with your program, add weight gradually by the smallest increment possible so your body can adapt to the added stress slowly over time. You should feel mildly fatigued by the end of the set of eight to ten repetitions.

When it becomes easy to perform a single set of ten reps, you can add a second set or increase the weight so that your muscles feel fatigued by the end of eight reps. Each time this becomes easy, add reps (up to ten) or another set (up to three) or increase the weight.

Working with an Expert

Particularly if you have not done strength training before, I recommend booking a few sessions with a certified personal trainer or physical therapist with specialty training in recovery from breast cancer treatment. Your doctor, a gym, other women, or nearby hospitals may be able to recommend someone, or you can find a certified fitness professional through the American Council on Education (acefitness.org) or use the personal trainer locator at IDEA (ideafit.com). Added to this, an at-home DVD program is available, entitled *Breast Cancer Survivor's Guide to Fitness* (see Resources). The four-hour DVD details the survivor's anatomy before and after surgery and illustrates what occurs during a mastectomy, node dissection, and breast reconstruction with an implant, TRAM flap, and latissimus dorsi flap. Four customized exercise prescriptions, each tailored to a specific surgical procedure, are presented. Of note, the DVD is nonprofit and sales benefit breast cancer research.

Lymphedema and Strength Training

Fear of lymphedema causes some breast cancer survivors to shy away from many activities. It's true that if you had underarm lymph nodes excised (other than during a sentinel node biopsy) or had radiation beneath the arm or around the collar-bone, you need to approach rehabilitation judiciously. Nonetheless, you can and should still exercise. Observing certain precautions, particularly during strength training, will help.

Years ago, many doctors believed even slight exertion of the arm would trigger lymphedema. New thinking suggests a gradual, progressive strength-training program may actually minimize the risk of lymphedema by helping dilate, or widen, remaining lymphatic channels around the shoulder. These channels would be better able to handle increases in the flow of lymph from the arm into the body prompted by exercise or a problem like an arm infection, if necessary.

What to Do. If you are at risk for lymphedema, you'll need to strike a careful balance during strength training—you want to work the arm enough to help widen remaining lymphatic channels while limiting the increase in lymph flow. You do not want lymph fluid to back up into the soft tissues of the arm, thus starting the cycle of lymphedema. To this end, try the following:

• Wear a full arm and hand compression sleeve during arm strength-training exercises, exercises where the arm is used in a repetitive movement (such as swimming, rowing, or racket sports), or more rigorous physical activities that may place stress on the arm (such as raking or scrubbing a large floor). Appearance boutiques in hospitals and other shops that sell breast forms and durable medical goods often can fit you for a compression sleeve. See Resources or call the American Cancer Society (800-ACS-2345 or cancer.org) for suggestions.

• Let your weaker side dictate the pace of strength training. Begin with no weight at all so you can focus on proper body alignment and slow, steady, purposeful movements.

• Err on the side of safety by doing no more than ten repetitions of arm exercises per set.

• Alternate between upper-body exercises and core and leg exercises. Thus, do a set of arm exercises or back exercises where the arm is used and then a set of an exercise that works the legs or abdomen. This allows lymph fluid and lactic acid to clear from the arm. When choosing upper-body exercises, first work the larger muscle groups (pectorals, latissimus dorsi, trapezius) before moving to the smaller ones (biceps, triceps). *Never* spend an entire strength-training session only on your arms. Such prolonged stress might initiate lymphedema.

• Each time you return to arm exercises, choose a different muscle group to work on. That is, if you first worked on your biceps and then on your abs, you might now move to triceps.

• Before doing a second set of all of the exercises, rest for one to two minutes to allow lymph fluid and lactic acid to clear from the arm.

• Leave at least two days between strength-training sessions.

• Only do arm strength training twice a week.

For more information on lymphedema precautions, see Chapter 3.

12

NOW SERVING: A
HEALTHY APPROACH
TO EATING

◉

Summing up her grocery list nowadays, Rose ticked off a few foods she stocks up on and those that she downplays. She is bullish on whole grains, fruits, and vegetables but tries to steer clear of white flour and plentiful sources of animal fats.

"I feel good about that," she said. "I never know if those cancer cells are floating around." Now finished with her treatments, she has adopted a three-prong strategy to deal with this concern: she eats well, exercises, and tries to control stress that pops up. To this I would add, get a good night's sleep.

For many years, scientists have tried to identify foods that fuel or fend off breast cancer. While current data fail to strongly associate breast cancer with any specific foods, vitamins, or nutrients, this is a rapidly evolving area of research.

After a diagnosis of breast cancer, you may wonder what allowed aberrant cells to gain a firm foothold in your body, especially if you usually tried to make healthy choices.

"I've always eaten well," said Sloan. "You know what my response was after I found out I had cancer? *Bring on the french fries*. Because I had been such a good mindful eater and I thought, 'A lot of good it did me.'"

Plenty of my patients echo her frustration. However, it is possible that years of healthy eating and regular exercise may have moderated the disease. Without these habits, their breast cancers may have been more aggressive or advanced. Certainly, taking care of yourself this way helps you weather cancer treatment. And we may yet learn that fruits, vegetables, and other healthy foods will actually minimize the odds of developing recurrent breast cancer.

We do know that staying within a healthy weight range appears to help boost the odds of survival and that bone loss, which can be the prelude to debilitating

LOOKING FOR ADVICE ON NUTRITION?

Registered dietitians have completed course and clinical work on nutrition and passed quali-fying exams. Some states have *licensed dietitian/nutritionists*, who also pass qualifying exams in nutrition but needn't undertake the full spectrum of training required for registered dieti-tians. Some people who freely hand out advice on diet and supplements have no training. When seeking advice, ask for credentials: R.D. (registered dietitian) or L.D.N. (licensed die-titian/nutritionist) or both. The National Cancer Institute (cancer.gov) and the National Cen-ter for Complementary and Alternative Medicine (http://nccam.nih.gov/health) also offer well-vetted information on cancer, nutrition, and supplements.

fractures, is one possible side effect of certain anticancer drugs. We also know that the majority of women outlive their breast cancer, which tells us that breast can-cer survivors—like all women—need to be concerned about heart disease and osteoporosis. This is why I firmly believe that a heart-healthy, bone-building diet combined with the active lifestyle covered in Chapter 11 is the way to go. No eso-teric eats or lengthy list of supplements comes close to matching the power of these two familiar prescriptions.

This chapter describes a healthy approach to eating that reaches well beyond breast cancer. The role excess weight may play in breast cancer and other serious ailments is explained, too. Whether you are currently undergoing treatment or have moved beyond it, the suggestions here aim to help you maximize your chances of staying healthy and living well.

EATING WELL DURING TREATMENT

Eating as well as possible during treatment will help you heal, fight infection, and cope with side effects, as well as protect against treatment-related bone loss. Choose foods that give your body the raw materials needed for healthy cell growth: whole grains, lots of vegetables and fruits, and protein sources such as beans, fish, and poultry as described later in this chapter. Be aware that appetite fluctuations are

VITAMIN D AND BREAST CANCER

Sure, vitamin D plays a role in keeping bones healthy, but could it also help block breast cancer? Some data suggest it might. Currently, much of this research stems from test tube or animal studies, but a few human studies already published or under way hint at the ability of vitamin D to retard the growth and spread of various cancer cells, including breast cancer. A daily dose of 800 I.U. (international units) from sources like a multivitamin, calcium supplements paired with vitamin D, and low-fat milk may be good insurance for women who have breast cancer.

common for a variety of reasons. The following strategies and others offered by your nurse or a registered dietitian can help.

Protecting Your Bones

One healthy step you can take immediately is to get enough calcium and vitamin D every day to help keep bones strong (vitamin K, magnesium, phosphorus, and other nutrients assist to a lesser extent). Vitamin D enables your body to absorb available calcium in the digestive tract rather than stealing it from the bones.

This is especially important for women undergoing chemotherapy. One study of women with early-stage breast cancers found rapid, significant bone loss occurred in the spine (7.7 percent), sites on the thigh bone (4.6 percent), and the hips (4.1 percent) during the first year after chemotherapy-induced menopause. There was a trend toward accelerated bone loss even among the women who did not go into menopause. Anticancer drugs known as aromatase inhibitors—anastrozole (Arimidex), exemestane (Aromasin), and letrozole (Femara)—can also cause bone loss. Other research suggests women with a breast cancer diagnosis are five times more likely than age-matched peers to fracture a spinal vertebra.

Less important but still helpful is minimizing alcohol and drinking only moderate amounts of caffeinated beverages like coffee—studies differ, but that's probably three to five cups a day—which may have indirect effects on hip fractures and calcium loss, respectively.

I recommend having a baseline bone density test before you start treatment. That way, you'll know right away whether you need to consider medication to help shore up bones or whether a healthy diet, supplements, and weight-bearing exercise should suffice. Plus you can track changes in bone mass over time and address them as necessary.

Daily Recommendations

Because bone loss is a serious issue for women who have chemotherapy, nutrition experts at Dana-Farber Cancer Institute usually recommend a daily dose of 1,200 mg. (milligrams) of calcium and 400 I.U. of vitamin D, says senior clinical nutritionist Stacy Kennedy, M.P.H., R.D./L.D.N. Depending on your age, this may be slightly more than is usually recommended, but it remains well within safe limits. If you do not have chemotherapy, the daily recommendation for calcium is 1,000 mg. between ages thirty-one and fifty and 1,200 mg. for age fifty-one and older. The daily adequate intake for vitamin D is 200 I.U. between ages thirty-one and fifty, 400 I.U. between the ages of fifty-one and seventy, and 600 I.U. for people older than seventy.

Every morning, I take a multivitamin that has 200 mg. of calcium and 400 I.U. of vitamin D. Every evening, I have a calcium chew supplement that supplies 600 mg. of calcium and 100 I.U. of vitamin D; these come in chocolate or caramel and have the added boon of sliding down more easily than pills. Cheese and other

---

CHOOSING CALCIUM SUPPLEMENTS

Calcium paired with vitamin D is the best choice in a supplement, particularly if you live in latitudes that see little sun in winter. Which form of calcium should you buy? Top honors go to calcium citrate (Citracal), which is most easily absorbed by the body and has relatively low traces of lead. Calcium carbonate (Tums, Viactiv) tends to be less expensive but not as easily absorbed. Skip supplements that list calcium carbonate derived from oyster shells. It sounds pleasantly natural but can have higher lead levels. Coral calcium is questionable, too, due to pollution and environmental concerns. Take calcium supplements in divided doses at different times of day (preferably with meals) because your body can only absorb about 500 to 600 mg. of calcium at a time.

calcium-rich foods, including broccoli, yogurt, and eggs, make up the difference. Equally important, I get regular weight-bearing exercise (see Chapter 11). Some women also may need to take medications that block bone loss or help build bone. Ask your doctor about this.

Handle Appetite Surges

During the first four days or so after a chemotherapy session, I felt so hungry due to a side effect of the steroid prednisone that I certainly ate more than I normally would. Yet I was well aware of research discussed later in this chapter that indicates that keeping weight from creeping upward significantly during treatment offers a survival benefit.

It's hard to be careful about calories when you're feeling miserable, but a range of appealing, healthy snacks can help keep appetite surges or nausea-inspired nibbling from adding too many unwanted pounds. Before you embark on chemotherapy, I suggest you clear the decks by tossing out less healthy items that may prove too tempting and filling your cupboards with healthy, easy foods. I stocked up on low-fat string cheese, dried apricots and raisins, bananas, nuts, and other quick, nutritious items that I enjoy.

Spotlight Protein and Calories

Surgery, chemotherapy, and radiation eradicate cancerous cells but also harm some normal cells in their path. After these treatments, your body works hard to heal and replenish cells. Protein, the building block of every cell, and energy-giving calories are poured into this effort. Try to get sufficient amounts of both without overdoing it. On days when it's hard to eat, try the strategies suggested for nausea.

Take a Multivitamin

Appetite swings, skewed eating habits, and various discomforts can conspire to keep you from obtaining the broad range of nutrients your body needs. A daily multivitamin provides insurance. It's best to take your multivitamin and calcium supplements at a different time of day to give your body the best chance of absorbing these nutrients. A store-brand basic multivitamin is liable to be as good as more costly brands.

Deal with Discomforts

Anticancer drugs may cause nausea, vomiting, dry mouth, mouth sores, an altered sense of taste or smell, constipation, or diarrhea, all of which have an impact on appetite and nutrition. Usually, these problems disappear fairly quickly once treatment ends, though taste troubles sometimes linger. Meanwhile, try the following tips and ask your cancer care team or a registered dietitian if they can tailor these suggestions specifically for your needs.

Nausea

Chemotherapy is a major player in nausea, but dehydration, hunger, and changes in taste and smell also may contribute. Talk with your nurse or doctor about drugs to control nausea. If one fails to work, another may help. According to a National Institutes of Health Consensus Statement on Acupuncture, this form of traditional Chinese medicine also has shown promise in relieving chemotherapy nausea. Four days before each of my chemotherapy infusions, I had an acupuncture session. I never once vomited during treatment. Acupressure, such as that supplied by pressing on a pressure point on the wrist with your fingers or wearing a wristband designed to do so (Sea Bands, sea-band.com, is one brand) may work, though this is less certain.

Start the day with a few bedside crackers and flat ginger ale if you usually wake up feeling nauseous. Divide three square meals into six smaller sittings or nibble frequent snacks throughout the day so that hunger doesn't amplify your nausea. Some good snack choices are crackers with cheese or hummus, peanut butter on a banana, nuts, sliced fruit and vegetables, granola, a hard-boiled egg, or a few spoonfuls of custard or pudding.

During treatment, said Luz, her appetite dwindled. "I wasn't eating a lot." She talked with a nutritionist, asking, "What's most important here that I should make sure not to drop off the list?"

Bland foods—toast, crackers, potatoes, noodles, oatmeal, broth—usually sit better in the stomach than greasy, fatty, ultrasweet, or spicy foods, but eat what

---

GINGER TEA

Fresh ginger tea stands a better chance of easing nausea than packaged products that vary in strength and shelf life. Grate a tablespoon of ginger root into a cup of hot water. Add a squeeze of lemon or lime, if you like.

---

appeals to you. I found oatmeal, Cheerios, and crackers helped ease the background buzz of nausea that followed my prednisone-induced hunger four or five days into each chemotherapy cycle. Sloan, who suffered mightily with nausea during chemotherapy, craved fruit when she felt too sick to eat much of anything. "Every day my husband would bring up a bowl with fruit and toast," she said. The loving gesture and the food comforted her while helping settle her stomach.

If solids are unappealing, pour a meal. Soup, liquid meals replete with vitamins and calories like Ensure or powdered "instant breakfast" mix, milkshakes, or fruit and yogurt smoothies are a few choices. Cooler foods, such as cold soups or ice cream, may slip down easily. Freeze flavored yogurt or even Ensure in ice cube trays or small paper cups with a Popsicle stick.

Sip liquids during the course of the day rather than drinking large amounts. Water on an empty stomach can make you feel worse; fruit juice, Jell-O, soup, milk, or a sports drink may be better choices to help you get enough fluids. Some women find ginger tea (see recipe in the sidebar), ginger ale, or even ginger candies help; others do not.

Odors can set off nausea, so ventilate your kitchen and rooms well. Some women mention that the smell of meat or poultry cooking turns their stomachs; once it has been cooked, they may be happy to eat it, however. If possible, have someone else cook (or buy healthy take-out foods) and handle other odorous tasks when you're feeling queasy.

Vomiting

Often, nausea is the prelude to vomiting, so try the tips given earlier, including medication and acupuncture. Many of my patients find that, over time, certain sights or smells associated with their breast cancer treatments—hospital odors, perhaps, or a soda often sipped to settle the stomach—begin to trigger nausea and vomiting. The bright red color of doxorubicin (Adriamycin) has put plenty of women off beverages that share its brilliant tint. "To this day I can't drink cranberry juice because it looks like the Adriamycin," noted one patient. "I can't drink Diet Pepsi because I drank that during one of my chemo sessions." For exactly this reason, some women suggest avoiding foods and beverages you really enjoy on days surrounding treatment.

Worrying about whether you're going to throw up can feed into the cycle, making it more likely to happen. Sometimes, relaxation techniques like deep breathing and visualization can help.

If you do vomit, wait until your stomach stops pitching before trying to eat or drink anything. Then start with little sips of a clear liquid like water, carbonated drinks, sports drinks, bouillon, or strained broth. The National Cancer Institute suggests drinking just a teaspoon of such liquids every ten minutes. Once you can tolerate that, try bumping it up to a tablespoon (three teaspoons make a tablespoon) every twenty minutes and then two tablespoons every half hour. Gradually move on to small amounts of a liquid diet or soft diet. Go back to eating normally when you feel ready to do so. Tell your nurse or doctor about any episodes of vomiting.

Dry Mouth

Soup, stews, smoothies, and soft purees of fruit or vegetables slip down more easily. Marinate foods in salad dressing or juice before cooking, braise foods (cook in liquid), or add gravy or dressings afterward. Taking small sips of water or other beverages between bites helps, too. Squirts of lemon or vinegar and tart foods can help generate saliva (these sting, though, if your mouth is tender). See additional tips on dry mouth in Chapter 10.

Mouth Sores

Soft or liquid foods are easiest to eat; these include applesauce, bananas, canned peaches; cottage cheese; soup; mashed potatoes; custard or pudding; scrambled eggs; cream of wheat; pureed fruit or vegetables; and filet of sole. Little pieces and little bites taken with a small spoon can help. Fibrous or rough-edged foods like raw vegetables, crackers, or toast can hurt. Avoid spicy or acidic foods and beverages (tomato sauce, citrus fruits or juices) if they sting tender mouth tissues. Review additional tips for mouth sores in Chapter 10.

Changes in Taste and Smell

Adding spices helped me counter the unpleasant metallic taste that plagued me during chemotherapy. I kept the Tabasco bottle handy and shook on amounts that would normally send steam shooting from my ears. Half a jar of jalapeños would vanish in one meal. Vats of salsa seemed to help, too. I put it on tortilla chips, of course, but also on scrambled eggs. I also squeezed a ton of lemon or lime juice into the water I drank. Some women find dried herbs—oregano, basil, rosemary—provide the punch their food lacks. Go lightly on salt, though, because most of us do not need more. All of these tricks to crank up the volume on flavor may help with dulled taste buds, too.

If smells trouble you, ask someone to prepare food or buy take-out. Take your meal well away from kitchen scents to eat. Ventilate the kitchen well and keep bedroom doors shut tightly so smells won't sneak in. Sometimes, a spray of lemon or another light scent helps.

Constipation

Anesthesia used during surgery, chemotherapy, narcotic agents given for pain or nausea, antidepressants, dehydration, and inactivity all may contribute to constipation. In my case, my first round of chemotherapy most assuredly did so. It wasn't until four to five days afterward that I finally had a bowel movement. By that point, I just wanted someone to shoot me and put me out of my misery. After that experience, I began taking Colace, a stool softener, on the day my chemotherapy cycle started. Discuss this approach with your nurse.

You can also try the following:

- Eating fiber-packed foods like whole grains, vegetables, and fruits. Bran cereals and dried or stewed prunes, raisins, apricots, and other fruits are especially helpful.

- Drinking plenty of fluids, including fruit juices, such as apple and prune.

- Taking fiber supplements, such as Metamucil.

- Increasing your activity. Even brief walks can help a great deal.

Diarrhea

Some women find chemotherapy causes diarrhea, not constipation. Infection, food-borne illnesses, or anxiety are other possible culprits. The artificial sweeteners sorbitol and mannitol can trigger diarrhea, cramping, and gas in some people. Lactose, the sugar in milk and some dairy products like ice cream, also is hard for some women to digest. Usually, yogurt with active cultures is easily digested, and hard cheeses, which have less lactose than soft cheeses, cause less of a problem.

Replenish losses due to diarrhea by drinking lots of fluids and eating foods that contain sodium and potassium, two minerals essential to your body. The National Cancer Institute suggests broth for its sodium content and bananas, boiled or mashed potatoes, and peach or apricot nectar for potassium. Both minerals are

WHEN TO AVOID ANTIOXIDANTS AND OTHER SUPPLEMENTS

Antioxidant supplements throng the shelves of health food stores, but some experts say they don't belong in your dietary repertoire during chemotherapy or radiation. *Antioxidant* is a catchall term for any compound that can counteract unstable molecules like free radicals that are thought to have a hand in cancer, heart disease, and many other ailments. Yet taking large amounts of certain supplements—particularly vitamins C and E and beta-carotene (a form of vitamin A)—could potentially counteract the oxidation that chemotherapy and radiation use to kill off cells. They can also interact with anticancer drugs and other medications in unexpected ways. Unlike drugs, supplements are not regulated by the FDA. They vary widely in strength and purity despite what their labels may boast. Before taking any supplement other than a basic multivitamin, talk with your cancer care team to make sure it won't interfere with any aspect of your treatment. A dietitian or a pharmacist may have helpful information, too.

Once active treatment ends, a healthy dose of skepticism should still prevail. Currently, the National Cancer Institute notes, no scientific evidence shows that vitamin or mineral supplements or herbal remedies can cure cancer or prevent it from recurring.

By contrast with supplements, a varied, colorful diet of fruits and vegetables offers a plentiful, safe source of antioxidants during and after treatment. Eating this way may not specifically block breast cancer, but it can contribute to your health in many ways. Paired with these antioxidants are countless other helpful nutrients in food that can never be bottled.

found in sports drinks, like Gatorade, and products designed to replace electrolytes, like Pedialyte fluid or ice pops.

Eating small snacks frequently rather than three large meals may help keep diarrhea in check. Read food labels and consider cutting out items with sorbitol and mannitol to see if this helps. At least temporarily, avoid fatty or greasy foods and foods that are very high in fiber, such as corn, cabbage, peas, and beans. If lactose-intolerance is a problem, you can avoid milk entirely, drink only small amounts of it, or try brands like Lactaid milk. Lactase enzyme supplements can be taken as well.

Careful food preparation is important. Wash hands before and afterward. See that vegetables and fruits are well washed, too. Using one cutting board for vegetables and fruits and another for meats and fish can help avoid cross-contamination with bacteria. Wash utensils and cutting boards with hot, soapy water. Cook meat, poultry, and fish completely.

Report severe or frequent bouts of diarrhea to your cancer care team. A liquid diet or a course of bland foods may be recommended; medications may also be suggested, if necessary.

EATING WELL AFTER ACTIVE TREATMENT ENDS

One day the active phase of your treatment sputters to a halt and the rhythms of your life gradually begin to reassert themselves. It may be comforting to hang on to some lessons learned, but it's best to let go of any nutritional dodges that may have helped you get through treatment, such as eating only a few foods that would reliably stay put or nibbling frequently throughout the day. Likewise, as more energy returns it's a good idea to shun the couch and boost your activity. Now is the time to go over your diet and the exercise plans covered in Chapter 11 with an eye toward adopting healthy changes.

Why Weight Matters

Several studies show a greater risk of breast cancer and lower survival rates after diagnosis among women who are overweight and obese, particularly once women reach menopause. What's more, additional pounds raise your risk for heart disease and diabetes.

Before you reach menopause, your ovaries produce most of the estrogen circulating through your body. Fat cells are another source of estrogen. After menopause—whether natural or induced by chemotherapy—these cells continue to churn out small amounts of it. This can add up significantly, depending on how heavily you tip the scales and how much of your weight is fat versus muscle. Because estrogen is believed to fuel some breast cancer cells, excess fat is troubling.

You might imagine that chemotherapy is a sure bet for weight loss, but research shows between 50 and 96 percent of women with early-stage breast cancer gain weight in the course of it. Usually, this ranges from five to fifteen pounds, but it's not uncommon to see greater gains. What's more, fat replaces some muscle, which means calories are not burned as efficiently. A healthy forty-year-old woman who undergoes chemotherapy experiences a 2.5 percent increase in body fat within a year—the equivalent of what would normally happen over the course of a decade.

The reasons for these changes are not completely understood. Inactivity stemming from the fatigue that can accompany chemotherapy, frequent snacks to help keep nausea at bay or for comfort, and hormonal changes that tip a woman into menopause each may play a role. Longer chemotherapy regimens, receiving chemotherapy in pills rather than through IV, the steroid prednisone, and being premenopausal contribute to greater weight gains.

This weight gain has a more worrisome aspect than any outward changes you might notice in the mirror, even though some may find that alone pretty disheartening. According to one study, premenopausal women who gained more than thirteen pounds during chemotherapy were 1.6 times as likely to die sooner as those who put on fewer pounds. Some, though not all, studies bolster these findings, and a similar trend has been noted among postmenopausal women.

Knowing all of this spurred my efforts to preserve muscle and keep weight off by eating carefully and pushing myself to exercise when possible. I purposely don't own a scale, but during my treatment, I checked my weight frequently at the gym. My weight fluctuated—fortunately, just by ten pounds—and it was easy to see that skipping activity on bad days and nibbling more on many days could add up over the course of several chemotherapy cycles.

Healthful Eating

Can a handful of ingredients affect breast cancer recurrence and survival? At this writing, no strong data support any such claims, despite plenty of popular works

BEYOND BREAST CANCER

The health implications of weight go well beyond its role in breast cancer. According to my research colleagues at the Harvard School of Public Health, three measures that help determine whether you currently fall within a healthy range are a ratio of height to weight known as *body mass index* (BMI), waist circumference, and the amount of weight gained since you turned twenty-one.

BMI

Body mass index offers a snapshot of total body fat for the average person, though the results can be thrown off if you are especially well muscled or well padded. A reasonably simple calculation of BMI can be done with a calculator as you fill in the following blanks:

_____ (number of pounds you weigh)

Divide by _____ (number of inches tall) = _____.

Divide the answer again by _____ (number of inches tall).

Multiply by 703.

_____ = Your BMI

The National Heart, Lung, and Blood Institute website offers a quick on-site calculator and charts (nhlbisupport.com/bmi). A substantial number of studies drawing on data collected from more than a million adults shows that a BMI higher than 25 raises the risk for many ailments, including cancers, heart disease, diabetes, and stroke. Although your fears may center on dying early from breast cancer, the odds of shaving years off your life due to one of these other health problems rise, too, once your BMI goes above 25.

Waist Circumference

Where you put on pounds may also matter. Some studies suggest that abdominal fat contributes to high blood sugar, blood pressure, and cholesterol and has a hand in heart disease, too. (Of course, a thickening waist may just be a marker of overall fat rather than a unique form of fat.) Measure your waist at the point where your sides dip in, which is generally at belly button height. According to the National Institutes of Health, a healthy waist circumference for women is less than thirty-five inches; Harvard researchers warn that this

(continued)

is a generous estimate. Beyond that, risk rises for diabetes, heart disease, high blood pressure, high cholesterol, and cancer.

Weight Gained

If you've gained more than ten pounds since you turned twenty-one, your health could probably profit from slimming down. Data from the Nurses' Health Study showed women who added eleven to twenty-two pounds in middle age were far more likely to develop heart disease, type 2 diabetes, gallstones, and high blood pressure than those who put on five pounds or less.

that suggest eating one food and avoiding another could change the course of breast cancer. Two large randomized, controlled trials on women living with breast cancer may give us more information on certain foods very soon. The Women's Intervention Nutrition Study looks at lowering dietary fat; the Women's Healthy Eating and Living Study considers whether boosting vegetables, fruit, and fiber and decreasing fats has any effect.

Meantime, I recommend the healthful eating plan described next. Developed by researchers at Harvard Medical School and the Harvard School of Public Health, it goes beyond breast cancer to encompass eating strategies that can help slow or prevent heart disease, diabetes, and other chronic health problems. That said, don't lose sight of the joy of eating well—the crisp snap of green beans or crunch of mixed greens, the richness of poached salmon or tomatoes sautéed in olive oil, a sharp whiff of garlic, or a bowl of ripe blueberries all pack pleasure as well as health benefits.

A New Food Pyramid

Large-scale nutrition studies from Harvard and other sites have drawn a new face on the once familiar USDA food pyramid, which is currently scheduled for much-needed revision. The Harvard Healthy Eating Pyramid (Figure 12.1), originally adapted from *Eat, Drink, and Be Healthy* by Walter C. Willett, M.D., with P. J. Skerrett, has been modified slightly to reflect advice for women who have had breast

BREAST CANCER EATING PYRAMID

The Harvard Healthy Eating Pyramid distills key points in current nutritional science. The widest parts of the pyramid showcase the most important categories. Foods in the top should be eaten sparingly. Thus, daily exercise and weight control are spotlighted in the wide base. Fats from healthy sources such as plants also appear in a wide wedge of the pyramid, indicating that they are healthy. Refined carbohydrates such as white bread and white rice are at the narrow top, indicating that you should eat them sparingly, if at all. Likewise, red meat should be eaten sparingly, while fish, poultry, and eggs are healthier choices.

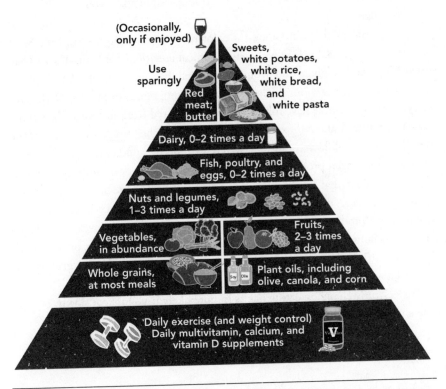

Figure 12.1 Adapted from *Eat, Drink, and Be Healthy* by Walter C. Willett, M.D., and P. J. Skerrett.

cancer. Several nutritional issues are discussed in the sidebar "Breast Cancer Eating Pyramid," too. Your cancer care team or a nutritionist can provide more in-depth information plus recipes and snack ideas that carry these points into your kitchen.

Changing Habits

Cancer experts recommend a general cancer-prevention diet high in fruits and vegetables and low in saturated fats. The World Health Cancer Research Fund and the American Institute for Cancer Research stress five to ten fruit and vegetable servings daily; U.S. recommendations shoot for five to nine servings. Aim at consuming no more calories than needed to maintain a healthy BMI (see earlier in this chapter) or, if necessary, try to lose weight until you are within the healthy range.

When grocery shopping, look for colorful, pungent produce, suggests Stacy Kennedy, M.P.H., R.D./L.D.N., a senior clinical nutritionist at Dana-Farber Cancer Institute and Brigham and Women's Hospital, because it's likely to have plenty of beneficial *phytochemicals* (biologically active compounds in plants). Dark green leafy vegetables, which have folic acid, and orange-red fruits and vegetables abundant in vitamin A and antioxidants may be especially helpful. Cruciferous vegetables (broccoli, cauliflower, radishes, watercress), berries, and citrus fruits are good choices, too. Frozen produce is fine and sometimes packs more nutritional punch than perishables that languish too long on grocery shelves. Steaming or gently sautéing vegetables can help release nutrients by breaking down cell walls. Searing, grilling, and broiling can char meat, creating *carcinogens* (cancer-causing chemicals), especially when fat flames up. Braising meat in liquid, boiling, or steaming is healthier, although choosing lean meats and cutting off fat before grilling also will help.

Successfully changing eating habits is more likely if you take it slowly, perhaps one change a week or every two weeks. For example:

- Check off calcium, vitamin D, and your multivitamin on the calendar each day.

- Add at least one extra fruit and vegetable serving a day—a breakfast fruit smoothie, lunch salad, or dinner stir-fry with lots of veggies could make that a snap.

- Drink a glass of water before each snack or meal if you need to lose weight.

- Try a new whole grain (brown rice, barley, quinoa, or even old-fashioned oats) or substitute a whole-grain product for one made with white flour. The American Cancer Society recommends buying a new whole grain—or fruit, vegetable, or low-fat item—each time you shop. However, avoid low-fat items that are high in sugar and calories.

- Proportion your plate: one-half vegetables, one-quarter protein, one-quarter whole grain.

Healthy Fats

Currently, no evidence links breast cancer to high total dietary fat despite past reports (although if excess fat means added calories and pounds, it may be another matter). Research bolsters the idea that certain fats are healthy while others speed development of heart disease and, possibly, breast cancer. High consumption of red meat and high-fat dairy products that have plenty of saturated fat, for example, was associated with a slightly greater risk for initial breast cancer development in a study of women ages twenty-six to forty-six published in 2003 in the *Journal of the National Cancer Institute*. Saturated fats and trans fats like partially hydrogenated vegetable oils used in many prepared foods are linked to heart disease. Try to eat fewer saturated fats by choosing skim or low-fat milk and dairy products and replacing red meat with lean poultry, fish, and plant protein sources. Try to cut out (or at least cut down) trans fats, which do not occur naturally.

Polyunsaturated and monounsaturated fats are considered healthy fats. Some controlled European studies suggest monounsaturated fats, especially olive oil, reduce the risk for breast cancers and other cancers. Antioxidant compounds called *phenolics*, which are plentiful in olive oil, seem to inhibit breast cancer in animals. Thus far, though, these findings are preliminary.

The ratio of two fatty acids called *omega-3* and *omega-6* appears to be out of balance in modern diets. Both of these polyunsaturated fats are essential to your diet because your body cannot make them. Some preliminary evidence supports a hypothesis that boosting omega-3s might reduce the risk for breast cancer. Most American diets lean heavily on sources of omega-6 fats and only rarely include foods rich in omega-3s, which have proven to suppress heart disease. Adding a daily source of omega-3s to your meals will help adjust this imbalance.

A FEW FAT SOURCES

The predominant fat in certain foods appears in the following list; many foods combine smaller amounts of several types of fat.

- **Saturated fats:** Meat, poultry, full-fat dairy products, and coconut milk or oil
- **Trans fats:** Partially hydrogenated vegetable oils used in many prepared foods, margarines, baked goods, and deep-fried or fast foods
- **Monounsaturated fats:** Canola, olive, and peanut oils, peanuts, and avocados
- **Polyunsaturated fats:** Corn, cottonseed, safflower, and soybean oils, cold-water fish, flaxseed, and walnuts
- **Omega-3:** Flaxseed (seeds or oil, but not meal), walnuts (especially English) and walnut oil, butternuts, pecans, anchovies, salmon, tuna, trout, sardines, and other fatty, cold-water fish or fish oil capsules, and Country Hen eggs and some other organic brands (but not usually standard eggs)
- **Omega-6:** Corn, safflower, canola, and cottonseed oils and soybeans

Organic Versus Conventional Foods

While I prefer to buy organic foods, there is no scientific evidence that it will improve my health. Organic foods are grown without the use of most conventional pesticides, petroleum- or sewage-based fertilizers, genetic engineering, or radiation. The USDA seal of organic approval is given to foods that are at least 95 percent organic or 100 percent organic. At this writing, shifts in the way the National Organic Program standards are interpreted, however, may permit more pesticide use than many advocates for organic foods feel is warranted.

Organically raised animals are given feed without antibiotics, growth hormones, or rendered remains of other animals—except possibly fish—which may prevent the spread of diseases such as mad cow disease (bovine spongiform encephalopathy). I also like to buy wild salmon because it has fewer potentially carcinogenic chemicals called PCBs and other toxins than much of the farm-raised salmon does.

Do organically raised fruits and vegetables have more vitamins and minerals or antioxidants and other helpful phytochemicals than conventional crops? Some preliminary research suggests this might be true in some instances, but no firm conclusions can be drawn.

Whether your grocery dollar goes toward organic or conventional foods, don't let worries about pesticides keep you from eating plenty of fruits and vegetables. The proven health benefits outweigh risks from ingesting pesticides. You can reduce your exposure to pesticides in other ways. The Environmental Working Group, a nonprofit organization, says more than half of the dietary risk from pesticide residues comes from twelve foods: strawberries, red and green bell peppers, spinach, cherries grown in the United States, peaches, cantaloupe grown in Mexico, celery, apples, apricots, green beans, grapes grown in Chile, and cucumbers. Check labels for country of origin or ask at your supermarket. Choosing organic versions of these fruits and vegetables and washing all produce carefully can help, too.

Blood Sugar Spikes

Easily digested foods cause sudden spikes in blood sugar that prompt your body to send out a gush of insulin to clear the sugar from your blood. Blood sugar then plummets, resulting in hunger pangs just a few hours after you ate. Repeated time and again over years, this may also spur the development of type 2 diabetes. Adopting eating strategies that smooth out blood sugar spikes and dips may help you avoid that and may keep you from gaining weight, too.

Glycemic load is a measure of how swiftly and how dramatically a single serving of food makes blood sugar rise. It puts a practical handle on the *glycemic index*, which ranks the effect on blood sugar of a fixed amount of a food compared to that elicited by fifty grams of white bread or fifty grams of pure sugar mixed into water. That practicality pays off. Although carrots are high on the glycemic index, well over a pound of them go into that measurement—hardly a standard serving.

How does this translate into healthy meals and snacks? It's a good idea to eat more foods with a lower glycemic load (brown rice, bran, and other whole grains; lentils, beans; most fruits and vegetables) and fewer with a higher glycemic load (refined grains like white rice and white flour, white bread, potatoes, soft drinks, sugar). As you must have noticed, these lower glycemic choices happen to be healthy foods as well. Changing the acidity of a food by adding vinegar or lemon reduces its glycemic load, though by exactly how much would be difficult to know. Even adding fat to a food ranked high on the glycemic index can help by slowing digestion. Choose a healthy fat, of course! Spread half a whole wheat bagel with peanut butter, for example. The University of Sydney in Australia has a website (glycemic index.com) that offers information on glycemic index and glycemic load as well as a searchable database that includes a wide variety of foods.

Alcohol

Alcohol is a double-edged sword for women. One to two drinks a day—five ounces of wine, twelve ounces of beer, or one and a half ounces of hard liquor per drink—appear to help prevent heart disease, which kills far more women than breast cancer annually. Yet pooled findings from many large studies indicate that women who have two or more alcoholic drinks a day are 40 percent more likely to develop breast cancer than women who don't drink at all. The Nurses' Health Study found that as little as half a drink a day increased a woman's breast cancer risk by 30 percent. Thus far, studies do not show that alcohol affects the risk of breast cancer recurrence or prognosis, but more research directly on these questions is needed.

Why alcohol changes breast cancer risk is debated. Possibly, it temporarily raises the amount of circulating estrogen in the blood, which might add up over time. It may make cells more vulnerable to cancer-causing agents. Another possibility is that alcohol interferes with the body's capacity to use folic acid, a B vitamin that has been linked to cancer prevention. The Nurses' Health Study found women who take 600 mcg. (micrograms) of folic acid a day and also drink more than one alcoholic beverage a day do not have a higher risk of breast cancer than women who drink less. Some other research supports this.

An occasional celebratory drink is unlikely to matter, but otherwise it is probably safest to avoid alcohol. If worry about heart disease makes you wonder whether regularly raising a glass might be a good idea, Dr. Walter C. Willett may send you on a different tack. In *Eat, Drink, and Be Healthy*, he points out that starting to exercise regularly—or increasing the intensity and length of exercise sessions—could supply the very same beneficial effect on your heart without raising other risks.

Soy

Isoflavonoids are a weak plant estrogen abundant in soybeans, tofu, soy milk, and similar soy products. Laboratory studies show that isoflavonoids seem to protect breast cells from becoming cancerous by blocking the cancer-initiating action of other estrogens. Recent human studies, however, have found that women who took soy supplements—which are an easier way than diet to ingest large amounts of isoflavonoids—experienced greater growth in breast cells, which might increase the potential for development of breast cancers. Animal experiments showed transplanted human breast cancer cells multiplied when mice were fed doses of soy isoflavonoids. Before any conclusions can be drawn about the link between isoflavonoids, soy, and breast cancer, more human studies are needed. Some researchers feel that women with ER+ tumors should probably avoid soy products due to phytoestrogens. Other experts believe that is going overboard, suggesting instead that it is sensible to enjoy soy occasionally as part of a healthy diet but not eat unusually large amounts of it and not take any soy supplements.

13

MENDING THE MIND: COGNITIVE CHANGES

◉

After ten years spent hammering out a dissertation while shuttling between dusty archaeology sites and the hushed halls of the British Museum, Sophie knew her subject intimately. Yet after surgery and chemotherapy for a fairly aggressive breast cancer that has recently recurred, she can't recall the details of a topic that had consumed her life for a decade.

"I know my IQ hasn't dropped," she said. "I'm back in a very demanding job. It's not my smarts, it's my memory. I could not give a paper on my dissertation. It would take me a year to do that. That's pretty much gone and it was ten years of my life."

Chemobrain. Chemofog. Many women who have had chemotherapy use pithy terms like these to describe changes in mental sharpness and abilities experienced during and after treatment. The medical community calls this condition *cognitive dysfunction* (or sometimes, cognitive impairment or cognitive sequelae). Both the President's Cancer Panel and the National Coalition for Cancer Survivorship have recognized it as a genuine problem and a challenge for survivors of breast cancer.

Earlier detection of breast cancer combined with continuing advances in treatments ensures that the number of long-term breast cancer survivors will continue to grow. That's certainly good news. The not-so-good news is that some of these women may experience difficulties with concentration—needing to read the same passage over and over or losing a thought in midsentence—as well as forgetfulness, distractibility, and trouble dredging up words. These are common experiences.

A growing body of research suggests that 16 to 75 percent of women undergoing chemotherapy for breast cancer experience certain cognitive problems, such as memory deficits, comprehension difficulties, or trouble learning new information. Most of these studies are flawed because they did not establish baseline assessments of cognitive abilities before women received chemotherapy, relying only on assessments made afterward. Thus, the research might underestimate the extent of

Common Symptoms of Chemobrain

A broad spectrum of cognitive changes has been reported. Not every woman who has chemotherapy will experience these changes, but some undoubtedly will run into one or more of the following:

- Difficulty concentrating or paying attention, especially when multitasking
- Slowed ability to process information
- Trouble learning and remembering new information
- Trouble recalling words
- Losing one's train of thought midsentence
- Increased forgetfulness
- Difficulty remembering planned events
- Difficulty interpreting and recalling visual patterns
- Decreased mental flexibility so that small, unanticipated changes seem overwhelming and irritability with others occurs more often as a consequence

Changes like these may be short-lived or may last a decade. Many women observe that problems are most likely to surface when their daily work or household routines resume and there is a need to multitask. Simply put, getting through the day can be a confusing, overwhelming struggle.

the problem in very high-functioning women whose mental capabilities now lie within normal bounds, albeit at a level far lower than usual for them. Similarly, the studies could overestimate how much of the problem was due to chemotherapy in women who would normally perform poorly on standardized tests.

While women have traded stories about chemobrain for years, cognitive dysfunction is a field of study still in its infancy. This chapter—which seeks to describe the problem and offer some solutions based on current knowledge—reflects that. In the coming years, much more on these topics should be revealed.

Overview: A New Field of Study

In 2003 a scientific think-tank session in Banff, Canada, funded by Hurricane Voices, a breast cancer foundation in Newton, Massachusetts, brought together international experts ranging from medical oncologists, radiologists, and clinical and experimental psychologists to patient advocates. Their task was to better define cognitive dysfunction. They tried to scope out the extent of the problem and its characteristic symptoms. They also considered the potential mechanisms through which chemotherapy might trigger declines in mental abilities and explored possible methods of treatment and rehabilitation.

Although truly definitive research has yet to be done, published studies consistently identify cognitive deficits—not always the same ones, however—in subsets of women who receive chemotherapy. The combination therapy CMF (cyclophosphamide, methotrexate, and 5-fluorouracil) and regimens containing anthracycline drugs, such as doxorubicin (Adriamycin), have been implicated in these problems. So, too, have high-dose chemotherapy regimens, which appear to impair mental functioning more than standard-dose chemotherapy.

To date, little has been published on tamoxifen (Nolvadex). Available evidence is mixed, ranging from reports that it has a protective effect on mental abilities or no effect or triggers a decline in narrative writing tasks or visuospatial performance, described later in this chapter.

No information is available yet on cognitive changes in women who receive taxanes, such as paclitaxel (Taxol) or docetaxel (Taxotere), or trastuzumab (Herceptin).

CULPRITS BEHIND THE CHANGES

"What I found during chemotherapy was that I forgot words," said Sophie. "Simple words. Like, 'I want a glass of _____.' That stuff. It was rare, but it did happen."

Like many other women who have chemotherapy, Sophie definitely experienced some changes in her mental abilities during the course of her treatment. *Chemobrain* or *chemofog* seem fitting labels. After all, for any given woman, it could indeed be that the effects of chemotherapy on her brain were the sole cause of forgetfulness or other changes. However, there are other possibilities, too. Chemotherapy might be just one of several underlying causes, or the problem might have nothing to do with chemotherapy at all. What's more, the culprit or culprits for cognitive changes might vary during and after treatment—at one point, changes in mental abilities could indeed be tied to chemotherapy, while at another, lack of sleep, general fatigue, aging, medications, or other factors might be prompting them.

While factors like aging cannot be modified, others can. That's why it's so important to identify possible causes and contributors. By changing modifiable factors—perhaps eliminating a medication that causes drowsiness or getting hot flashes under control to achieve a good night's sleep—women may be able to improve mental abilities considerably.

Chemotherapy: The Direct Effects

Studies of the brain show that women who experience verbal declines, such as trouble with speech and word fluency, also exhibit sluggishness called *hypometabolism* in corresponding areas of the brain. At the 2003 meeting of the American Society of Clinical Oncology, a small but intriguing study from UCLA was presented on twelve women in their early fifties who were evaluated using positron-emission tomography (PET) scans of the brain, which measure metabolic activity. Most of the women had a college education. Two had received local therapy only for breast cancer, and two had never been treated for breast cancer. Eight had received chemotherapy; four of those eight also received tamoxifen. These eight women had experienced declines in verbal abilities following chemotherapy, including word fluency.

All twelve women underwent PET brain imaging of twenty-six distinct brain regions, followed by neuropsychological tests. In the women who received chemotherapy, PET imaging demonstrated a decrease in metabolic activity in two regions of the brain. These areas are involved with verbal memory for new stimuli, speech, and verbal fluency (the ability to express oneself). Women who were treated with both chemotherapy and tamoxifen demonstrated the greatest decrease in brain activity in those two regions. These imaging findings were not observed in the four women who did not receive chemotherapy.

How might chemotherapy affect the brain? Currently, there are theories but no firm conclusions. Exposure to chemotherapy may directly or indirectly cause cognitive changes in some women.

In small amounts, various chemotherapeutic agents may cross the blood-brain barrier. Once in the brain, the agent may prove toxic to neurons (nerves) and particularly to synapses. The *synapse* is the area where one nerve transmits chemical signals called *neurotransmitters* to the next nerve.

Alternatively, chemotherapeutic agents may work indirectly by first creating unstable molecules called *free radicals*, which could damage the nervous system.

Another indirect mechanism may involve the body's own immune system. Chemotherapy affects the immune system and could potentially affect intercellular messengers called *cytokines* that modulate the body's immune response, such as by amplifying it. Cytokines are produced by several types of cells and include interleukins, interferons, and lymphokines. Affected cytokines might establish a neurotoxic environment that in turn affects the brain. Animal studies offer some support for this theory. Animals treated with the cytokine interleukin-1 (IL-1) exhibit fatigue, a need for increased time sleeping, and less interest in their environments. In another study, animals exposed to the interferon class of cytokines exhibited a decrease in activity that suggests some impairment in learning and depressed mood.

Other theories draw from research on humans treated for heart disease or stroke. These people experience inflammation and damage to the lining of the blood vessels. Chemotherapy may cause similar damage to the blood vessel walls in the brain, predisposing small vessels particularly to develop clots called *micro-infarcts*. These tiny clots deprive small regions of the brain of needed oxygen. An irritated blood vessel lining also may more readily enable chemotherapy drugs to cross the blood-brain barrier.

Genetic influences could modulate any of these potential variables. It may turn out that women who share certain genetic characteristics might be susceptible to the effects of chemotherapy through a given pathway, while those with a different makeup are not affected. In 2003 a study of patients given chemotherapy to treat breast cancer or lymphoma was done by the Dartmouth-Hitchcock Medical Center. The researchers found that those who carried a modification of the APOE gene scored lower in tests of visual memory and spatial ability compared with those who did not.

Other Medications: Possible Interactions

Did you take narcotic medications or a drug to help control nausea or vomiting during your breast cancer treatment? Are you taking an antidepressant? If so, you're certainly in good company, because these supportive medications can ease side effects considerably.

Yet many of the helpful medications commonly used during and after chemotherapy are able to cross the blood-brain barrier and thus are active in the central nervous system. Narcotics may be prescribed after a surgical procedure for pain control. Antiemetics such as ondansetron hydrochloride (Zofran) and steroids such as prednisone are prescribed during chemotherapy to minimize nausea and vomiting. The use of antidepressants may predate a breast cancer diagnosis or may be introduced as a new medication during a time of heightened stress.

These medications can be sedating, causing fatigue and drowsiness, or may contribute to anxiety, agitation, depression, and insomnia, all of which may compromise mental sharpness and reaction time. When alcohol is combined with narcotics, antiemetics, or antidepressants, such side effects can be boosted further.

Usually, the effects of these drugs are short-lived. Once you stop taking them, fogginess stemming from the medication should begin to lift relatively soon. Meantime, rather than being stoic and forgoing medications that can help you get through your breast treatments more comfortably, I recommend temporarily cutting back on your daily routine to accommodate any dampening of mental abilities.

It is also worthwhile to periodically review your medication list with your doctor, nurse, or pharmacist. Perhaps certain drugs could safely be discontinued or exchanged for other medications with fewer side effects. Often, one class of antidepressants can be substituted for another, for example. If one does not agree with you, speak with your doctor about alternatives.

Hormonal Therapies

Sometimes, the problem lies not with supportive drugs but with the actual therapies used in breast cancer treatment. Tamoxifen, a selective estrogen receptor modulator (SERM), is given to women with hormone receptor–positive cancers. SERMs bind to estrogen receptors in the breast, the uterus, bones, the brain, and other sites throughout the body. By competing with estrogens circulating in the bloodstream that would otherwise attach to the receptor, SERMs lower the amount of estrogen that certain cells receive.

In the brain, tamoxifen may behave as an estrogen antagonist; that is, it may bind to estrogen cell receptors so that the brain perceives there is less estrogen in its environment. To date, there are limited data published on tamoxifen. Some data do not support the theory that it might cause a decline in cognitive function. Other studies suggest that tamoxifen could cause a decline in visuospatial performance key to hand-eye coordination and trigger difficulties with a narrative writing task as well as prompt more frequent doctor visits for memory problems. Of note, though, one small study using proton magnetic resonance spectroscopy to assess brain metabolism in women ages sixty-five to eighty suggests that tamoxifen may protect the brain to some degree.

Another hormonal therapy, anastrozole (Arimidex), significantly reduces the circulating estrogen level. It does so by blocking the enzyme aromatase, which converts hormones from the adrenal glands to estrogen. Anastrozole, one of a promising new class of drugs called *aromatase inhibitors*, thus cuts down production of estrogen. It is approved to treat postmenopausal women with early-stage breast cancer that is ER+.

An exploratory study from the United Kingdom looked at cognitive tests performed on ninety-four women during a well-known breast cancer treatment trial in which women received anastrozole, tamoxifen, or both treatments. These were compared with cognitive test results from thirty-five women who had not been treated for breast cancer. The women receiving anastrozole, tamoxifen, or a combination of the medications had scored significantly lower on the verbal memory task of recalling a paragraph. They also scored lower in manual dexterity speed compared with the women who were taking neither of the medications. The results remained constant when reanalyzed for past use of hormone replacement therapy. The trial was not designed to evaluate how much of the reduced test score may have been due to either medication alone.

Fatigue

Fatigue, which plagues many women during breast cancer treatments, can certainly drain brain power. Prior to my own treatment, I slept merely six hours or so a night and could not remember the last time I napped. I was in good physical condition before starting chemotherapy and managed to shoehorn in a workout at my gym on most days. After a five-year surgical residency with many sleepless nights, I was well used to working through fatigue.

Although this side effect of chemotherapy was described to me, the extent of my fatigue caught me off guard. During my treatment, I slept twelve to fourteen hours a night. I napped for several hours each afternoon. Still, I did not feel refreshed. Instead, I dragged myself through the day and on many occasions could barely muster the energy to operate the remote as I lay on the couch.

I have since learned that my experience is not at all unusual and that doctor after doctor consistently recommends the same treatment for fatigue. This is a time to give in to fatigue, they say. This is a time to rest and sleep. During and immediately after chemotherapy when fatigue is most intense, the body is channeling its energy into repairing normal cells in the body that were affected by chemotherapy. Sleep and rest help with this repair process.

Remedies for Fatigue

Because many factors can contribute to fatigue—such as anemia, depression, or poor appetite and nutrition—you should discuss the problem and possible solutions with your nurse or doctor. You may also wish to try the suggested solutions that follow:

- **Exercise and be active.** Rest is essential, but it is also important to try to be active during times when your energy level rises a bit. That might mean taking a walk in the early morning or whenever you feel most energetic. Do more if you feel the urge. Some of my patients have reported that running, biking, inline skating, and playing tennis were not only possible at times during the course of their chemotherapy but lifted their spirits and helped them feel more in control of their lives while toning their bodies. A sedentary lifestyle can beget fatigue. Exercise, which is recommended to help counter fatigue, also helps in minimizing weight gain, muscle wasting, and bone loss. According to the National Cancer Institute, some small, preliminary studies suggest that light to moderate walking or other activities may boost energy, mood, and flagging appetite, as well as having other benefits.

- **Sleep tight.** Not being able to obtain a good night's sleep can contribute greatly to fatigue. Physicians in training now have their workweek limited to eighty hours by federal law for good reason. Adequate sleep facilitates an alert mind, and fuzzy thinking can accompany fatigue. Medications, menopausal hot flashes, and general anxiety over your diagnosis and treatment all can interfere with a good night's sleep. That, in turn, affects your mental alertness and sharpness during the day. For premenopausal women, chemotherapy can initiate the abrupt onset of menopause. With plummeting estrogen levels, hot flashes can be severe and can disrupt sleep. Women on tamoxifen may experience hot flashes, too. Periodically review your medications and emotional well-being with your physician to pinpoint other factors that will help you sleep tight. Recommendations for minimizing hot flashes and optimizing sleep are described in Chapter 14.

- **Identify and address other issues.** Caffeine and alcohol can disrupt sleep cycles. Anxiety, stress, and depression can be addressed through relaxation techniques, exercise, counseling or therapy, or medications. Anemia, a decrease in the red blood cells that carry oxygen in the blood, is a common side effect of chemotherapy and can be treated. Your physician may also check and, if necessary, treat you for an underactive thyroid gland (hypothyroidism), which is fairly common in women. Nutritional deficiencies, diabetes, heart disease, and other conditions can contribute to fatigue, too.

Changes in Mood

Under many circumstances, stress, anxiety, and depression can trigger cognitive impairment. In some studies, these mood disturbances were not found to increase the cognitive changes observed with chemotherapy.

Other studies found there was a stronger correlation between cognitive decline and changes in mood, particularly anxiety and depression. If you do experience such mood changes, it's a good idea to speak with your physician and consider treatment, whether or not these mood changes are affecting memory or other mental abilities.

Menopause: Falling Estrogen Levels

In many women who have not been diagnosed with breast cancer, the decrease in estrogen and progesterone hormone levels that comes with menopause is associated with declines in attention, learning, and memory. Verbal fluency and word recall appear particularly sensitive to declines in estrogen levels. In the brain, estrogen receptors are densely concentrated in the hippocampus and amygdala, two regions involved with learning and memory. Furthermore, in animal models, estrogen has a hand in maintaining or expanding neural circuits in areas of the brain that are key to cognitive abilities.

As women get closer to the average age of menopause, which is fifty-one in America, the possibility of chemotherapy-induced menopause rises. For women receiving CMF, menopause will occur in 35 percent of women younger than thirty-five years of age. It occurs in 85 percent of women between ages thirty-five and forty-four and 94 percent of those forty-five or older. Unlike natural menopause, where hormonal levels slowly decrease over several years, chemotherapy-induced menopause produces an abrupt and rapid hormonal decline, especially in estrogen. In addition, women in their thirties or forties who still may be years away from natural menopause experience an extended, early preview of reduced circulating hormone levels, which may potentially lead to premature cognitive aging.

Studies continue to explore the potential relationship between chemotherapy, premature menopause, and declines in ovarian function. From a practical stand-point, women with a breast cancer diagnosis are strongly cautioned against taking hormone replacement therapy. Thus, hormonal decline is not a modifiable factor when a woman is pushed into early menopause by chemotherapy.

THE REAL WORLD: HOW WOMEN ARE AFFECTED

Scientific research fuels the medical community, but many women who have under-gone breast cancer treatment need no hard data on cognitive impairment. They know firsthand how these changes challenge household routines, daily tasks, career objectives, and personal lives. Simply put, forgetfulness, impaired decision-making abilities, and other cognitive changes negatively affect quality of life.

Something as simple as crossing the street may become difficult when a glitch in interpreting visual patterns occurs. A woman might stand on the street corner, looking at the traffic lights. Seeing one light that is red and another that is green, she feels pretty sure it's safe to cross. Once she leaves the safety of the sidewalk, however, a car comes zooming along, nearly hitting her.

Even if a woman finds she can often conceal deficits, concerns bubble to the surface. Are you worried that others might notice the changes? Frequently racking your mind for the right words to express a thought? Finding it impossible to con-centrate on more than one person or concept at once? Misplacing keys and other important items? Anxious about staying employed? Forgetting meetings? It's not too big a leap from here to avoiding going out with friends and colleagues and min-imizing face-to-face interactions at work.

One city dweller who often met friends for dinner began looking up restaurant menus online before venturing out. "It was just too overwhelming for me to have to read the menu, conjure up meaning from the written words, and make a selec-tion while my friends chatted about their days and asked questions about my life," she said.

Certain symptoms occur more often than others, and some symptom categories are so interrelated that a change in one will affect the other. The most frequently reported symptoms are trouble paying attention and concentrating, learning new information, and recalling recently learned information. Activities that call for multitasking lead the list of challenges. Simultaneous juggling of multiple tasks, generally routine in the past and executed without thought, now looms as an impossibility.

"At its worst," said one woman, "I was incapable of washing the dishes and carrying on a conversation with my children. I needed to stop doing the dishes, turn my body, and look directly at my son. I also found—and my son noticed this, too—that after he would say something, I would repeat it back to myself to process the information before responding to him."

Difficulty concentrating can show itself as attention fatigue. A thought can be lost in midsentence. The same passage needs to be read over and over before it is understood, then read yet again to commit it to memory. Word finding—whether for sophisticated words, short words, or common words—can stop a conversation in its tracks. Calculating a restaurant tip can be embarrassingly impossible. Problem solving can be . . . well, problematic. Even manual dexterity can be impaired, so that a woman takes longer than usual to do a task and may find herself dropping items or fumbling.

Forgetfulness and difficulty remembering planned events are common. For more than a decade, my dear friend Barbara and I have attended several productions each year of the Boston Lyric Opera. We were season ticket holders for so long that we have had front row, center seats for several years. I am well aware that these seats are not deemed first choice from an acoustic perspective; however, I enjoy seeing the facial expressions of the singers and the orchestra members in the pit (and I don't have an exacting ear for music).

Each season, I purchase our tickets and Barbara treats us to dinner before the performance. On rare occasions, when one of us is unable to make a show, we will give our tickets to a friend. Several months after my chemotherapy ended, Barbara called to catch up and see how I was doing. As the conversation was winding down, she gently inquired about the opera the preceding weekend. She had thought I had given the tickets to someone else. In point of fact, after a decade of reliably attending with her, I had totally forgotten our date.

Declines in visuospatial performance can make it hard to figure out where objects lie in relation to you or other points in space. For example, that could affect your ability to reach for the keys you dropped on the hall table, catch a ball flying toward you, or chart a course through a crowded space without bumping into people or objects. It might make you clumsier than usual or even affect your handwriting.

Another change, less often mentioned, is a shift in mental flexibility. This may manifest itself as irritability with others. "Sometimes, even the smallest unplanned change in the day is too overwhelming to cope with," admitted one woman. "If that change involves a person, he or she may be the recipient of cross words or a roll of my eyes and shake of my head."

Handling the Challenges

The following tips have been gleaned from the 2003 Banff meeting and strategies from other sources on strengthening memory. Right now, although research continues, many recommendations focus on how a woman can adapt her environment and lifestyle to address her specific challenges and ease the stress they cause.

- Structure your day and environment to minimize the need to multitask, and avoid being plunged into emergency situations that call for a quick reaction.

- Decrease your workload as much as is reasonable and feasible. At home, that might mean asking others to take on specific tasks. At work, this is trickier. Although not always possible, temporarily shortening your workdays or working fewer days may help.

- Get a good night's sleep every night. That may mean going to bed earlier and sleeping later than usual for a while.

- Make lists and remember where you put them! Putting them in a prominent place each time—clipped to the refrigerator or tacked to a special bulletin board put up for just this purpose—may help. Cross tasks off your list when you accomplish them.

- Jot down all important information, even where you parked your car.

- Use a handheld organizer or a simple personal calendar to keep track of plans and meetings.

- Use a tape recorder for important conversations so that you can go over the information as often as you like.

- Try focusing strategies. If you're having trouble in one area, such as misplacing your keys, visualize what you are doing every time you put them down.

- Repeat new information. After reading or hearing complex information, repeat it to yourself in your own words several times to reinforce it in your mind.

Talk with other women who are experiencing similar problems. Knowing that you're one of many and gaining useful tips from others negotiating the same challenges can effectively reduce your stress. Be reassured that the symptoms do improve. Many, perhaps even all, will resolve with the passage of time.

HONING THE STUDIES

Research in this field is relatively new. The ideal study on cognitive impairment has yet to be formulated, never mind launched, analyzed, and published. When reading in the newspaper about studies, you might want to keep in mind the following concerns that compromise much of the currently available data.

Baseline Testing

Once a woman is told she has breast cancer, stress descends. Stress alone can cause cognitive impairment, as underscored by a 2004 study on eighty-four breast cancer patients at the University of Texas M. D. Anderson Cancer Center. Prior to starting chemotherapy, 35 percent exhibited cognitive impairment, specifically in verbal learning and memory. Compared to tests performed on women from the general population matched for age, education, and other variables, this is a much higher percentage than expected. Stress from the diagnosis and its effect on test-taking capabilities, the cancer itself, or other factors might be at work. Ideally, baseline tests would predate cancer diagnoses. However, that's not feasible because it would require periodic testing on a subset of the population thought to be at particularly high risk for breast cancer.

Follow-Up Testing

Periodic follow-up tests would be needed, too. A study from Dartmouth-Hitchcock Medical Center of breast cancer and lymphoma survivors showed that even after five to ten years of follow-up, 39 percent of those treated with chemotherapy appeared to have cognitive deficits compared to 14 percent of those whose treatment did not include it. In an analysis of a subset of women from the Texas study who completed one-year follow-up testing, 50 percent of those who showed declines immediately after chemotherapy showed improvements one year after its completion. Follow-up tests must be designed to minimize the so-called practice effect—meaning that one becomes a good test taker, thus raising the possibility that improvements are due to practice and not to actual changes in cognitive function.

Real-World Tests

Women who report cognitive changes don't always find these reflected in formal testing results, as several studies have demonstrated. There are several possible reasons for this.

First, tests validated in people with Alzheimer's disease or brain injuries may not be appropriate for detecting subtle changes experienced by women treated for breast cancer.

Second, many women find changes crop up when they attempt to resume daily activities—running a household, returning to work, and so on—and are expected to perform multiple tasks. That's when a woman realizes that she is unable to process many pieces of information at once and is overwhelmed. A psychologist's office tends to be a quiet environment where the only focus is the test.

Third, studies can miss changes in high-functioning women if tests are measured only at a single point in time. Eighteen women underwent periodic neuropsychiatric tests before chemotherapy (baseline), six months later, and one year after completing chemotherapy in another study from the University of Texas M. D. Anderson Cancer Center. During the postchemotherapy evaluations, 46 percent of the women tested at normal limits, but when these tests were compared to their baseline evaluations, it was clear they had experienced cognitive declines that would otherwise have remained hidden.

14

HANDLING
MENOPAUSE

◉

When I was diagnosed with breast cancer, I was forty-two and had not yet entered menopause. At the time, it seemed hard to believe that I might hope to hurry that life stage along. Yet my chemotherapy-induced menopause offered important benefits. My pathology report showed estrogen receptor–positive cancer cells. When hot flashes started and my periods ceased for six months, I knew that my ovaries were producing less of the estrogen that could help fuel the growth of cancer cells. I was also aware of research suggesting that suppressing the ovaries, even temporarily, benefits women with estrogen receptor–positive breast cancers like mine.

Because 80 percent of women diagnosed with breast cancer are fifty or older, many have already passed through menopause at the time of their diagnosis. If you are among them and do not feel you need any more advice on this topic, you can skip this chapter. If you had been taking hormone replacement therapy for any reason—or if you had not reached menopause and now need advice on easing hot flashes, vaginal dryness, insomnia, or other symptoms—read on.

ANTICANCER TREATMENTS
AND MENOPAUSE

Generally, a woman is declared menopausal after a year without menstrual periods. In the United States, most women reach menopause between the ages of forty-five and fifty-five. On average, menopause occurs at fifty-one. Not every anticancer treatment prompts early menopause in women who have not yet gone through it. Radiation to the breast or chest wall, for example, will have no such effect, nor will

NEED BIRTH CONTROL?

While you might find it tempting to forgo birth control if your periods cease, think twice about doing that if you are a sexually active, heterosexual woman. Instead, choose reliable, non-hormonal birth control and use it. It's hard to know whether or when your cycle might start up again, so getting pregnant may be easier than you think. In fact, the drug tamoxifen (Nolvadex) sometimes enhances fertility in premenopausal women despite causing hot flashes that would seem to suggest just the opposite result.

Even if you're hoping to have a child after treatment, it's best to discuss this with your oncologist and let your body recover after finishing anticancer drugs. Many drugs used to combat cancer may cause birth defects if taken during the first trimester. Some stay in your system longer than others do.

breast surgery. However, chemotherapy or hormonal therapies can cause a woman's periods to stop. Called *amenorrhea*, this is a key sign of menopause. In this context, it may prove temporary or permanent, depending largely on a woman's age, the medications taken, and the dosage given. Although the data are imperfect, reports consistently show that older women are less likely than younger women to have their periods resume after treatment.

For example, a standard six-month course of the combination of cyclophosphamide (Cytoxan), methotrexate (Mexate), and 5-fluorouracil (Adrucil, abbreviated as 5-FU), called CMF, permanently prompts menopause in about 30 to 40 percent of women younger than forty, and 80 to 95 percent of those older than forty. Other data show that the combination of doxorubicin (Adriamycin) and Cytoxan, known as AC, does the same in about 5 to 15 percent of women younger than forty, and 55 to 70 percent of women older than forty.

Sometimes, periods return when chemotherapy or hormonal therapy ends. That's far more common in younger women but can happen in older women, too. Annette started having her period again roughly five years after she had finished chemotherapy. At the time, she was fifty-one and had just stopped taking tamoxifen. Another woman, who was in her early forties when diagnosed, had her periods resume within the year after she finished chemotherapy even though she had started taking tamoxifen.

HANDLING CHANGES

If you do seem to be tipping into menopause, what sort of changes can you expect? The truth is, menopause differs from woman to woman. For some, the changes may be easily brushed aside; for others, symptoms seriously affect quality of life.

"My mother was nutty when she went through menopause," observed Audrey. Her own experience has been much easier, creating only a few truly bothersome symptoms. When awakened by hot flashes, she has trouble falling back to sleep. That's a problem, especially because she's a nurse whose beeper frequently goes off in the wee hours. During the day, Audrey fans herself frequently to cool hot flashes, and she definitely notices sudden heat waves at night. Although she keeps a window wide open, there are times when she's ready to strip off her nightgown. "My husband says, 'You couldn't have done this when we were younger?'"

The following tips can help you handle a variety of menopausal challenges.

Osteoporosis: A Long-Term Issue

One troubling, largely silent change of menopause is a speedier decline in bone density. If not addressed, this may pave a path toward osteoporosis and, eventually, debilitating fractures. No matter what your age or menopausal status, a healthy diet paired with calcium and vitamin D supplements, regular sessions of weight-bearing exercise, and in some cases, bone-saving medications are essential. Declines in bone density can occur especially rapidly with certain treatments, such as chemotherapy and the hormonal therapy anastrozole (Arimidex). Tamoxifen, by contrast, slows bone loss, particularly in the hip area. Ideally, you would have a baseline bone density test done before starting treatment. See Chapters 11 and 12 for information on nutrition and exercise, and talk with your doctor about the best approach for you.

Hot Flashes: Conventional Approaches

Like sun suddenly striking through clouds during the dog days of August, hot flashes can send a mild or major heat wave streaking across your upper body. Your heart speeds up, blood vessels dilate, skin may redden, and perspiration flows to cool you down. The sensation may dissipate quickly or stretch out for minutes; it may occur occasionally or many times a day.

Many women find hot flashes an annoying but not insurmountable bump in the road. Sometimes, however, hot flashes are severe or occur very frequently, or they may be accompanied by drenching sweats, notable palpitations (a racing, erratic heartbeat), anxiety, or confusion. Hot flashes brought on by surgically removing the ovaries or suppressing them with chemotherapy or hormonal therapy tend to be more intense than those that occur over time with natural menopause.

During the six months following chemotherapy when I was not having periods, I experienced hot flashes virtually every hour and could count on waking up a few times a night slick with sweat. My hot flashes seemed to be served with a dash of irony. When temperatures dropped well below zero last winter, I never once enjoyed a personal heat wave while trudging along the icy streets of Boston's Back Bay. My hot flashes would hold off until I entered a heated building, clad in twenty layers of winter warmth, which I would want to instantly strip off. On days when I wore makeup, I also noticed my hot flashes didn't start until I applied the finishing touches. Then the makeup would bead up on my face atop the sheen of sweat.

Fortunately, hot flashes do not last forever. It may seem that way, though, especially if you are taking tamoxifen or anastrozole for five years after chemotherapy. While these medications successfully reduce recurrence and new cancers in the opposite breast in women with early-stage breast cancer (and are also used for women with advanced cancer), they often trigger hot flashes.

Hormone Replacement Therapy

The estrogen in hormone replacement therapy (HRT) relieves hot flashes, possibly by tinkering with the body's temperature and sweating thresholds via hormonal pathways. Because estrogen appears to speed the growth of some breast cancer cells, though, this is a controversial option for survivors. Recently, a randomized trial of women who had completed chemotherapy and radiation after breast cancer surgery, some of whom were taking tamoxifen, underscored these fears. The researchers reported in the *Lancet* in 2004 that they had halted the study early after twenty-six women in the group receiving HRT had a recurrence or new breast cancer compared to seven women with a new cancer or recurrence in the group not given HRT. A few earlier observational studies—which do not carry the scientific clout of randomized trials—recorded no effect on recurrence rates.

As you might know, the Women's Health Initiative's long-term trials of hormone replacement came to an abrupt halt before completion because of increases in breast cancer, cardiovascular disease, and blood clots in women taking estrogen plus progestin and increases in strokes in women taking estrogen alone or estrogen plus progestin. The benefits—fewer hip fractures for both forms of HRT and fewer cases of colon cancer in women who took estrogen plus progestin—simply didn't outweigh the risks for most women. Follow-up reports slated for 2007 may tell us more.

Cooling Down Hot Flashes

The following options may offer some reprieve from hot flashes. Try them alone or in combination (also see the information under "Insomnia" later in this chapter). If you still cannot find relief, speak with your doctors about whether a low dose of HRT for a short while makes sense in your situation.

- **Trace the triggers.** Keep a diary for a week. Note when you have hot flashes, how long they last, and what you were wearing and doing, as well as what you've been eating and drinking. Alcohol, caffeine, spicy foods, stress, and heat in general—from a shower, a hot tub, a sauna, or the atmosphere—trip off hot flashes for some women. Try avoiding your triggers.

- **Wait it out.** Often, it simply takes your body some time to adjust to a medication that affects hormone levels. Hot flashes due to tamoxifen, for example, may lessen in intensity and frequency over three to six months. Luz, who took anastrozole for five years as part of a clinical trial, noticed that her hot flashes subsided somewhat over time.

- **Dress lightly, carry cold water, and wield a fan.** Dressing in layers, especially during the winter, allows you to peel down or open an outer shirt, as needed. Avoid turtlenecks, which trap heat. Sips from a cold water bottle and cooling breezes from an inexpensive paper fan or a handheld battery-operated fan or a tabletop model can help.

- **Relax.** Daily sessions of relaxation therapy may ease hot flashes, too, as described later in the sidebar "Relax: It's Good for You."

- **Consider medications.** When all else fails, certain medications may bridge the gap. Potential side effects may outweigh benefits, however. Some, though not all, of the medications may dampen sexual desire.

  - Venlafaxine (Effexor), an antidepressant, reportedly cooled off some breast cancer survivors whose hot flashes were tracked by filling out a daily questionnaire in a 2002 trial of 102 women. At the end of the study, daily hot flash activity—that is, the number of hot flashes and a score combining number and severity—was averaged. Taking 75 milligrams a day reduced hot flashes by 60 percent within four weeks. A placebo reduced hot flashes by 27 percent. Venlafaxine may cause short-term nausea, drowsiness, dry mouth, and dizziness.

  - Fluoxetine (Prozac), another antidepressant, when given at 20 milligrams a day, lessened frequency and severity of hot flashes by 50 percent, according to a 2002 study of eighty-one breast cancer survivors who recorded both measures in a daily diary. Women taking a placebo experienced a 36 percent reduction in hot flashes. Fluoxetine may cause nausea, diminished libido, dry mouth, weight gain, and headaches.

  - Gabapentin (Neurontin), an antiseizure drug, given at 900 milligrams a day reduced the frequency and severity of hot flashes by 54 percent versus 29 percent for those taking a placebo. Reported in 2003, this study of fifty-nine postmenopausal women who did not have breast cancer required participants to track hot flashes in a daily diary.

  - Megestrol acetate (Megace), an anticancer drug, given at 40 milligrams a day cut the frequency of hot flashes in half in 74 percent of participants in a short-term 1994 study of ninety-seven women with a history of breast cancer and sixty-six men with prostate cancer treated with androgen-deprivation therapy. A follow-up study suggested the medication continued to offer relief in patients who kept taking it for approximately three years at a lower dose of usually 20 milligrams a day. Megace may cause chills, increases in appetite and weight, vaginal bleeding, and symptoms of carpal tunnel syndrome.

  - Medroxyprogesterone (Depo-Provera), a progestin sometimes employed for birth control at lower doses, was compared to Megace in a 2002 study of seventy-one women with a history of breast cancer who recorded hot flash frequency and severity daily. One group received injections of 500 milligrams of medroxyprogesterone every other week for six weeks; the other group took 40 milligrams a day of Megace. There was an 86 percent reduction in hot flashes on average at week six with no significant difference between the drugs. After discontinuing the drugs, 89 percent of those who responded to medroxyprogesterone still experienced relief at twenty-four weeks compared with 45 percent of those who had taken Megace.

- Clonidine (Catapres), a high blood pressure medication, is probably the most widely prescribed nonhormonal treatment for hot flashes. Yet trials suggest that the magnitude of relief offered does not outweigh possible side effects, which include drowsiness, dry mouth, constipation, and insomnia.

Hot Flashes: Natural Approaches

So-called natural approaches to menopausal symptoms include vitamin E, soy, black cohosh, red clover, evening primrose oil, and dong quai, an ingredient in many Chinese herbal remedies. Some of these remedies, such as soy and red clover, are classified as phytoestrogens (plant estrogens). Black cohosh, however, appears to exert leverage through other means.

Natural or not, dietary supplements may deliver variable doses of the ingredients stated on the label. While the Food and Drug Administration oversees safety and efficacy of medications, it does not do the same for supplements.

Vitamin E

Like most natural remedies for hot flashes, vitamin E has not been widely evaluated in clinical trials. One study of one hundred breast cancer survivors experiencing menopausal symptoms had women take 800 I.U. of vitamin E each day for four weeks and then take a daily placebo look-alike for four weeks. According to the researchers, the women averaged only one fewer hot flash a day while taking vitamin E compared to placebos. The women reported feeling no better during the weeks taking vitamin E compared to the weeks taking placebos.

The bottom line? A 2004 analysis of nineteen vitamin E trials in which many participants had a variety of ailments other than breast cancer has raised some doubts about the safety of high doses because of a rise in mortality rate among those who regularly took 150 I.U. or more of vitamin E. Not all experts agree with these findings, however. If you wish to try taking 800 I.U. of vitamin E a day, speak with your doctor about potential risks and benefits and find out whether any other medications that you take, such as the blood-thinner warfarin (Coumadin, Warfilone), might interact with it. Vitamin E is a fat-soluble vitamin, which means it can build up in your body, so it is important to check your multivitamin to see how much it offers before adding another supplement.

Black Cohosh

No dearth of studies on black cohosh exists, but lack of consistency in design and results makes it hard to evaluate its effectiveness and safety, especially for women who have had breast cancer. An analysis of controlled trials on a variety of alternative products touted for their ability to quash menopausal symptoms appeared in the *Annals of Internal Medicine* in 2002. In ten trials of herbal products—including ginseng, red clover, dong quai, evening primrose oil, and an herbal mixture—only black cohosh appeared to cut the intensity and frequency of hot flashes. The following year, a review of studies in *Menopause: The Journal of the North American Menopause Society* that considered eighteen randomized clinical trials of several herbal products concluded there was no truly convincing evidence for any of the treatments. The investigators noted that evidence favoring Remifemin, a widely sold black cohosh preparation, was promising but limited by the study designs. According to GlaxoSmithKline, which manufactures Remifemin, this supplement delivers a standard dose equivalent to 20 milligrams of black cohosh per tablet, though there is no independent agency that confirms standard dose. Dosages of other black cohosh supplements may differ.

Test-tube studies show black cohosh does not hook up with estrogen receptors on cells. Some intriguing research suggests it acts on the hypothalamus, a part of the brain that regulates hormones and body temperature. Lab studies show black cohosh can bind to serotonin receptors in the hypothalamus—the very same receptors targeted by certain antidepressants, which relieve hot flashes in some women.

Because it is not considered estrogenic, black cohosh theoretically might be safe for women with breast cancer to use in quelling hot flashes. Recently, though, a preliminary study reported at a meeting of the American Association for Cancer

LOOKING FOR ALTERNATIVES?
Current evidence on alternative therapies for menopausal symptoms is available to the public through the National Center for Complementary and Alternative Medicine (http://nccam .nih.gov or 888-644-6226), which is part of the National Institutes of Health.

Research found that black cohosh increased the risk of cancer spread in mice bred specifically to develop breast tumors. Whether this would be true in women is not known, but a few cases of liver toxicity in humans have raised another concern.

The bottom line? Currently, safety has only been assessed for six months in healthy women, although two yearlong National Institutes of Health trials in the same population are under way at this writing. Talk with your doctor about how the risks and benefits of black cohosh stack up for you.

Phytoestrogens

Red clover, dong quai, and soy contain weak plant estrogens called *phytoestrogens*. Right now, there are more questions than answers concerning phytoestrogens. If they quell hot flashes by acting like an estrogen in the body, might they also fuel the growth of breast cancer cells, at least in some women? Could a phytoestrogen like soy interfere with tamoxifen, a drug that blocks the action of estrogen in the breast? Might women react differently to phytoestrogens based on individual body chemistry or the features of their particular breast cancers? Will tablets that do not contain the full spectrum of chemicals found in the plant affect the body in the same way?

The bottom line? Currently, there is insufficient definitive research to answer these questions satisfactorily. Cancer experts usually suggest erring on the side of caution. Red clover and dong quai appear to have little effect on hot flashes anyway, as noted earlier, so skipping them may be no loss. Studies disagree over whether eating several servings a day of soy helps with mild hot flashes. However, eating a lot of soy or taking soy supplements is not advised. Occasionally eating soy as part of a healthy diet is probably fine.

Vaginal Changes

The vagina is a wondrously pliable organ with plump walls richly supplied with blood vessels. Declines in estrogen due to menopause cause vaginal walls to thin and become drier as secretions diminish. Itching and burning that are generally uncomfortable, but especially so during sex, may occur. Thinner vaginal walls are more easily irritated, so much so that some women find intercourse painful or notice light bleeding that shows up as spotting after sex. Sometimes, vaginal membranes become inflamed, a condition called *atrophic vaginitis.*

In response to less estrogen, the vagina also becomes less acidic and more alkaline, which can encourage the overgrowth of organisms that normally exist quite peaceably inside you. Sometimes, this leads to a vaginal infection, especially if cancer treatment suppresses your immune system. Symptoms include unusual discharge with a distinct odor (fishiness, yeast), burning, or itchiness. An odorless, thin, clear discharge can also be an annoying side effect of certain medications, such as tamoxifen.

Needless to say, none of these changes will boost your sex life or general happiness. You needn't sit still for them, though. There are a number of ways to address problems that may crop up.

Discuss Solutions

Report any dryness, discomfort, spotting, or unusual discharge to your doctor or nurse, so she or he can consider possible causes and suggest appropriate solutions. Some women feel quite comfortable talking with their oncologist about gynecological and sexual concerns; others may prefer to speak to a nurse on their cancer care team or their gynecologist.

Add Moisture

Some women swear by personal lubricants and moisturizers. Others swear at them, disliking the drippiness of certain products and possible need for panty-liners or not liking the chemical approach. Try a few different products to see what works well for you. Your doctor or nurse may be able to supply samples.

- Water-based personal lubricants, such as Astroglide or K-Y Silk-E, can be applied before sex or during foreplay and at other times when dryness is bothersome. These products offer temporary relief.

Urinary Tract Infections

Diminished estrogen also thins and dries urinary tract tissues, which can contribute to urinary tract infections (UTIs). Symptoms include pain, burning, or irritation while urinating; frequent, urgent need to urinate; and sometimes blood in the urine. Although an infection usually occurs in the bladder or the urethra (the tube that carries urine from the body), back pain and fever suggest the infection may have spread to the kidneys. Report any of these symptoms to your nurse or doctor so that the problem can be properly diagnosed. Usually, antibiotics are used to stop an infection and a painkiller may be given for discomfort.

Estring may help prevent recurrent UTIs. If you wish to skip prescription preventatives, you might try drinking ten ounces of cranberry juice a day. According to a small Harvard study, this makes the bladder more acidic and therefore less hospitable to certain bacteria. This may help prevent bladder infections in women at high risk for them. Wiping yourself from front to back will help keep bacteria that normally live in the digestive tract from making the small jump to the urinary tract where they can cause an infection.

- Moisturizers, such as Replens and Silken Secret, draw moisture to the vaginal walls. When regularly applied a few times a week, these products help relieve dryness and discomfort but may not be sufficiently slippery during sex. (If not, add a personal lubricant.)

Consider Prescription Products

Prescription products that deliver very low doses of estrogen directly to the vagina help thicken vaginal walls and boost lubrication but will not quell hot flashes. Very little of the estrogen is thought to reach the bloodstream. Discuss prescription products with your cancer care team.

- Estring, a flexible plastic ring that sits at the top of the vagina around the cervix, gradually releases a very low dose of estrogen. A slight rise in blood estrogen occurs during the first twenty-four hours after inserting the ring. Many experts believe this is unlikely to affect breast cancer. At Dana-Farber Cancer Institute, Estring has been used for years to help reverse uncomfortable vaginal changes in women who have breast cancer. This is a key reason why I chose to try it after suffering several urinary tract infections when my periods had stopped during the first six months after chemotherapy (see the sidebar "Urinary Tract Infections"). Once in place, the ring cannot be felt at all and is effective for three months. The first time I used Estring, I had my gynecologist place it to be sure it was in the right spot. After that I was able to remove and replace it myself. The sensation of dryness that had been bothering me disappeared within a few weeks. Overall, I'd say this solution worked for me, although not every woman who tries it will agree.

- Vaginal creams or tablets containing a very low dose of estrogen are also available. Because variable amounts of the estrogen in these products can be absorbed into the bloodstream, Dana-Farber Cancer Institute does not recommend them.

Keep Trying

"Use it or lose it" is a classic phrase where sex is concerned. Sexual play boosts vaginal blood flow, which increases lubrication. Regular intercourse helps keep vaginal walls elastic, too. It's possible, though not certain, that similar actions, such as with a vibrator, might do the same. If you need a nudge toward sex—with a partner or by yourself—consider this a prescription.

Insomnia

When insomnia occurs, sleep may seem impossible to attain or simply not refreshing. While sometimes attributed to hormonal changes of aging and menopause, the roots of insomnia can extend in several other directions as well. Worries about breast cancer or other concerns often keep sleep at bay for hours or make it hard for a woman to fall back to sleep if she awakens. Naps taken during the day can impinge on lengthier sleep sessions at night. Hot flashes also can wake a sleeper, as I can personally attest, especially if the sudden rise in temperature leads to soaked nightclothes and sheets. Occasionally, insomnia may be a side effect of a medication that helps quell cancer cells, such as trastuzumab (Herceptin).

Consider what might be prompting your insomnia before trying these tips:

- Accept fears as normal at this point and explore ways to handle them. Speak with an oncology social worker or another mental health professional, or join a support group in person or online (see Chapter 2). It may help to set aside a

RELAX: IT'S GOOD FOR YOU

Relaxation techniques help ease stress, tension, and anxiety. They can help you slip off to sleep more easily and may cool down hot flashes a bit. Tests and treatments may also seem less upsetting if you consciously try to relax. When practiced regularly, relaxation techniques may offer other benefits, too, as described next. Three easy approaches follow.

The Relaxation Response

Chronic stress boosts blood pressure and the risk of heart disease and may also suppress the immune system. Landmark research done by Dr. Herbert Benson, a cardiologist who founded the Mind/Body Medical Institute in Boston, shows that inducing a deep state of relaxation helps erase many of the effects of chronic stress. Some women find it has an effect on hot flashes, too. A two-month study of women bothered by tamoxifen-induced hot flashes found that a group who practiced a relaxation technique daily had significantly fewer hot flashes than usual. Meanwhile, the intensity of hot flashes increased for a control group of women who did not receive relaxation training. Here is one step-by-step way to induce the relaxation response:

1. **Choose a word or phrase to help you focus.** Silently repeat a word, sound, prayer, or phrase (such as "one," "peace," "Om," or "breathing in calm"). You may close your eyes if you like or focus your gaze upon an object.
2. **Adopt a passive attitude.** Disregard distracting thoughts or concerns about how well you're doing. Anytime your attention drifts, simply say, "Oh, well," to yourself and return to silently repeating your focus word or phrase.
3. **Now slowly relax your muscles, moving your attention gradually from your face down your body to your feet.** Breathe easily and naturally while using your chosen phrase for ten to twenty minutes. After you finish, remain quiet for a minute or so with your eyes closed. If you are doing this to relax yourself in bed, you can allow yourself to drift off to sleep. Otherwise, open your eyes and continue to remain quiet for a minute before standing up.
4. **Practice daily to reap the full health benefits (or use as needed to relax).** Try to meditate for ten to twenty minutes or longer, preferably at a specific time of day.

Paced Breathing

According to *Mind over Menopause*, which Dr. Benson coauthored with Leslee Kagan and Bruce Kessel, paced breathing done for fifteen minutes twice a day may help relieve hot

(continued)

flashes. To learn this technique, you should first practice breathing deeply. When you do so, the air coming in through your nose fully fills your lungs, and your lower abdomen should actually rise slightly. The first few times you try this, place your hand beneath your navel so you can feel the gentle rise and fall of your belly as you breathe. Sit or lie down comfortably. Breathe in slowly while silently counting to five. Breathe out slowly while silently counting to five. This technique can be used whenever a hot flash starts.

Breath Focus

Sit or lie down comfortably. Blend deep breathing with helpful imagery and a focus word or phrase that will help you relax. Imagine that the air you breathe in washes peace, calm, and healing into your body. As you breathe out, imagine that the air leaving your body carries tension and anxiety away with it. Inhale, saying to yourself, "Breathing in peace, calm, and healing." Exhale, saying to yourself, "Breathing out tension and anxiety."

specific time during the day to air worries instead of continually trying to swallow fears, which may then reappear when you feel most vulnerable, such as at night.

- If you experience soaking hot flashes, keep a change or two of nightclothes handy and perhaps even a folded sheet that you can slip beneath yourself so you needn't rouse yourself much to find dry bedding. A fan clipped near you or a cool, damp washcloth you can apply as needed may help, too. These suggestions won't solve the problem but may make dealing with it a bit easier. Also try the other solutions for dealing with hot flashes.

- Relaxation tapes or techniques, such as invoking the relaxation response using self-hypnosis or biofeedback, or tightening and relaxing muscles progressively from head to toes (*progressive muscle relaxation*), may ease your entry to sleep or help you fall back to sleep.

- Inactivity often contributes to trouble sleeping, so try to be active during the day if possible. Even a brief walk may help. Late afternoon exercise may encourage deeper sleep, according to the National Center on Sleep Disorders Research, although it's best to avoid strenuous exercise for three to four hours before going to bed.

- Practice good sleep habits. Get up at the same time each day. Limit caffeinated beverages during the day and avoid alcohol and caffeine within several hours of bedtime. Don't smoke, especially near bedtime or in the middle of the night, because nicotine is a stimulant. A light bedtime snack, but not a heavy meal, may make you sleepy. A pleasantly dark, quiet bedroom kept at a comfortable temperature fosters sleep. Keep naps short and preferably finish napping by midafternoon.

- Make your bedroom a haven for sleep and sex, not the spot for restless tossing and turning. If you truly can't sleep, it may be best to curl up elsewhere to read a book, listen to calming music, or watch TV.

- Review medications with your doctor to see if any drugs you take might cause insomnia, and find out whether adjustments are possible.

- Discuss sleep medications with your doctor.

Sexual Desire

Sexual desire waxes and wanes for many reasons. Surely, a breast cancer diagnosis and the varied trials of treatment could be among them. So, too, could vaginal changes due to menopause. Ways to cope with vaginal changes are discussed earlier in this chapter, and suggestions for handling dips in desire can be found in Chapter 16.

Skin

Skin changes, such as wrinkles, fine lines, blotches, broken capillaries, and dry patches, usually owe a tip of the hat to many factors, including tobacco use, sun exposure, and aging. Smoking, for example, harms blood vessels that bring oxygen and nutrients to the skin and may damage underlying fibers like collagen that give skin its elasticity, too. Some research notes that less water is apparent in the skin of smokers. Sun exposure also breaks down collagen. Over time, it leaves blotchy, uneven pigmentation in its wake. With age, the skin's ability to retain water and produce oil diminishes.

Skin changes can also be accelerated by chemotherapy and hormonal therapy, as well as by an earlier than usual menopause that is sometimes prompted by these treatments. Estrogen levels seem to affect collagen and may contribute to dry skin, too, although this is less certain. Estrogen may also help the skin retain fluid, which makes it appear plumper and less wrinkled.

Whether wrinkles, fine lines, blotches, or other skin changes are due to menopause, chemotherapy, sun exposure, or another cause, there are plenty of ways to combat them if you choose to do so. The options range from moisturizers and cover-ups to skin peels. See Chapter 8 for more information.

Weight Gain

Stepping on the scale alarms many women, but weight gain tends to be an especially tricky issue for women undergoing breast cancer treatments because fat tissue, when overly abundant, can be a significant source of estrogen after menopause. And, as we know, chemotherapy and some other treatments for women with breast cancer may push a woman into menopause earlier than usual.

A study published in the *American Journal of Preventive Medicine* in 2004 offers us some information about midlife weight gain. Study subjects included 2,850 white women and 711 African American women who were ages fifty-one to sixty-one. Over the course of eight years, average weight gain among the white women was roughly four pounds. However, 10 percent gained eleven to twenty-two pounds and 4 percent gained more than twenty-two pounds. Over the same span of time, average weight gain among the African American women was a little bit more than two pounds; however, 11.5 percent of these women gained eleven to twenty-two pounds and 7.9 percent gained more than twenty-two pounds.

While weight gain in midlife is not believed to be a direct result of hormonal changes or menopause or even age, it is probably tied to a variety of factors, including the fact that older women tend to be less physically active. If you continue taking in the same number of daily calories while doing less daily activity, the pounds will slowly accumulate. Furthermore, with less physical activity, muscle thinning ever so slowly occurs. Muscle metabolizes calories twice as efficiently as fat does. Less muscle combined with a constant daily calorie intake further accelerates weight gain.

Certainly, hormonal factors play into weight distribution. In addition to estrogen, every woman's body also has small amounts of male steroid hormones called *androgens*. Although androgens decline with age, estrogen declines to a greater degree. At menopause—whether induced by chemotherapy or the natural course of life—the marked shift in the proportion of androgen to estrogen can change the distribution of body fat so that some women thicken around the waist. Unfortunately, the layer of abdominal fat that can change a pear-shaped figure to more of an apple shape is linked with a rise in heart disease, diabetes, and other health problems.

My experience has been that keeping my weight in a healthy range truly has been a battle since chemotherapy started. Perhaps that's not surprising. Research shows that, on average, roughly 85 percent of women gain a bit more than five pounds during chemotherapy. A healthy forty-year-old woman who receives chemotherapy experiences a 2.5 percent boost in body fat within a year—the equivalent of what would normally happen over the course of a decade. This often is compounded by a loss in muscle mass, because during chemotherapy, many women simply do not feel well and are less physically active. Less muscle means calories are not burned as efficiently.

Whether tamoxifen might add pounds or not is debatable and may be highly individual. A large trial of women at high risk for breast cancer showed no difference in weight gain between the group that received tamoxifen and the control group given a placebo. Yet many women on tamoxifen feel convinced that the drug is one cause of added pounds.

The underlying reasons for creeping weight gain or stalled attempts at weight loss are not completely understood. Inactivity stemming from the fatigue that can accompany chemotherapy or during recovery from surgery, frequent snacks to help keep nausea at bay or quiet a ravenous hunger tripped off by steroids, and hormonal changes that prompt menopause may all have a hand in it. Then, too, aging brings some loss in muscle tissue. *Hypothyroidism* (an underactive thyroid gland) is a medical problem that slows metabolism and prompts general sluggishness and fatigue. It is also one more reason why some women gain weight. According to the Thyroid Foundation of America, about 10 percent of all women experience signs of hypothyroidism by age fifty; by age sixty, that rises to 17 percent. It is not unreasonable to ask your treatment team whether you need to be tested for this.

When my periods ceased because of chemotherapy, the scale crept upward. I had seen a nutritionist, who offered me many tips on making changes in my diet during treatment. I ate sensibly and truly watched my portions. During the course of my chemotherapy, when I could rise from the couch, I took a walk with my pedometer strapped on or went to the gym. Yet, only when my periods resumed did the weight start to fly off again. It's true that my energy had rebounded somewhat, too, but this certainly made me more aware than ever of the issues breast cancer survivors face.

All of us have a hand in our own destiny. If you have had breast cancer, do your best to attain or maintain a healthy weight. Although this may be difficult, it is really important. No one can exercise or eat well for you.

Staying active and eating well are essential for every woman, whether she has had breast cancer or not. Eat the healthy foods first—with luck, they will help fill you up so that there is less room for less healthy choices. Aerobic exercise, such as regular walks, running, or biking, can help pare your waistline and burn off calories. Strength training builds muscle that burns calories more efficiently than fat. See Chapters 11 and 12 for more information on exercise and a healthy diet that can help you achieve your goals.

15

FERTILITY AND PREGNANCY AFTER BREAST CANCER

◉

When Amanda found out she had breast cancer, she was only thirty-one and had been married for less than a year. One of the biggest blows in a series of knockouts was the thought that she and her husband, Daniel, might never have the chance to have children. Amanda had a lumpectomy, radiation, and chemotherapy, and Daniel did what he could to ease the strain of this radically new life. Afterward, Amanda began taking tamoxifen (Nolvadex) to lessen the risk of recurrences and new cancers but experienced unusually marked side effects, which made it hard for her to stay on the medication. Gradually, and with great trepidation, she and her husband began to talk seriously again about having children.

"He really wanted to move forward and I was scared to death," she said. "We had these talks: What happens if the cancer comes back and I don't make it? Are you ready to be a single parent? What happens if you have to make a choice between me and the baby?"

The two also talked with Amanda's general practitioner, who was awfully worried about the idea, and her oncologist, who helped her consider the minimal available research most relevant to her circumstances. Eventually, said Amanda, she and her husband did indeed decide to move forward. Half a year later, they learned she was pregnant. Slightly less than nine months after that, the two of them welcomed a wondrous, healthy baby girl to the world.

By far, most women diagnosed with breast cancer will never have to frame the questions that Amanda faced. After all, the vast majority of women are fifty or older when they first hear that diagnosis. Yet according to the most recent figures available from the American Cancer Society, an estimated 1,000 women under thirty, 10,500 women in their thirties, and 35,500 women in their forties were first diagnosed with invasive breast cancer in 2003. Additionally, an estimated 14,800 women spread over those age groups learned they had breast cancer in situ, such as ductal carcinoma in situ. Embedded in these diagnoses for those who may have wished to have a child or more children was an extra layer of hurt and shock.

Once a woman has had breast cancer, concerns about fertility and pregnancy rightly mount. Will treatments cause infertility? Can anything be done to protect against this? If a woman is able to get pregnant after breast cancer treatment, will the rise in hormones during the pregnancy awaken dormant cancer cells or encourage the development of a new, second breast cancer? Are recurrence and survival rates different among women who have become pregnant and those who haven't? Available research is slim and certainly flawed, but this chapter touches on what little is known currently in the hope that it offers some guidance.

Choices to Make Before and During Treatment

If you know you wish to have children, discuss your options with your oncologist, preferably before treatment. Only she or he is acquainted with your specific circumstances and thus can guide you through the possibilities. Only you can decide how important having a biological child is to you and how much you are willing to potentially gamble in order to fulfill your dream. No woman who has had breast cancer should undertake pregnancy lightly. That said, some women who have weighed the risks against the strong pull of long-held hopes—and some who became pregnant accidentally—have quite joyfully gone on to have children. Others have decided to consider different options for forming the family they dream of, such as adoption or surrogacy.

Eggs, Ovaries, and Anticancer Treatments

Every baby girl starts life with hundreds of thousands of eggs stored in her ovaries. Many of these eggs will no longer be there by the time she reaches puberty. Once a girl starts having periods, hormones begin to ripen a number of eggs each month, although generally only one is released midcycle during ovulation. Eggs that never

CHEMOTHERAPY AND MENOPAUSE

Natural menopause, defined as having no periods for a year, usually happens between ages forty-five and fifty-five in America; only 4 percent of healthy women younger than forty start menopause prematurely. Chemotherapy may temporarily or permanently halt a woman's periods, however. The drug, the dose, and a woman's age make a difference here. Some data show that cyclophosphamide (Cytoxan, which is part of the combinations CMF and AC) and doxorubicin (Adriamycin, which is part of the combination AC) can cause periods to stop in some women. Yet different doses of particular drugs and rest periods in various chemotherapy regimens may play into how often this occurs. Although the data are imperfect, reports consistently show that a younger woman is less likely to have her period cease during treatment and more likely to find that if this does happen, her period will resume after treatment is completed.

For example, approximately 30 to 40 percent of women younger than forty, and 80 to 95 percent of those older than forty who receive the combination CMF (Cytoxan, methotrexate, and 5-fluorouracil) for six months permanently enter menopause. By contrast, roughly 5 to 15 percent of women younger than forty, and 55 to 70 percent of women older than forty who receive four cycles of AC (Adriamycin and Cytoxan) over three months will experience the same.

Separately, methotrexate (Mexate) and 5-fluorouracil (Adrucil; abbreviated as 5-FU) are considered somewhat less likely to affect the ovaries. Most likely, the higher total dose of Cytoxan in CMF versus AC make the difference here. Less is known about paclitaxel (Taxol) and docetaxel (Taxotere) and other chemotherapy drugs. Some research on tamoxifen suggests periods are likely to cease in less than 5 percent of women in their thirties and between 5 and 30 percent of women older than forty. Because it's hard to know whether or when your cycle might start up again, it's best to use reliable nonhormonal birth control to avoid pregnancy if you are a sexually active, heterosexual woman.

If you wonder what might happen in your case, speak with your oncologist. Sometimes, it is possible to choose a drug regimen that will be less likely to affect fertility and still successful at quashing cancer cells.

fully mature and those not fertilized by a sperm simply die off. Eggs in the ovaries die for other reasons, too, so that their numbers dwindle with each passing year.

Thirty-five is often spoken of as the tipping point after which women have increasing trouble conceiving and are more likely to experience spontaneous miscarriages. Older eggs that do get fertilized are less likely to be viable than younger eggs. Thus, the likelihood of a successful pregnancy that culminates in a healthy birth naturally declines for every woman long before she reaches menopause.

Not all anticancer treatments affect the ovaries. Surgery or radiation to the breast or chest wall will not affect fertility, although the fact that you've had breast cancer still requires that you consider how safe a pregnancy is for you. Chemotherapy may damage eggs directly and may also harm fertility by tampering with the hormones needed to start and support a pregnancy. Certain types of chemotherapy often cause a premenopausal woman's periods to cease and may put her into menopause permanently. Whether that happens depends on the drugs, the dose, and her age (see sidebar).

The hormonal therapy tamoxifen, which many women take for up to five years after other treatments, may not affect a woman's periods at all or may cause periods to become irregular or stop. Some women start to menstruate again after they stop taking tamoxifen. However, the years since their diagnosis may push them closer to menopause or actually into it and generally affect fertility. Other hormonal therapies, such as leuprolide (Lupron), are chosen for their ability to shut down the ovaries, a strategy sometimes employed protectively during chemotherapy, as described later in this chapter.

Keep in mind that, according to the American Society for Reproductive Medicine, infertility is attributed to difficulties that a woman has about a third of the time and those that a man has a third of the time. Ovulation disorders, blocked fallopian tubes, and uterine fibroids or structural defects that make miscarriages more likely are common sources of trouble in women; few or no sperm cells or sperm that are damaged are common causes in men. More than one factor is often at play. The remaining cases of infertility stem from a combination of problems such as those already explained or from unknown factors.

Embryo Banking

Sometimes, women choose to use the span of weeks between breast cancer surgery and the start of chemotherapy to do embryo banking. This in vitro fertilization

(IVF) technique generally requires a woman to take drugs like clomiphene (Clomid, Serophene) that stimulate her ovaries to produce many mature eggs at once. Less often, eggs are removed from a woman with breast cancer after her ovaries are stimulated by tamoxifen or simply during a natural menstrual cycle.

Eggs are retrieved by a doctor using laparoscopic surgical techniques and then mixed with sperm at a lab. Usually, a woman's partner supplies the sperm, although a lesbian couple, single woman, or woman whose male partner is infertile can choose to use donor sperm.

After several days, successfully fertilized eggs should have started dividing into a mass of cells that will form an embryo. Not all will reach this point, but those that do can then be frozen. The embryos remain frozen during the time a woman undergoes cancer treatments. Later, they can be thawed and placed in her uterus or a surrogate's uterus. Not all embryos survive the thawing, but with luck one or more embryos that do may then burrow into the uterine lining and go on to create a viable pregnancy that ends successfully in a healthy birth. Often, hormones are required to start and maintain such a pregnancy.

Embryo banking in women with breast cancer raises many important questions that have yet to be answered through large, well-controlled studies. Among them are these key issues:

- Most of the drugs that stimulate the ovaries raise blood levels of estrogen dramatically for a few weeks. Could this fuel cancer cells remaining in the body after surgery that have not yet been treated by systemic therapies?

- How often do banked embryos result in pregnancy, and how often do those pregnancies end in the birth of a child?

Potential pitfalls abound. When a woman who does not have breast cancer undergoes IVF, it's not unusual to go through several cycles to maximize the odds of a successful pregnancy and birth. One cycle takes four to six weeks, and delaying treatment to go through more than one cycle is uncommon in the midst of breast cancer treatment. The deliberate estrogen boost that stimulates many eggs to "ripen" during a few weeks of the cycle could theoretically be feeding residual cancer cells while they are still strong and untouched by cancer treatments.

Youth also counts here: the younger the woman and her eggs, the more likely that embryos started through IVF will result in pregnancy. "Having only three embryos frozen for a thirty-eight-year-old does not give her a terrific chance of getting pregnant," observes Dr. Elizabeth Ginsburg, medical director of the in vitro

SAVING EGGS ALONE

Thus far, saving eggs alone is not a truly viable option. No protocol for freezing eggs has been shown to later produce a pregnancy with any consistency, notes Dr. Ginsburg, although sporadic case reports and tiny studies occasionally report success. The eggs seem to freeze nicely. The hitch comes in thawing and fertilizing them, so the embryo quality is usually quite poor. Given this, it's unlikely to be worth taking the risks of ovarian stimulation simply to freeze eggs (see "Embryo Banking").

Another experimental approach taken—mostly with animals, but recently also in women—is removing part or all of an ovary, freezing it, and returning it to the body. At that point, the ovary or ovarian tissue may begin to work again as it once did, churning out hormones and releasing eggs, and possibly resulting in a pregnancy. In 2004, a single, celebrated case made the news in which a thirty-two-year-old woman in Belgium, who had undergone cancer treatments for Hodgkin's lymphoma, gave birth to a child using this approach. At this point, however, the techniques involved are not ready for general use just yet.

fertilization program at Brigham and Women's Hospital in Boston and associate professor at Harvard Medical School.

One avenue being explored relies on tamoxifen to stimulate the ovaries. Because tamoxifen blocks the action of estrogen in the breast, theoretically it might help a woman avoid the potential effects of the estrogen surge from standard fertility medications should remaining cancer cells exist. However, no solid data back the safety and efficacy of this approach, and while certain doses of tamoxifen may help mature eggs in the ovaries, this technique produces far fewer eggs than standard fertility drugs.

The little data available suggest that relying on tamoxifen to stimulate the ovaries, or simply retrieving eggs after a natural cycle, results in few or no embryos so that the odds of a pregnancy culminating in birth are slim. In the best possible world, a woman would have a number of embryos ready so that more than one attempt at pregnancy could be made—a chance optimized with standard fertility drugs.

All of these issues should be discussed with a knowledgeable reproductive endocrinologist or obstetrician and your oncologist. How much you (and your partner, if you have one) desire a child counts greatly. How old you will be after completing treatment, especially if you are taking tamoxifen, should be considered, too. You'll also want to think through how likely it is that you will later be able to have a pregnancy and a child through embryo banking. This depends partly on your age, as well as your oncologist's best estimate of the relative safety or danger of having fertility treatment before you have received a full course of cancer treatments.

Protecting the Ovaries During Chemotherapy

It would be wonderful to be able to protect the ovaries from harm during chemotherapy. One strategy occasionally employed requires a woman to take Lupron or goserelin (Zoladex). These hormonal treatments shut down the ovaries, which may lessen the harm to follicles, where eggs grow and mature. This is experimental and the jury is still out on whether it does or doesn't work, notes Ann H. Partridge, M.D., M.P.H., a medical oncologist at Dana-Farber Cancer Institute specializing in breast cancer.

PREGNANCY AFTER TREATMENT

"Cancer is such a controlling force," said Eva, who was thirty-one when first diagnosed. "For that whole time you're going through it, you're all about it. Once it was over, I thought, 'I just really want to get past this.' It was always part of my plan to have another baby."

Her husband agreed. The couple had few reservations after talking the issue over with her doctors. Eva's cancer had been caught at an early stage. Her treatments had been successful. And, despite chemotherapy, her periods were most definitely on track. Within months—sooner than recommended, Eva noted—she had a positive pregnancy test. And within the year, the two had a third child, a dream they'd put aside indefinitely during the early weeks after her diagnosis.

As Eva and Amanda found, women do go on to have children after breast cancer and feel that these children enrich their lives enormously. Whether or not women have had breast cancer, some conceive naturally, while others need varying amounts of assistance. Amanda used ovulation kits to track her fertile days in order to maximize her chances of getting pregnant. Because she had had previous abdominal surgery entirely unrelated to her breast cancer treatments, she had an imaging procedure that sends dye through the fallopian tubes to make sure there were no obstructions that would compromise fertility.

The decision to get pregnant and have a child after breast cancer is intensely personal. There are no guarantees about whether or when the cancer might return; the possibility that this could happen during a pregnancy or even many years after a child is born is clearly unsettling.

The good news is that babies born to women who have gone through chemotherapy or had radiation to the breast or chest wall do not seem to have higher than usual rates of birth defects.

Yet some of the questions that women and their doctors ask are still largely unanswered at this point in time. Will a pregnancy, which causes nine months of high estrogen levels, feed residual cancer cells? Could it speed a recurrence of cancer and shorten survival time? For women who banked embryos or who choose to use donor eggs or donor embryos, will the need to support the pregnancy in its early weeks with an outside source of estrogen and progesterone affect prognosis? Is pregnancy safer in some women—depending on characteristics of their cancer—than in others? The truth is, the available data are seriously flawed.

Generally speaking, the studies that have been done are likely to have looked at a very selective population. Perhaps women who go on to become pregnant after cancer are almost exclusively those with better prognoses. Certainly, women with more advanced breast cancers are likely to be strongly advised against getting pregnant. And a randomized study—in which some women who have been treated for breast cancer are randomly assigned to become pregnant, while others with the same treatments and cancer characteristics serve as a control group—is clearly impossible to do.

Still, some oncologists feel there is room for cautious optimism. When talking to patients who very much want to have children, comments Dr. Partridge, "I say that the data are reassuring, but not definitive." Taken as a whole, the preliminary research suggests that pregnancy after a full course of breast cancer treatment does not negatively affect prognosis. How this might fit into your personal situation depends on many factors known only to you and your oncologist, so a serious discussion with your doctor is warranted.

A few further points are in order:

• If you are at least thirty-five or have reason to believe that you may have trouble getting pregnant (such as having irregular periods or a history of pelvic surgery, endometriosis, or pelvic inflammatory disease), a consultation with a fertility specialist is probably a good idea. Likewise, it is prudent to consider consulting with a reproductive endocrinologist to begin an evaluation once you have tried to conceive for three months without success. Studies have shown that 60 percent of couples who conceive on their own do so within the first three months of unprotected intercourse. Remember, though, fertility problems need not be related only to breast cancer treatments. They may involve the male partner, as well.

- Generally, women are urged to wait to get pregnant for at least two to three years or, ideally, five years after diagnosis. This is partly because if cancer is going to recur, it does so most often during that span of time. No data suggest that low-risk women court harm by becoming pregnant sooner that this, however. Waiting means more time ticked off on the fertility clock, so this should be weighed with your doctors.

- If you are urged to take tamoxifen as part of your treatment, it is best to do so for five years, but if you have fertility (or other) concerns, discuss this with your doctors. Research cautiously suggests that taking tamoxifen for two or three years still provides a measure of protection against recurrence and new cancers, although less so than a five-year course. Tamoxifen may cause birth defects, however, so you should avoid getting pregnant while on it. Because it stays in your system for a while, it's safest to wait at least two months after stopping the medication before you start trying to conceive.

- If you are considering IVF or other assisted reproductive technologies, ask about the live birthrate using that particular approach. The number of successfully fertilized eggs and even embryo transfers to the uterus is often much higher than the number of children born via these efforts. One hitch, of course, is that these percentages are likely to be drawn from women who have not been treated for breast cancer. Currently, there are no data on safety and efficacy of IVF after breast cancer.

Breast Screening During Pregnancy and Breast-Feeding

Changes in breast density and lumpiness that accompany pregnancy and breast-feeding can make it harder to pick up a recurrence or new cancer. Forethought and

NEED MORE INFORMATION?

The nonprofit organization fertileHOPE (fertilehope.org or 888-994-HOPE) was launched to help cancer patients facing infertility. Its website has publications, helpful resources, and message boards. The American Society for Reproductive Medicine (asrm.org or 205-978-5000) is a multidisciplinary professional organization devoted to reproductive medicine. Its website offers referrals to qualified physicians, including reproductive endocrinologists and reproductive surgeons; it also has publications and links to assisted reproductive technology clinics and mental health professionals. The Centers for Disease Control and Prevention track fertility clinic success rates and other information. The CDC Reproductive Health Information Source website is cdc.gov/reproductivehealth (or you can call 770-488-5200).

vigilant screening are essential. Speak with your doctor about tailoring the approach I take with my patients to your particular circumstances.

- **Before pregnancy:** I ask my patients to tell me if they are contemplating a pregnancy, so that I can make sure they have an up-to-date breast exam and mammogram. Sometimes, that means having an annual mammogram earlier than usual. Talk with your breast surgeon about this.

- **During pregnancy:** As many physicians do, I hover over patients who are pregnant. During this time, they have a breast exam by me or one of their other physicians every two to three months. Other tests may be done, if necessary. Eva, for example, needed to have a biopsy to check out a suspicious lump. Fortunately, it was benign.

- **If breast-feeding:** Surgery and radiation to the breast can make breast-feeding difficult or impossible with the affected breast. A few of my patients have breast-fed—for as long as several weeks or a year or more. For those who do so, I recommend a breast exam by me or one of their other physicians every two to three months. Also speak with your doctors about whether and when to schedule a mammogram or another imaging test. One of my patients, who had very dense breasts while lactating, had a mammogram alternating with a breast MRI every six months during the two years that she breast-fed her child. Just prior to these screenings, she pumped her breasts. That won't ensure a clear image, but it may help.

- **After pregnancy or breast-feeding:** Usually, a mammogram is scheduled within three to six months after pregnancy or breast-feeding ends.

When Pregnancy Isn't an Option

Sometimes, pregnancy ends in miscarriage, never happens, isn't deemed a wise path, or simply is not chosen. Loving families are created in many different ways. Some possibilities are surrogacy arrangements, sometimes using a donor egg matched with a partner's sperm or donor egg and donor sperm. Private and public adoptions in the United States and elsewhere are well worth consideration. Some countries are more open than others to international adoption by families in which a parent has had health problems. The U.S. Department of Health and Human Services sponsors the National Adoption Information Clearinghouse (http://naic.acf.hhs.gov or 888-251-0075). Another website with helpful information on certain domestic and international agencies is run by the National Council for Adoption (adoption council.org or 866-212-3678), a nonprofit, nonsectarian advocacy group that promotes adoption.

The pain of having dreams about the family you wished for derailed can be very sharp. You may wish to speak with a therapist or social worker who has experience working with people around these issues. Doctors and friends may be able to suggest someone, or you might try a referral through the American Society for Reproductive Medicine.

WHO PAYS?

Assisted-reproduction technologies like IVF and embryo banking are quite expensive. Some states, including Massachusetts and California, have laws requiring health insurance companies to pay for certain procedures. Some health care plans are a good deal more generous in what they cover than others. Check with your health care plan or the insurance commissioner's office in your state for specific information.

16

SEXUALITY: CHANGING BODY, CHANGING NEEDS

◉

Not long into the first numb days of wondering whether she'd survive breast cancer and worrying about her children and what her treatment would entail, Natalie started thinking about what all of this might do to her sex life. She and her husband talked about it. "He said, 'Don't worry, we'll work it out. We'll get through it.'"

Dallas, who had lived with her partner, Paul, for years, also had her worries. Her tumor had been fairly large when finally diagnosed. When she knew that she needed a mastectomy, she had hoped to have immediate breast reconstruction, but that wasn't possible. She didn't have enough extra padding on her body for a TRAM flap reconstruction nor, as it turned out, enough healthy breast skin remaining after surgery to cover an implant. At first, said Dallas, her sex life sputtered. "I just didn't feel pretty. I didn't want Paul to see me. I'd hurry up and put pajamas on and jump into bed."

Paul's response was blunt and loving. "I used to tell her, it didn't matter if she had one breast or two or three breasts—it wouldn't make a difference to me. Sexually, she turned me on anyway." What's more, he added, "I love her. She's my world."

Such reassurances can certainly ease a woman's mind and maybe even put a smile on her face, although they can't speak to women who don't happen to be in warm, committed relationships. Nor can they provide a detailed blueprint of just how to scramble over obstacles ranging from sadness over body changes and treatment-induced fatigue to nitty-gritty troubles like vaginal dryness and the numbness or discomfort that breast surgery may have left behind.

Research tells us that a substantial number of women struggle with sexual issues after breast cancer treatment. (See the sidebar "Sizzle or Fizzle.") Still, statistics are only a small part of this story. After all, sexuality is a bit of a chameleon. As life

SIZZLE OR FIZZLE

Several intriguing points came out of a 1998 study exploring changes in sexuality among more than eight hundred women who had had either a mastectomy or a lumpectomy roughly three years earlier. Two out of five of these breast cancer survivors had received chemotherapy, and, at the time of the study, half were taking tamoxifen (Nolvadex).

It's worth noting that 65 percent of the women reported being sexually active at the time of their diagnosis—a number similar to that found in an age-matched group of women. Among those who were sexually active, 88 percent considered their sex lives moderately to extremely satisfying before their treatment. After treatment, 75 percent felt that way. So, while there was a change, many clearly continued to enjoy themselves.

In a subsequent study, when the researchers delved into predictors of sexual interest, satisfaction, and dysfunction, several issues proved to be at least somewhat open to change. Body image, vaginal dryness, emotional well-being, the quality of the relationship, and a partner's sexual problems all played into sizzle or fizzle—that is, where a woman stood along the spectrum of desire and a satisfying or dysfunctional sex life. Two other factors that couldn't be changed—whether a woman had undergone chemotherapy and whether she had a new partner since diagnosis—had a negative impact.

goes on and circumstances change, it may shift shape and colors, hide and reappear. Perhaps every woman who has been affected by breast cancer ends up writing her own story about how this slice of life might proceed, one that requires her to figure out what obstacles she needs to overcome. This chapter, while by no means exhaustive, is designed to set you on your way.

QUESTIONS, FEARS, AND FEELINGS

"Who do you ask about sexual questions?" Amanda wondered after being diagnosed with breast cancer. At thirty-one, she had been married for about six months when she discovered a lump in her breast. None of her friends had been through this experience. As time and treatment unfolded, questions inevitably arose. "Do you ask your fifty-year-old male oncologist, who might not be comfortable answering these questions? Your surgeon who you see once a year? Do you ask a girlfriend?"

The answer is bound to vary. While some cancer specialists are quite adept at fielding questions about sexuality, others may not be. Sometimes, conversations in the doctor's office may seem too clinical in comparison to life itself. And, truth to tell, depending on the question and your own sexuality, broaching the subject might make *you* feel distinctly uncomfortable. Rather than keep the questions bottled up, though, consider where you can go for good advice. Here are a few sources:

• **Your cancer care team or gynecologist:** Despite the vignettes sketched, doctors and nurses hear these questions all the time and will often be able to give you answers tailored to your specific health situation.

• **A therapist or social worker:** Preferably find someone who has worked with breast cancer survivors. If your doctor or a friend cannot refer you to anyone, the American Psychosocial Oncology Society (apos-society.org or 866-APOS-4-HELP) may be able to help.

• **A sex therapist:** Sex therapists have varied backgrounds—they might be psychologists or social workers, for example—but all should have special training in sexuality and sexual dysfunction. Your doctor or nurse may have names to suggest, or you can contact the American Association of Sex Educators, Counselors, and Therapists (aasect.org or 319-895-8407).

• **Support groups:** A good match between you and the group makes it easier to raise intimate questions. As a lesbian, Jody found she felt uncomfortable in the first group she attended, which appeared to be all heterosexual women. While they talked readily about their husbands, she felt ill at ease raising any issues concerning her relationship with her partner of twenty years. "I just felt like we were on two different planets," she said. Sophie, who was thirty-six when first diagnosed, reported feeling equally out of place amongst a group of women who were many years older and whose concerns differed from hers. Ask your cancer team about support groups that might meet your needs, or try the American Cancer Society (cancer.org or 800-ACS-2345); Young Survival Coalition (youngsurvival.org or 212-206-6610); the national lesbian health organization, The Mautner Project (mautnerproject.org or 202-332-5536, voice and TTY); or other organizations listed in Resources. Local hospitals and health care centers may also sponsor helpful groups.

Mirror Image

Body image is a tricky subject. Often, research on it focuses on how a woman feels about her body after a lumpectomy or mastectomy without delving too deeply into how she felt about herself beforehand. Sometimes, it seems that the veneration of youth and perfection that saturates this culture leaves little room for real bodies with curves, lumps, bumps, and, yes, even scars. Whether you loved the way your breasts looked or never gave them much thought, breasts are such an enduring symbol of femininity that this cancer strikes many women especially hard. While the changes in your body literally occur overnight, the march toward acceptance can take quite a lot longer.

"I lived with my other body for forty-seven and a half years. I've had this one for the last two and a half years," said Jody, who had a double mastectomy with TRAM flap reconstructions. Her new breasts are smaller than her natural breasts were. Her scars are still visible, though time and silicone sheets have helped to minimize them. The pleasing sensations once supplied by a network of nerves have been numbed in the wake of her surgeries. "I think in my mind, I try to pretend that the area doesn't exist."

Whether you had a lumpectomy or a mastectomy with or without reconstructive surgery, it takes a while to come to terms with a new body. Ways to enhance this process include the following:

- **Looking at your body:** Think about what you like about your body, not just what you don't like. Think about the whole picture, too—what's appealing about you is so much more than the shape of your body or its curves.
- **Touching your body:** Touching your own breast or chest can tell you much about what does and does not feel pleasurable. It can also help reawaken you sexually. If you'd like a medical reason to do it, a gentle daily massage on the surgery scar once new skin has covered the wound appears to help promote healing and settle down scars. Use a dab of vitamin E, Mederma cream, or a product your surgeon recommends and try massage for the first six months or longer. Check with your surgeon beforehand.
- **Involving your partner, if you have one, in your treatment and recovery early on:** Paul helped change bandages and handle surgical drains. Kim smoothed soothing cream onto the tender skin of her partner's chest during radiation therapy. You may not think of these tasks as the sort of intimacy you'd like to encourage, but believe it or not, it sometimes makes people on both sides of the relationship feel closer to one another, as well as loved and wanted.

- **Breast cancer survivors:** Reach to Recovery (part of the American Cancer Society) and other breast cancer organizations can connect you with women who have been down this road before you. While their experiences are individual, it may help to speak one-on-one with other women who understand your situation.

- **Breast cancer organization websites:** Many organizations, such as the Susan G. Komen Breast Cancer Foundation (komen.org or 800-IM-AWARE), Young Survival Coalition (youngsurvival.org), and the Wellness Community (wellness-community.org), offer online chat groups and bulletin boards where questions about sexuality are often discussed. Be a bit wary about these venues. While they can be invaluable forums for sharing experiences, you have no way of knowing how reliable the information gleaned is. And while it's nice to know you're not the only person who has had to deal with annoying discharge or who has noticed a slackening in desire, it can be hard not to add to your worry list when someone reels off five more possible side effects that had never occurred to you. Check what you learn against a reliable source.

THE OBSTACLES

Months after her mastectomy for early-stage breast cancer, Natalie was pleased to find her sex life largely unchanged. Yet not every woman would say the same. Even more than the experts, many women who have breast cancer treatments can reel off obstacles thus created. It can be hard, however, to know whether treatments are the sole source of changes or whether a woman has gotten closer to menopause and thus would experience some of the symptoms anyway. Growing older creates the same conundrum: is sexual desire waning because of breast cancer treatments, body image, or simply because it can with time? Whatever the answer, there are generally steps you can take to improve your sexual life, if you would like to do so. First, it helps to identify which obstacles, if any, are getting in your way.

Surgery

Surgery changes body image, of course. How radically depends on whether you had a mastectomy or a lumpectomy and whether you decided to have reconstructive surgery and, if so, what type. As detailed earlier in this book, some reshaped breasts look and feel very nearly the same as the original when you're nude, while others—such as implants—can be perfect under clothes but don't feel or look as much like your natural breasts. That can affect how you feel about sexuality and whether you want your partner to look at or touch you. After having had a double mastectomy and reconstructive surgery, Jody found her partner, Brooke, didn't have any problems at all with how her new body looked. The problem was reversed: Jody didn't want to touch her partner's breasts, because this reminded her painfully of her own loss.

Surgery of any kind tampers with nerve endings, so it's likely you'll feel some numbness and possibly discomfort that may or may not ease with time. Some women report dysesthesia, pain or tingling, in the affected breast or chest wall that can make even a light touch uncomfortable. Surgery can also affect many different muscles and your range of motion, so that lifting your arms up, holding them in certain ways, or assuming certain positions may be uncomfortable or pretty much impossible.

Chemotherapy

During chemotherapy, your sex drive might wane for a number of reasons. Fatigue can be a powerful dampener, as can nausea and overall feelings of illness. You may be coping with side effects that keep you from looking or feeling like yourself, such as a complexion that appears washed out or develops blotches or blemishes. Side effects of supportive medications like steroids or sometimes chemotherapy itself may make you gain weight.

Temporary or not, losing the hair on the head and elsewhere on the body is a big blow to many women who experience it. After being urged to think about whether she might like to wear a wig, one woman kidded, "I'm bald, I'm forty, my breasts are smaller, not bigger, and you're telling me now that having this on is going to help me attract men?" Yet as more than one woman noted, some husbands and partners find the lack of pubic hair appealing. A woman may enjoy it herself or may find it disturbing.

Women who are still having their periods may find chemotherapy sets off a temporary or permanent menopause, especially if they are within a decade or so of when menopause would naturally occur. Having less estrogen floating freely around your body may be cause for celebration if your cancer is hormone receptor–positive, but the symptoms that may accompany this are not. Every woman's experience is different, but some report more urinary tract infections, vaginal dryness and thinning of vaginal tissues that can make sex uncomfortable, and changes in sex drive. Hot flashes and night sweats are frequent complaints that may be mildly annoying or vividly so; they can also make it hard to get a decent night's sleep, which is no one's idea of an aphrodisiac.

Hormonal Therapy and Herceptin

The effects of hormonal therapies vary. Those that shut down the ovaries like leuprolide (Lupron) and goserelin (Zoladex) can trigger the menopausal symptoms just mentioned under "Chemotherapy," including particularly intense hot flashes. So, too, can removing the ovaries surgically.

Tamoxifen competes with estrogen for hormone receptors on the surface of cells. To some women, taking tamoxifen is truly like taking a vitamin pill—practically unnoticeable. The most common complaints that other women have are hot flashes and vaginal discharge. A smaller group of women experience irregular periods, vaginal itching or irritation, fatigue, headaches, nausea, and skin rashes. In a large study of thousands of women at high risk for breast cancer, tamoxifen didn't affect depression or weight. Other data suggest it doesn't have a negative impact on sexual functioning either. Yet there are certainly women on tamoxifen who struggle with these problems. It's hard to know whether the drug or other sources or a combination may be at the root of this.

For some women, aromatase inhibitors—anastrozole (Arimidex), letrozole (Femara), and exemestane (Aromasin)—may trip off hot flashes. The first two medications may also cause joint and muscle pain, which could dampen desire; the first and third may cause mild nausea, which could certainly do the same.

Like many of the hormonal therapy medications, the monoclonal antibody trastuzumab (Herceptin) has far fewer notable side effects than chemotherapy. The most serious problem is an allergic reaction that sometimes happens with the first dose. Lesser problems may include nausea, vomiting, diarrhea, weakness, headaches, and rashes, though actual side effects will vary from woman to woman.

Radiation

Radiation is a bit of a wild card. Some women pass through it entirely unscathed, while others experience changes in how the skin on the breast or chest feels and looks, which can certainly affect body image. For example, women who have radiation after a lumpectomy sometimes notice that the remaining breast tissue shrinks or swells. The skin of the nipple and areola may lighten or darken in color. During the course of treatment, a mild to severe burn similar to sunburn may occur, leaving skin very tender for weeks. Redness, peeling, skin thickening, and discoloration are also possible. Some of these changes are temporary, while others may be long lasting.

Because radiation affects blood vessels, the skin may not heal as easily. Muscles on the chest wall may stiffen, too. The ribs may become irritated due to radiation skimming the top of these bones, a condition called *costochondritis*. This can trigger pain, particularly near the breast bone, which worsens with even slight pressure on the area.

Fatigue builds as radiation treatment continues. The body is focusing a great deal of its energy on repairing normal cells and building new cells, leaving little energy for other pursuits, including sex. It can take months for this fatigue to completely lift. Some women rebound in a matter of months, and most report feeling like themselves again by the time a year has passed.

Medications

Sometimes, breast cancer patients need to take strong painkillers called *opioids*, which are known to dampen sex drive. Both newer and older medications for depression can do the same, as can some other drugs. Ask your cancer care team whether drugs you are taking might have this effect. Sometimes, changing medications—from one antidepressant to another, perhaps—helps.

Growing Older

Celebrating birthday after birthday can be especially sweet and poignant if you've had breast cancer. But passing years also bring all of us that much closer to aches and pains and other changes related to aging. Some women, who were relatively young when first diagnosed with breast cancer, are bound to find themselves facing menopause and, consequently, its symptoms. They may have had a preview of this, of course, depending on which treatments they had. While libido by no means disappears with age, many people experience less sexual urgency as they grow older, particularly if they have been in the same relationship for a while. "We're old," said Rose comfortably about herself and her partner. "We've been together a long time."

Anxiety and Depression

Worries abound around breast cancer. Even women who have successfully navigated treatment may have anxiety about recurrence. Depression, which strikes many thousands of women in the general population, can be a potent force here, too. Either mood can affect libido. According to the National Cancer Institute, in fact, about half of depressed patients who are not on medication report problems with lowered sex drive and trouble achieving orgasm. Anxiety may work on sex drive indirectly by keeping you tense, irritated, and sleepless. As noted, medications designed to ease these problems may contribute to sexual difficulties, too, in which case switching medications can be helpful.

PLEASURE AND COMFORT

Quite possibly, sex is the furthest thing from your mind these days, but unless you're truly ready to give it up, it's wise to consider ways to bring it back into your life. Whether alone or with a partner, sex can be one of the great joys in life. It doesn't add a single calorie; in fact, it strips a few off. It can be an expression of love and a reaffirmation of your deepest sense of self. It cements many relationships. It also can be just plain fun.

What sex shouldn't be is fraught with fear, tension, or unexpected physical and emotional land mines. Perhaps some of the following suggestions may help you enhance pleasure and comfort alike.

Communicate

Sex can easily fall by the wayside for long stretches of time amidst all the worries and side effects of breast cancer treatment. It's also easy for partners to misunderstand one another. Your partner may feel pushed away by your lack of interest or be fearful that initiating sex will hurt you somehow. Continued avoidance may set up a cycle that is difficult to break.

Acknowledging the losses—of the body you loved or appreciated, of the intimacy between you—and expressing a wish for change as you feel better can help. "I'd like to get a nice calm day when we're not trying to go anywhere to just say, 'Let's find each other's bodies again and see where we're at with this,'" said Rose.

It also helps to tell a partner honestly what hurts and explore together what might feel good. "Even now, when Paul touches my ribs, it hurts," said Dallas. "It doesn't feel good." Although she says he's a very gentle, considerate lover, she can recall pulling away sharply one night and saying, "I don't want you touching me because you're going to go over that part." Fortunately, she felt she could say that and he felt he could listen, so there was communication, rather than hurt feelings and misunderstanding.

Eva finds her reconstructed breast is quite numb. "When my husband and I have sex, he doesn't even go there. It's not going to give me any pleasure." However, she noted she really does enjoy having her other breast touched. "Thank God I have the other one," she said.

Slow Down

Maybe what you need is more cuddling and displays of affection. Maybe longer periods of foreplay would help. Try to communicate needs such as these to your partner. One way to take the pressure off is to temporarily agree to ban sex focused solely on orgasm or intercourse while continuing to kiss, stroke, hug, and touch a partner anywhere except the genitals.

Counter Dryness

Pleasure flies out the window if sexual play causes unwanted irritation and pain or light bleeding due to friction against vaginal walls that are dry and possibly thinning from lack of estrogen. Regular use of personal moisturizers, like Replens, can help ease dryness, although these products typically don't supply enough slipperiness during sex. Personal lubricants, such as Astroglide or K-Y Silk-E, do give you enough slipperiness when applied liberally before or during sex to your vulva and vagina and your partner's fingers or penis. Another option is Estring, a flexible plastic ring placed at the top of the vagina that releases a very low dose of estrogen. This plumps up thinning vaginal walls and counters dryness. Usually, the ring can be left in place during sex. Occasionally, in certain positions, your partner might notice it. If so, the ring can be removed before sex and replaced later. Just be sure to pick a clean spot for it to rest in the meantime.

Change Positions

A partner's full weight on your chest may be more than you can bear. It can actually hurt or just make you anxious that you might get hurt—too anxious to relax and enjoy yourself. A woman may prefer to be the partner on top in order to control touching and depth of penetration. A spooning position (one partner tucked behind the other) or a position where you each lie on your sides with legs intertwined may also be enjoyable.

Consider Clothes

In a perfect world, we might all make love with the lights on full and bodies abandoned to the joy of the moment, but in the real world, some women prefer to dim the lights and remain partly dressed during sex because of self-consciousness about how their bodies look. This is true for some women who have had breast cancer as well as for some who have not. If you wear a breast form, you might like to continue to do so during sex or you may find it gets in the way. A few companies, such as Still You Fashions (stillyoufashions.com), make lovely lingerie that may help you feel beautiful and sexy, too, while keeping a breast form in place. Pretty or sexy lingerie is also available at many stores, of course.

Change the Venue

Sometimes, memories of past lovemaking—and of how your body used to look and feel—intrude on present-day possibilities. Think about other places you might like to try. A brief holiday away from home and responsibilities (and children, too, if you have any) can be refreshing.

Enjoy Your Body

Bringing pleasure to your body can be accomplished in many ways. Some women prefer sensual approaches. Silken clothes, candles, warm baths, heady scents, delicious foods, or a light, trailing massage can all offer sensual pleasures that remind you of ways to enjoy the skin you're in. Mindfulness—the art of being in the moment while bathing in all of your senses—is another path. A classic mindfulness exercise is slowly peeling and eating an orange. As you do so, really experience the appearance, scent, and taste of the fruit and the textures beneath your fingers and in your mouth.

One wonderful route to reclaiming your body is exercise. Stretching can extend your range of motion and ease sore spots so that a variety of positions become more comfortable. Depending on your stamina, walks with a friend or regular visits to the gym can tone you up, or tough, sweaty workouts that really push your limits might be more satisfying. Working your body this way helps keep you healthy by shaving off extra pounds and, sometimes, adding muscle. It can lift your spirits and help you feel more attractive and energized. What's more, it can allow you to regain a trust in your body that may have been shaken hard by your experience with breast cancer.

"Every time I had treatment, it would knock me lower and take me longer to rebound," said Amanda, an athletic woman who continued her workouts on bad days and good days. "This was something I could do. I felt good when I exercised."

A few years after completing her treatment, Sloan chose to learn an entirely new sport. "Now that I've started rowing, I feel like a warrior woman," she crowed. With the fog of fatigue that had dogged her throughout her treatments truly gone, getting out on the river to row provided a way to learn to trust her body again and revel in the pleasure it could bring her. "I didn't totally mistrust my body, but I did lose enjoyment of it. I wanted to move back to feeling connected. Rowing did that."

PARTNERS

While you bore the brunt of the experience, the repercussions of breast cancer reach far beyond you. Partners grieve, too. If you're involved in a relationship, it would be strange, indeed, if the changes in your body went entirely ignored. "I'm not saying at first it wasn't shocking to see it, because it was," said Paul. Yet, he added, "I think she had more of a problem with it than I did, to be honest. Whatever I had to do to make her feel right, I wanted to do."

Dallas admits she shied away from sex for a while. She felt tired, ill, and anxious. She worried about her responses and his. "I don't feel pretty. I don't feel like a woman," she remembered thinking. "Am I still going to have the same sexual feelings? Am I still going to get excited when he touches me?"

Sometime during her chemotherapy, the two of them broke through the ice. "I didn't have a stick of hair." It didn't matter. "I'm going to pretend I'm me six months ago," she decided, "and after that everything went back to normal."

"When we make love, a lot of times she doesn't take her shirt off," noted Paul. If that makes her feel more comfortable, he said, so be it. "Everyone changes in life as you get older. You're not going to look the same at fifty as at twenty." His body has gone through some changes, too, through illness and added pounds. "Ten years ago, I was thirty or forty pounds lighter. She hasn't thrown me out."

It's natural to worry about whether the strains of breast cancer treatment and a changed body will drive a partner away. A shaky relationship can indeed founder on these rocks. A reasonably strong marriage or partnership may grow still stronger as two people united by urgent needs become closer and consider what truly matters to them and what doesn't. Two studies looking at marriage have found similar rates of separation or divorce among couples dealing with breast cancer as in control groups. Distress can ebb and flow, however, as the needs of one partner or the other fail to be met at different times. It's no defeat to call in a counselor or therapist when distress ratchets up or you need help improving communication.

ON BEING SINGLE

Not every woman who goes through breast cancer has a partner standing steadfast behind her. If you're single, breast cancer treatments can be harder to handle in some ways and possibly easier in others. Katherine rounded up friends, neighbors, and even acquaintances to help her during her lumpectomy and radiation treatments. People were pleased to do so, particularly since she wasn't shy about asking.

Sophie ended a hot affair the day after she was diagnosed with breast cancer. "I didn't want to go through that with him," she said simply. She didn't date again for more than a year.

Thinking about launching into love and relationships anew after breast cancer may seem discouraging or make you fearful. Dating can be hard enough by itself. How and when do you tell your story to a casual date? Are you ever going to find someone who will love you anyway?

Two years after she had had a lumpectomy for breast cancer that was fortunately caught very early, Mia lost her partner of many years to his own battle with illness. Starting over was enormously hard, not least because she had loved him so much and thus missed him endlessly. "I felt petrified," she said, when she finally started dating another man two years later. "Do you tell people you've had cancer? Some people would be out the door in a New York second. I told him I was in remission and the chance of recurrence is very low."

As it happened, her experience with cancer didn't seem to rattle him. In fact, he'd dated a woman before who had had breast cancer.

"He helped me move forward because the whole thing moved very, very slowly," said Mia. When it came to sex, though, she felt terrified. "The gift he gave me was this: when you're ready, let me know."

She did. Now, said Mia, she's not sure this relationship will last, but it clearly isn't foundering on sex or breast cancer. Rather, she's not sure he can be as present emotionally and deeply caring as she'd like him to be. Having experienced a long, loving relationship, she doesn't want to settle for less.

EPILOGUE

Moving Forward

◉

Shortly after I was diagnosed with breast cancer, the 2003 Pan-Mass Challenge (PMC) took place. This two-day, 190-mile bike ride is sponsored by Dana-Farber Cancer Institute to raise funds for cancer research. Fresh from my two initial breast surgeries, I rode the first day of it. I began in the heat and ended in the rain, halting finally at the last water stop. Despite the two sports bras I had layered on under my jersey, the railroad track bumps got the better of me, and after seventy-five miles, I needed to call it a day.

After months of treatment, summer again rolled around and my family and I went to stay at my long-time friend Lisa Clark's beach house on the coastline of Massachusetts. The house held many fond memories of my friendship with Lisa, the warm bonds between our children, and the slower, more introspective pace of life a summer cottage on the beach brings. The house also held the mirror in which, after a bike ride one year earlier, I had noticed the minor change in my breast that proved to be cancer. Walking into the bathroom and seeing this mirror again was like seeing an old friend, a friend who is honest and frank, caring and genuinely concerned about you. One who clearly sees the beauty and the imperfections, reflecting both while remaining steadfast and true. The best type of friend to have.

Just a few weeks after we had taken up residence at the beach house, I would again wheel my bike to the starting line of the 2004 PMC. Between chemotherapy, reconstructive surgery, and the general rush of life, I hadn't been able to train very hard in the months leading up to the ride. Yet I tried my best, going to the gym whenever I felt up to it and attending three bicycle pace-line training clinics taught by my close friend Jim Decaprio. Jim had come to every one of my chemotherapy sessions to sit and talk with me; his wife, Leslie, had made delicious, home-cooked dinners for my family and me. I also went out on two training rides with my colleague and now good friend Ann Partridge who slowed her pace, too, when my new top speed proved nowhere near as fast as usual.

This time around, the day slated for the PMC was bright, crisp, and sunny— probably the best weather ever and quite fitting for the twenty-fifth anniversary of the ride. At the starting line, I met Ann. Stacey Lucchino and Lee Nadler were there, too. Stacey had been there for me and for my family on many occasions over the past year and our daughters are friends and schoolmates. Lee had been there for me, too. We ride together every PMC, and I was pleased that this year Lee and I would be together again at the starting line. Meredith Starr, a new friend who supported me in many quiet ways during my treatment, helped launch all of the riders with her warm, inspiring, and rousing words. She waved and smiled at me as I rode past her to start my ride.

As different stretches of roadway rolled by beneath my wheels, I rode alongside many other close friends and colleagues who had helped see me through a difficult year. I savored the breeze on my face and the feeling of my muscles working hard to push me up hills and along miles of unfurling road. At the last water stop, where I had had to end my ride the year before, I was met by my husband, Bill; my children, Kathryn Grace and Tripp; my parents; and cousins and extended family who had traveled from near and far to cheer me on.

This time I reached my goal—the finish line. Although sweat-streaked, tired, and one of the last riders in, I felt exultant. I had come full circle and that night at a celebratory dinner I was surrounded by many of the people who had been my anchors throughout a difficult, sometimes overwhelming year.

MOVING FORWARD AFTER BREAST CANCER

Moving forward after breast cancer may conjure mixed emotions. Many women are enormously relieved to be finished with active treatments. Plunging back into aspects of life suspended for months is a joy. You may wish to mark a close to this chapter in your life. Greta, whose children had pinned up a homemade banner with numbers one to four representing her chemotherapy treatments, recalled how much they enjoyed tearing down the very last piece of it. A long-planned trip to celebrate her parents' anniversary helped punctuate the completion of her treatment. She felt exhausted but ultimately happy to go along.

Sometimes, women find the transition from treatment to recovery rocky. Suddenly, your cancer care team, which supported you throughout, is no longer a reassuring presence, although lingering reminders of treatment, such as assorted aches and pains, menopausal symptoms, and concerns about body image, may still be bothering you. Many people in your circle who pitched in readily with an outpouring of love and tangible assistance will have drifted back toward their own lives. Breathing huge sighs of relief, partners and children may expect life at home to magically return to normal, too. At a time when others expect you to celebrate, you might be too exhausted to do so or feel as if something is holding you back. Anxiety about recurrence may make you feel that declaring yourself a survivor is courting trouble.

Yet difficult times can have a brighter side. You might emerge from this experience with new priorities based upon the recognition of what is truly important to you. You might take better care of yourself by eating well, exercising, and carving out time to relax and enjoy yourself and life. Even little pleasures may seem disproportionately rewarding.

As you move back into the center stream of your life, be gentle with yourself. Life will never be exactly the same as it once was, and forging a new "normal" takes time. Speak with other women who have made this transition if you feel their experiences might help. Don't be afraid to seek professional help if anxiety and depression interfere with moving forward in your life (see Chapter 2 and Resources for more information).

PLANNING FOR THE FUTURE

Whether you find this time challenging or a release, it helps to have a plan in place with your cancer care team. Guidelines issued by the National Comprehensive Cancer Network, a coalition of leading cancer centers, recommend regular follow-up every four to six months for five years and annually thereafter. During these follow-up visits, one of your doctors will take a medical history covering the months since your last appointment and perform a physical exam. A mammogram is recommended annually of the unaffected breast and every six to twelve months of the breast that has undergone breast-conserving surgery and radiation. If you are taking tamoxifen (Nolvadex) and have not had a hysterectomy, an annual pelvic exam also is recommended.

Between visits, if you have symptoms that might signal a recurrence, call your doctor for advice. Data suggest that in the absence of symptoms, tests aimed solely at checking for recurrences usually are not helpful. Two prospective, randomized trials, each of which enrolled more than twelve hundred women treated for breast cancer, compared intensive surveillance—which incorporated a battery of tests, such as bone scans, chest x-rays, and blood tests—to clinical surveillance similar to the follow-up visits just described. The trials demonstrated that recurrences were found slightly earlier in the group receiving intensive surveillance, albeit only about a month sooner in one study. Neither study showed that intensive surveillance improved survival time or quality of life, however. Extra tests tend to cause more anxiety for some women as well as needless expense.

A few weeks after the 2004 Pan-Mass Challenge, I took a much-needed and greatly enjoyed annual family vacation at The Tyler Place in northern Vermont. We reconnected with many summer friends. I biked every morning, swam every afternoon, went hiking, did yoga, and, importantly, spent time with my family. It was a glorious summer week in New England, a season that I love. These memories are fresh and alive in my mind, while those from the earlier seasons of my treatment and recovery are fading. I have made an important transition. For most hours of most days, breast cancer is nowhere near the front of my mind. Life at that moment in time, or planning for the future, is.

I have come to accept that breast cancer will forever be a part of my being. Yet as my own expertise and experiences show, its imprint can be eased. Each of us has the ability to make choices to help keep ourselves healthy. The pages of this book have been devoted to just that. I hope you found—and will continue to find—them helpful.

RESOURCES

⊙

GENERAL INFORMATION: WEBSITES

American Cancer Society
1599 Clifton NE
Atlanta, GA 30329
800-ACS-2345 (800-227-2345)
cancer.org

American Joint Committee on Cancer
633 N. Saint Clair Street
Chicago, IL 60611
312-202-5420
cancerstaging.org

The Breast Cancer Research Foundation (The Lauder Foundation)
654 Madison Avenue, Suite 1209
New York, NY 10021
646-497-2600
bcrfcure.org

breastcancer.org
111 Forrest Avenue
Narberth, PA 19072
610-664-1990
breastcancer.org

Centers for Medicare and Medicaid Services
Women's Health and Cancer Rights Act
7500 Security Boulevard
Baltimore, MD 21244-1850
877-267-2323
cms.hhs.gov/hipaa/hipaa1/content/whcra.asp

Hurricane Voices Breast Cancer Foundation
1340 Centre Street, Suite 208
Newton, MA 02459
866-667-3300
hurricanevoices.org

Lance Armstrong Foundation
P.O. Box 161150
Austin, TX 78716-1150
512-236-8820
laf.org

National Cancer Institute
9000 Rockville Pike
Bethesda, MD 20892
800-4-CANCER (800-422-6237)
cancer.gov

National Coalition for Cancer Survivorship
1010 Wayne Avenue, Suite 770
Silver Spring, MD 20910
877-NCCS-YES (877-622-7937)
canceradvocacy.org

National Comprehensive Cancer Network
500 Old York Road, Suite 250
Jenkintown, PA 19046
888-909-6226
nccn.org

National Institutes of Health
9000 Rockville Pike
Bethesda, MD 20892
301-496-4000
nih.gov

National Lymphedema Network
Latham Square, 1611 Telegraph Avenue, Suite 1111
Oakland, CA 94612-2138
800-541-3259 or 510-208-3200 (hotline)
lymphnet.org

Susan G. Komen Breast Cancer Foundation
5005 LBJ Freeway, Suite 250
Dallas, TX 75244
800-IM-AWARE (800-462-9273)
komen.org

GENERAL INFORMATION: BOOKS AND DVDS

After Breast Cancer: A Common-Sense Guide to Life After Treatment, Hester Hill
  Schnipper, L.I.C.S.W., Bantam Books (2003)
*Breast Cancer Husband: How to Help Your Wife (and Yourself) Through Diagnosis,
  Treatment, and Beyond*, Marc Silver, Rodale Books (2004)
Breast Cancer Survivor's Guide to Fitness (DVD) (Copies can be ordered through
  Brigham and Women's Hospital at brighamandwomens.org/breastcancerexer
  cisedvd.)
Eat, Drink, and Be Healthy: The Harvard Medical School Guide to Healthy Eating,
  Walter C. Willett, M.D., and P. J. Skerrett, Free Press (2002)
Facing the Mirror with Cancer: A Guide to Using Makeup to Make a Difference, Lori
  Ovitz with Joanne Kabak, Imaginis Corporation (2004)
The Hope Tree: Kids Talk About Breast Cancer, Laura Numeroff, Wendy S. Harpham,
  M.D., and David McPhail, Simon & Schuster Books for Young Readers (1999)
"Information for Women About the Safety of Silicone Breast Implants," Institute
  of Medicine, National Academy Press, Washington, DC (2000) (888-624-
  8422) (A free copy can be ordered through Y-ME National Breast Cancer Orga-
  nization, 800-221-2141.)

Mind over Menopause: The Complete Mind/Body Approach to Coping with Menopause, Leslee Kagan, M.S., N.P., Bruce Kessel, M.D., and Herbert Benson, M.D., Free Press (2004)

Show Me: A Photo Collection of Breast Cancer Survivors' Lumpectomies, Mastectomies, Breast Reconstructions, and Thoughts on Body Image, hmc.psu.edu/womens/showme to order

Surgery Choices for Women with Early-Stage Breast Cancer, National Cancer Institute (cancer.gov/cancertopics/breast-cancer-surgery-choices or 800-4-CANCER for a free copy)

The Year My Mother Was Bald, Ann Speltz and Kate Sternberg, Magination Press (2003)

CANCER CARE PROFESSIONALS AND FACILITIES

Accreditation Association for Ambulatory Health Care
3201 Old Glenview Road, Suite 300
Wilmette, IL 60091
847-853-6060
aaahc.org

American Academy of Dermatology
P.O. Box 4014
Schaumburg, IL 60168-4014
888-462-DERM (888-462-3376)
aad.org

American Association of Sex Educators, Counselors, and Therapists
P.O. Box 5488
Richmond, VA 23220-0488
319-895-8407
aasect.org

American Board of Medical Specialties
1007 Church Street, Suite 404
Evanston, IL 60201-5913
866-ASK-ABMS (866-275-2267)
abms.org

American College of Radiation Oncology
5272 River Road
Bethesda, MD 20816
301-718-6515
acro.org

American College of Radiology
1891 Preston White Drive
Reston, VA 20191
703-648-8900
acr.org
Radiology Info (patient website sponsored by American College of Radiology
and Radiological Society of North America), radiologyinfo.org

American College of Surgeons
633 N. Saint Clair Street
Chicago, IL 60611-3211
800-621-4111
facs.org

American Dental Association
211 E. Chicago Avenue
Chicago, IL 60611-2678
312-440-2500
ada.org

American Psychosocial Oncology Society
2365 Hunters Way
Charlottesville, VA 22911
866-APOS-4-HELP (866-276-7443)
apos-society.org

American Society of Clinical Oncology
1900 Duke Street, Suite 200
Alexandria, VA 22314
703-299-0150

asco.org
People Living with Cancer (patient website)
plwc.org

American Society of Plastic Surgeons
444 E. Algonquin Road
Arlington Heights, IL 60005
888-475-2784
plasticsurgery.org

Association of Oncology Social Work
1211 Locust Street
Philadelphia, PA 19107
215-599-6093
aosw.org

Casting for Recovery
P.O. Box 1123
3952 Main Street
Manchester, VT 05254
888-553-3500
castingforrecovery.org

Joint Commission on Accreditation of Healthcare Organizations
One Renaissance Boulevard
Oakbrook Terrace, IL 60181
630-792-5000
jcaho.org

National Cancer Institute–Designated Cancer Centers
301-435-3848
www3.cancer.gov/cancercenters

Society of Surgical Oncology
85 W. Algonquin Road, Suite 550
Arlington Heights, IL 60005
847-427-1400
surgonc.org

Additional Support Information and Resources

The Mautner Project
1707 L Street NW, Suite 230
Washington, DC 20036
202-332-5536
mautnerproject.org

National Alliance for Hispanic Health
1501 Sixteenth Street NW
Washington, DC 20036
202-387-5000
hispanichealth.org

Reach to Recovery (American Cancer Society)
1599 Clifton NE
Atlanta, GA 30329
800-ACS-2345 (800-227-2345)
cancer.org

Row as One Institute
P.O. Box 55
Newton, MA 02456
617-924-2120
rowasone.org

Sisters Network
8787 Woodway Drive, Suite 4206
Houston, TX 77063
866-781-1808
sistersnetworkinc.org

The Wellness Community
919 Eighteenth Street NW, Suite 54
Washington, DC 20006
888-793-WELL (888-793-9355)
wellness-community.org

Y-ME National Breast Cancer Organization
212 W. Van Buren, Suite 1000
Chicago, IL 60607-3908
800-221-2141
y-me.org

Young Survival Coalition
155 Sixth Avenue
New York, NY 10013
212-206-6610
youngsurvival.org

Nutritional Resources and Information

Glycemic Index (University of Sydney, Australia)
glycemicindex.com

Harvard School of Public Health
Department of Nutrition
665 Huntington Avenue
Boston, MA 02115
617-432-1851
hsph.harvard.edu/nutritionsource

National Heart, Lung, and Blood Institute Health Information Center
P.O. Box 30105
Bethesda, MD 20824-0104
301-592-8573
Calculating your body mass index:
nhlbisupport.com/bmi

Alternative Medicine

National Center for Complementary and Alternative Medicine
P.O. Box 7923
Gaithersburg, MD 20898
888-644-6226
http://nccam.nih.gov

FERTILITY AND PREGNANCY

American Society for Reproductive Medicine (ASRM)
1209 Montgomery Highway
Birmingham, AL 35216-2809
205-978-5000
asrm.org

CDC Reproductive Health Information Source
Division of Reproductive Health
National Center for Chronic Disease Prevention and Health Promotion
Centers for Disease Control and Prevention
4770 Buford Highway NE, Mail Stop K-20
Atlanta, GA 30341-3717
770-488-5200
cdc.gov/reproductivehealth

fertileHOPE
P.O. Box 624
New York, NY 10014
888-994-HOPE (888-994-4673)
fertilehope.org

ADOPTION

National Adoption Information Clearinghouse
330 C Street SW
Washington, DC 20447
888-251-0075
http://naic.acf.hhs.gov

National Council for Adoption
1930 Seventeenth Street NW
Washington, DC 20009-6207
866-212-3678
adoptioncouncil.org

PRODUCTS

Airway (breast forms and bras)
3960 Rosslyn Drive
Cincinnati, OH 45209
800-888-0458
surgicalappliance.com/airway.html

Amoena (breast forms, clothing)
1955 W. Oak Circle
Marietta, GA 30062
800-726-6362
amoena.org
thebreastcaresite.com (informational website run by Amoena)

Camp Healthcare (breast forms, clothing)
P.O. Box 89
Jackson, MI 49204
800-492-1088
camphealthcare.com

ContourMed (breast forms)
2821 Kavanaugh Boulevard, Suite 2
Little Rock, AR 72205
888-301-0520
contourmed.com

Especially Yours Catalog (wigs and hairpieces)
P.O. Box 105
South Easton, MA 02375
800-748-6910
especiallyyours.com

Look Good . . . Feel Better
c/o CTFA Foundation
1101 Seventeenth Street NW
Washington, DC 20036

800-395-LOOK (800-395-5665)

lookgoodfeelbetter.org

(Look Good . . . Feel Better was developed by the Cosmetic, Toiletry, and Fragrance Association Foundation in cooperation with the American Cancer Society and the National Cosmetology Association.)

Paula Young Catalog (wigs and hairpieces)

P.O. Box 483

Brockton, MA 02303

800-343-9695

paulayoung.com

Still You Fashions (breast forms, clothing)

2801 N. Turner Grove Drive

Greensboro, NC 27455

800-325-4548

stillyoufashions.com

The "tlc" catalog of the American Cancer Society (breast forms, clothing, wigs)

P.O. Box 395

Louisiana, MO 62253-0395

800-850-9445

tlccatalog.org

PROTECTION FROM THE SUN

Coolibar

4206 Park Glen Road

St. Louis Park, MN 55416

800-926-6509

coolibar.com

Solumbra

Sun Precautions

2815 Wetmore Avenue

Everett, WA 98201

800-882-7860

sunprecautions.com

CREDITS

◉

Figures 1.1, 1.2, 1.3, 1.4, 3.1, 3.2, 3.4, 7.1 by Harriet B. Greenfield, courtesy of President and Fellows of Harvard College

Figure 3.3 by and courtesy of Harriet B. Greenfield

Figures 4.1, 4.2, 4.3, 6.1, 6.2, 9.2 by Scott Leighton, courtesy of President and Fellows of Harvard College

Figures 6.4, 6.5 courtesy of Amoena/Coloplast Corporation

Figure 6.6 courtesy of ContourMed

Figures 7.2, 7.3, 7.4, 7.5, 7.6, 7.7, 7.8, 7.9 by Raoul Kim, courtesy of Carolyn M. Kaelin, M.D.

Figure 9.1 by Patrick Scullin, courtesy of President and Fellows of Harvard College

Figures 11.1, 11.2, 11.3, 11.4, 11.5 by Doron Ben-Ami, courtesy of President and Fellows of Harvard College

Figure 12.1 courtesy of President and Fellows of Harvard College, adapted with permission from Walter C. Willett, M.D. Dr. P.H., Harvard School of Public Health

INDEX

⊙